iPad and iPad Pro

2022 – 2023 Edition

by Paul McFedries

A Wiley Brand

iPad and iPad Pro For Dummies®, 2022 – 2023 Edition

Published by: **John Wiley & Sons, Inc.**, 111 River Street, Hoboken, NJ 07030-5774, www.wiley.com

Copyright © 2022 by John Wiley & Sons, Inc., Hoboken, New Jersey

Published simultaneously in Canada

For general information on our other products and services, please contact our Customer Care Department within the U.S. at 877-762-2974, outside the U.S. at 317-572-3993, or fax 317-572-4002. For technical support, please visit https://hub.wiley.com/community/support/dummies.

Wiley publishes in a variety of print and electronic formats and by print-on-demand. Some material included with standard print versions of this book may not be included in e-books or in print-on-demand. If this book refers to media such as a CD or DVD that is not included in the version you purchased, you may download this material at http://booksupport.wiley.com. For more information about Wiley products, visit www.wiley.com.

Library of Congress Control Number: 2022933147

ISBN 978-1-119-87573-4 (pbk); 978-1-119-88047-9 (ebk); 978-1-119-87857-5 (ebk)

SKY10042093_013023

Contents at a Glance

Table of Contents

Introduction

One of the nice things about an iPad is that you can start using one a few minutes after liberating the device from its box. After traipsing through a mercifully brief setup routine, you end up on the iPad's Home screen and you're good to go. Even if you'd never used an iPad before, you probably figured out lickety-split that tapping the screen make things happen and running your finger across the screen scrolls things here and there.

The iPad basics are intuitive and not hard to master, but you might also have learned a hard iPad lesson: Once you've got the easy stuff down, the rest of the iPad is less intuitive. How do you make the screen brighter? How do you get that app that all the cool people are using? How do you set up your email? How do you take amazing photos and videos?

These are all great questions, but they probably only scratch the surface of what you want to know, iPad-wise. Not only that, but the iPad is a wonderfully complex device with hidden depths that enable the tablet to perform tasks you've likely never thought of. How do you get your iPad questions answered and how do you explore your iPad's depths?

I thought you'd never ask.

About This Book

Welcome, therefore, to *iPad and iPad Pro For Dummies, 2022-2023* Edition. This book is designed to take you beyond the basics of your iPad and show you what your tablet can do. iPads aren't cheap, so you owe it to yourself to get the most out of your investment by learning not only the iPad's ABCs but also its XYZs. From mail to messaging, from Siri to settings, from contacts to calendars, this book covers all major iPad and iPadOS features (and quite a few minor ones, too).

I need to get one thing out of the way from the get-go. I think you're pretty darn smart for buying a *Dummies* book. To me, that says you have the confidence and intelligence to know what you don't know. The *Dummies* franchise is built on the core notion that everyone feels insecure about certain topics when tackling them for the first time, especially when those topics have to do with technology. The iPad is no exception.

This book is chock-full of useful tips, advice, and other nuggets that should make your iPad experience more pleasurable. I'll even go so far as to say you won't find some of these nuggets anywhere else. So keep this book nearby and consult it often.

Foolish Assumptions

Although I know what happens when one makes assumptions, I've made a few anyway. First, I assume that you, gentle reader, know nothing about using an iPad or iPadOS, that you want to understand your iPad and its operating system without digesting an incomprehensible technical manual, and that you made the right choice by selecting this book.

I do my best to explain each new concept in full and loving detail. Perhaps that's foolish, but . . . oh, well.

One last thing: I also assume that you can read. If you can't, please ignore this paragraph.

Icons Used in This Book

Little round pictures (or *icons*) appear in the left margin throughout this book. Consider these icons as miniature road signs, telling you something extra about the topic at hand or hammering a point home. Here's what the icons in this book look like and mean.

These juicy morsels, shortcuts, and recommendations might make the task at hand faster or easier.

This icon emphasizes the stuff I think you ought to retain. You may even jot down a note to yourself on the iPad.

Put on your propeller beanie hat and insert your pocket protector; this text includes truly geeky stuff. You can safely ignore this material, but if it weren't interesting or informative, I wouldn't have bothered to write it.

You wouldn't intentionally run a stop sign, would you? In the same fashion, ignoring warnings might be hazardous to your iPad and (by extension) your wallet. There, you now know how these warning icons work, for you have just received your very first warning!

Beyond the Book

I wrote a bunch of things that just didn't fit in the print version of this book. Rather than leave them on the cutting room floor, I've posted the most useful bits online in a cheat sheet for your enjoyment and edification.

To find them, go to www.dummies.com and type *iPad and iPad Pro For Dummies cheat sheet* in the Search field. Here's what you'll find: info on using the iPad's buttons and icons, tips for mastering multitouch, and where to find additional help if your iPad is acting contrary.

Where to Go from Here

Why, go straight to Chapter 1, of course (without passing Go).

Note: At the time I wrote this book, all the information it contained was accurate for all Wi-Fi and Wi-Fi + Cellular iPads that support iPadOS. The book is also based on version 15 of the iPadOS operating system. Apple is likely to introduce new iPad models and new versions of iPadOS between book editions, so if the hardware or user interface on your new iPad looks a little different, be sure to check out what Apple has to say at www.apple.com/ipad. You'll no doubt find updates on the company's latest releases.

1
Getting to Know Your iPad

IN THIS PART . . .

Get basic training for getting along with your iPad.

Enjoy a gentle introduction to your iPad.

Peek at your iPad hardware and software and explore the way it works.

Discover the joys of synchronization and how to get your data — contacts, movies, songs, podcasts, books, and so on — from a computer (or iCloud) to your iPad.

Chapter **1**

Unveiling the iPad

Are you familiar with the old proverb that says, "Well begun is half done"? Some say it comes from Aristotle, so if you mumbled to yourself that the phrase is "Greek to me," you'd be spot on! The proverb's meaning is straightforward enough: If you start a project well, the rest of it will proceed so swimmingly that it'll feel like you need to expend only half the effort to get it done.

This chapter is your chance to get your relationship with your iPad off to such a good start. Sure, you can dive right in and start tapping and scrolling stuff willy-nilly. If that's your style, go for it; I won't judge. However, one thing I've learned over the years is that if you approach a new piece of technology slowly and curiously, you'll end up with a solid grounding in the basics that will pay back your initial time investment manyfold.

To that end, in this chapter, I offer a gentle introduction to all the pieces that make up your iPad, plus an overview of its most useful hardware features and a few software features that come with iPadOS.

REMEMBER

iPadOS is the software that runs behind the scenes to control just about everything that happens on your iPad. The *OS* part of *iPadOS* is short for *operating system*, which tells you that iPadOS is the iPad equivalent of macOS on a Mac or even Windows on a PC.

In this book, I cover all iPad models that run iPadOS:

>> **iPad:** iPad fifth generation (2017) and later; iPad Air 2 (2014) and later

>> **iPad mini:** iPad mini 4 (2015) and later

>> **iPad Pro:** iPad Pro first generation (2015) and later

Because the first four generations of iPad, the first generation of iPad Air, and the first three generations of iPad mini can't run iPadOS, they're not covered in this book. If you're the owner of one of those models, you can still find a lot of handy information here, but some things might look or work differently.

The iPad: A Bird's-Eye View

The iPad has many interesting and useful features, but perhaps its most notable feature is that it doesn't come with a physical keyboard or stylus. You can get them as options (Apple's first-generation $99 Apple Pencil, the second-generation $129 Apple Pencil, and the Smart Keyboard, which starts at $159), but they aren't required to use your iPad. Instead, every iPad is designed to be controlled with a pointing device that you're intimately familiar with: your finger.

And I love the iPad's plethora of built-in sensors. It has an accelerometer that detects when you rotate the device from portrait to landscape mode — and instantly adjusts what's on the display. A light sensor adjusts the display's brightness in response to the current ambient lighting conditions. Then there's a three-axis gyro that works with the accelerometer and built-in compass. And all iPadOS-capable models also include Apple's Touch ID sensor or Face ID. These features let you unlock your iPad with your fingerprint (Touch ID) or just by looking at it (Face ID)! I talk about both in detail later.

Last, but definitely not least, all iPads include Siri, a voice-controlled personal assistant happy to do almost anything you ask.

In the following sections, it's time to take a brief look at the rest of the iPad's features, broken down by product category.

The iPad as a media player

The iPad's built-in speakers and sharp, clear display mean you can enjoy all your favorite media — music, audiobooks, audio and video podcasts, music videos,

YouTube cat videos, television shows, and movies — all from the comfort of your favorite armchair.

REMEMBER

If you can get a media file — be it video, audio, or whatever — on your iPad, you can watch or listen to it on your iPad. And, of course, you can always buy or rent content on your iPad in the iTunes Store. You can also watch streaming content from Netflix, Hulu, Apple's own Apple TV+ streaming service, and a host of others through apps.

The iPad as an internet device

The iPad is a full-featured internet device. For example, your iPad comes with the Safari app, which is a no-compromise web browser that makes navigating web pages intuitive and even fun. Check out Chapter 4 to learn how to surf the web using Safari.

TIP

Many other iPad web browsers are available, including Google Chrome, Mozilla Firefox, and Microsoft Edge, but I don't talk about them in this book. If you use the desktop equivalent of one of these browsers, you might want to try out the iPadOS version.

The iPad also comes with an email app (called, somewhat boringly, Mail) that's compatible with most mail services. For more on using your iPad for email, see Chapter 5.

If you're more into text messaging, your iPad has you covered with the Messages app. The details are in Chapter 6.

Another major internet feature is Maps, a mapping app that not only lets you see where things are located but also can provide directions to get from here to there. For the full scoop on Maps, see Chapter 13.

The iPad as an e-book reader

Download the free Books app if you don't already have it, or any of the excellent (and free) third-party e-book readers such as the Kindle app from Amazon, and you'll discover a new way of finding and reading books. The Apple Book Store and News app (covered in Chapter 7) are chock-full of good reading at prices that are lower than what you'd pay for a printed copy.

Better still, when you read an e-book, you're helping the environment and saving trees. Furthermore, some (if not many) titles include audio, video, or graphical content not available in the printed editions. Plus, a great number of good books are free. And best of all, you can carry your entire library in one hand. If you've never read a book on your iPad, give it a try. I think you'll like (or love) it.

The iPad as a multimedia powerhouse

Your iPad has built-in speakers and support for connecting external headphones or speakers (directly or via Bluetooth), so if you want to listen to some tunes, your iPad is happy to help, as I show in Chapter 7.

All iPads also come with a couple of cameras, so you can use your tablet as a (slightly bulky) video camera (see Chapter 8) or still camera (see Chapter 9).

The Retina display on all iPads since the third generation makes the experience of watching video a pleasure. You can use AirPlay to send your video out to Apple TV, too, and your iPad turns into a superb device for watching video on a TV, with support for output resolutions up to 4K. Chapter 8 talks about watching video on your iPad.

You can also use the iPad cameras and the FaceTime app to video-chat with family and friends. Chapter 8 gets you started with FaceTime.

The iPad as a platform for third-party apps

At the time of this writing, there were more than 4 million apps in the App Store, with hundreds of billions of downloads to date in categories such as games, business, education, entertainment, healthcare and fitness, music, photography, productivity, travel, and sports. The cool thing is that most of them, even ones designed for the iPhone, also run on the iPad (although, it must be said, they look a tad weird on the larger screen). And more than a million are designed *specifically* for the iPad's larger screen. Chapter 10 helps you fill your iPad with all the cool apps your heart desires.

The iPad as a multitasking content production device

Apple has made the iPad more and more of a device for creating content as opposed to only consuming it. Writing, taking and editing pictures, recording and editing music or videos, and even putting together full-scale presentations — all these tasks are doable with iPadOS, especially on the iPad Pro. Split-screen views, support for the Files app, and a fast processor give the iPad more than enough power to handle most tasks you throw at it. I talk more about multitasking in Chapter 2.

What do you need to use an iPad?

To *use* your iPad, only a few simple things are required. Here's a list of everything you need:

» An iPad (duh)

» An Apple ID (assuming that you want to acquire content such as apps, TV shows and movies, music, books, and podcasts, which you almost certainly do)

» Internet access — broadband wireless internet access is recommended

Several years ago, you needed a computer with iTunes to sync your iPad. That's no longer true; these days you can activate, set up, update, back up, and restore an iPad wirelessly without ever introducing it to a computer.

If you do decide to introduce your iPad to your computer (and I think you should), you need one of the following for syncing (which I discuss at length in Chapter 3):

» A Mac with a USB 2.0, 3.0, or USB-C port, macOS version 10.8.5 or later, and iTunes 12.7 or later (for macOS Mojave and earlier) or Finder (macOS Catalina or later)

» A PC with a USB 2.0 or 3.0 port, Windows 7 or later, and iTunes 12.7 or later

? iTunes is a free download, available at www.itunes.com/download.

Touring the iPad Exterior

The iPad is a harmonious combination of hardware and software. In the following sections, you take a brief look at the hardware — what's on the outside.

On the top

On the top of your iPad, you find the top button, headphone jack (iPad only), and microphone, as shown in Figure 1-1:

» **Top button:** This button is used to put your iPad's screen to sleep or to wake it up. It's also how you turn your iPad on or off. To put it to sleep or wake it up, just press the button. To turn it on or off, press and hold down the button for a few seconds. On some iPad models, the top button is used also as a fingerprint sensor for the Touch ID security feature.

Your iPad's battery will run down faster when your iPad is awake, so I suggest that you make a habit of putting it to sleep when you're not using it.

To wake it up, press the top button again, or press the Home button on the front of the device (as described in a moment), or on iPad Pro, tap the screen.

If you use an Apple Smart Cover or Smart Case (or any third-party case that uses the Smart Cover mechanism), you can just open the cover to wake your iPad and close the cover to put it to sleep.

In Chapter 14, you can find out how to make your iPad go to sleep automatically after a period of inactivity.

» **Headphone jack:** This jack lets you plug in a headset, although as I write this the latest models of the iPad Pro, iPad mini, and iPad Air no longer come with this feature. You can use pretty much any headphone or headset that plugs into a 3.5-mm stereo headphone jack. Apple no longer makes headphones with a headphone jack, but it does sell EarPods ($29), which connect via a Lightning connector, and AirPods (starting at $159), which connect via Bluetooth.

Throughout this book, I use the words *headphones, earphones,* and *headset* interchangeably. Strictly speaking, a headset includes a microphone so that you can talk (or record) as well as listen; headphones and earphones are for listening only. Either type works with your iPad, as do most wireless Bluetooth headsets and newer headsets with Lightning connectors.

» **Microphone:** The tiny dot — or two dots on some iPad Pro models — in the middle of the top of the device is a pretty good microphone. (*Hint:* You'll sound better if you use a headset — any headset.)

» **Speakers (iPad Pro only):** iPad Pro has four speaker vents, two on the top and two on the bottom.

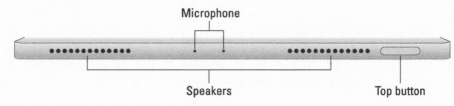

FIGURE 1-1:
The top edge of an iPad Pro.

Microphone

Speakers

Top button

On the bottom

On the bottom of your iPad are the speakers (two of the four speakers on iPad Pro models) and Lightning connector or USB-C connector, as shown in Figure 1-2.

>> **Speakers:** The speakers play audio — music or video soundtracks — if you don't have headphones or external speakers plugged in or connected via Bluetooth.

>> **Lightning or USB-C connector:** This connector has three purposes:

- *Recharge your iPad's battery:* Simply connect one end of the included cable to the iPad's Lightning or USB-C port and the other end to a USB or USB-C port, where appropriate.

- *Synchronize your iPad:* Connect one end of the same cable to the Lightning or USB-C connector and the other end to a USB or USB-C port on your Mac or PC.

- *Connect your iPad to a camera or television:* Make sure to use an adapter that works with the Lightning connector or the USB-C connector, depending on your iPad.

REMEMBER

If you connect your iPad to a USB port and get a *Not Charging* message, the USB port doesn't have enough power. Generally speaking, USB ports built into recent Macs and PCs, on powered hubs, or on the USB charging brick that came with your iPad will charge your iPad properly. Any USB data port connected to your Mac or PC will allow you to sync your iPad, whether or not it's charging.

FIGURE 1-2:
All iPad models
have speaker
ports and a
connection
port on the
bottom.

Speaker   Lightning or USB-C connector   Speaker

On the right side of your iPad are the volume up and volume down buttons, as shown in Figure 1-3. Press the upper button to increase the volume; press the lower button to decrease the volume.

TIP

The Camera app uses either volume button as an alternative shutter release button to the on-screen shutter release button. Press any of them to shoot a picture or start and stop video recording.

FIGURE 1-3:
The right side
of the iPad
features
volume
buttons, and
some feature a
SIM tray, too.

SIM card tray   Volume up and down buttons

On iPads with cellular capabilities, the SIM card tray is on the right side. Wi-Fi-only models do not have a SIM card tray.

TIP

Apple used to include a SIM card eject tool with iPads and iPhones. If you don't have one lying around, you can straighten a paper clip and use it as a faux SIM card eject tool.

On the front and back

On the front of your iPad, you'll find the following (labeled in Figure 1-4):

>> **Touchscreen:** I describe how to use the iPad's touchscreen in Chapter 2.

>> **Home button:** If your iPad comes with a Home button, then no matter what you're doing, you can press the Home button at any time to display the Home screen, as shown in Figure 1-4. The Home button also doubles as a Touch ID sensor, so you can use your fingerprint (or a passcode) to unlock your phone and authenticate purchases. Recent models of the iPad Pro, iPad mini, and iPad Air don't have a Home button. For these iPads, you swipe up from the bottom of the screen to go back to the Home screen.

>> **Front (FaceTime) camera:** You use the front camera for FaceTime video chats and taking selfies. You shouldn't use it much for taking regular photos because the back camera on all iPad models is much better.

>> **App icons:** Each of the icons shown on the screen (see Figure 1-4) launches an included iPad app. You read more about these apps later in this chapter and throughout the rest of the book.

The back of your iPad has a rear camera, just below the top button, which is better than the one in front. iPad Pro, iPad mini, and iPad Air models have a 12-megapixel rear camera with an f/1.8 aperture, and the iPad has an 8-megapixel rear camera with f/2.4 aperture. The iPad can record HD video at 1080p, and the iPad Pro, iPad mini, and iPad Air can record video at up to 4K.

Front camera   App icon

FIGURE 1-4:
The front
of the iPad
10.2-inch.

Touchscreen   Home button

Courtesy of Apple, Inc.

Status bar

The status bar, which is at the top of the screen, displays tiny icons that provide a variety of information about the current state of your iPad:

» **Airplane mode:** Airplane mode should be enabled when you fly. It turns off all wireless features of your iPad — the cellular, 5G, 4G, LTE, 3G, GPRS, and EDGE networks; Wi-Fi; and Bluetooth — so you can enjoy music, video, games, photos, or any app that doesn't require an internet connection while you're in the air.

Tap the Settings app and then tap the airplane mode switch on (so green is displayed). The icon shown in the margin appears on the left side of your status bar when airplane mode is enabled. You can also pull Control Center down from the top-right corner and tap the airplane mode icon to turn airplane mode on (the icon turns orange).

REMEMBER

Disable airplane mode when the plane is at the gate before takeoff or after landing so you can send or receive email and iMessages.

To use Wi-Fi in flight with a cellular iPad, first enable airplane mode and then reenable Wi-Fi.

» **Wi-Fi:** If you see the Wi-Fi icon, your iPad is connected to a Wi-Fi network. The more semicircular lines that are lit (up to three), the stronger the Wi-Fi signal. If your iPad has only one or two semicircles of Wi-Fi strength, try moving around a bit. If you don't see the Wi-Fi icon on the status bar, internet access with Wi-Fi is not currently available.

» **Personal Hotspot:** You see this icon when you're sharing your internet connection with computers or other devices over Wi-Fi, USB, or Bluetooth. Personal Hotspot is available for every cellular-enabled iPad but may not be available in all areas or from all carriers. Additional fees may apply. Contact your wireless carrier for more information.

» **Syncing:** This icon appears on the status bar when your iPad is syncing with iTunes on your Mac or PC.

» **Activity:** This icon tells you that some network or other activity is occurring, such as over-the-air synchronization, the sending or receiving of email, or the loading of a web page. Some third-party apps use this icon to indicate network or other activity.

» **VPN:** This icon shows that you're currently connected to a virtual private network (VPN).

» **Lock:** This icon tells you when your iPad is locked. See Chapter 2 for information on locking and unlocking your iPad.

» **Screen orientation lock:** This icon appears when the screen orientation lock is engaged.

» **Location Services:** This icon appears when an app (such as Maps; see Chapter 13 for more about the Maps app) is using Location Services (such as GPS) to establish the location of your iPad.

» **Do not disturb:** This icon appears whenever do not disturb is enabled, silencing incoming FaceTime calls and alerts. See Chapter 14 for details on do not disturb.

» **Play:** This icon informs you that a song is currently playing. You find out more about playing songs in Chapter 7.

» **Bluetooth:** This icon indicates the current state of your iPad's Bluetooth connection. If you see this icon on the status bar, Bluetooth is on and a device (such as a wireless headset or keyboard) is connected. If the icon is gray, Bluetooth is turned on but no device is connected. If the icon is white,

COMPARING WI-FI AND CELLULAR NETWORKS

Wireless carriers offer several data networks relevant to the iPad, all of which can take advantage of the speediest 4G or LTE networks. AT&T has a form of LTE the company misleadingly calls 5G. 3G is slower than 4G and LTE, and EDGE and GPRS are slower still. Your iPad starts by trying to connect to the fastest network it supports. If it makes a connection, you see the appropriate cellular icon on the status bar.

Most Wi-Fi networks, however, are faster than even the fastest 4G cellular network. So, because all iPads can connect to a Wi-Fi network if one is available, they do so, even when a cellular network is also available.

Last but not least, if you don't see 5G, 4G, LTE, 3G, GPRS, E (for EDGE), or the Wi-Fi icon, you don't currently have internet access.

Bluetooth is on and one (or more) devices are connected. If you don't see a Bluetooth icon, Bluetooth is turned off. Chapter 14 goes into more detail about Bluetooth.

>> **Bluetooth battery:** This icon displays the battery level of supported Bluetooth devices (while connected). Only certain devices — mostly headsets and speakers — support this feature. If you see this icon in your status bar, it's telling you the approximate battery level of whichever supported device is currently connected with your iPad.

>> **Battery:** This icon shows the level of your battery's charge and also indicates when your device is connected to a power source. It's completely filled when your device isn't connected to a power source and is fully charged. It then empties as the battery becomes depleted. You see an on-screen message when the charge drops to 20 percent or below, and another when it reaches 10 percent.

Exploring the Home Screen and Dock

The iPad Home screen refers to the screen you see when your iPad is unlocked and you're not working in an app. The Home screen is divided into multiple pages; you scroll to the next page by swiping your finger to the left on the screen and you scroll to the previous page by swiping right. With the exception of the first page, which contains a mixture of widgets and app icons, each Home screen page can hold up to 30 icons, with each icon representing a different built-in app or function.

Each Home screen page also displays the *dock*, which is a strip that runs along the bottom of the page. The dock can store up to 15 app icons, depending on your iPad model.

How you display the Home screen depends on your iPad model:

>> **If your iPad has a Home button:** Press the Home button. If your iPad was asleep, you see the unlock screen, so you need to press the Home button again. After you unlock your iPad, you see whichever app or page was on the screen when it went to sleep. If you see the Home screen page you want, you're golden. If not, press the Home button to summon your iPad's Home screen.

>> **If your iPad doesn't have a Home button:** If your iPad is asleep, tap the screen to display the unlock screen. Now use a finger to swipe up from the bottom edge of the screen. With your iPad unlocked, you see the app or page that was displayed when the tablet went into sleep mode. To get to the Home screen (if it's not displayed already, that is), swipe up from the bottom of the screen again.

REMEMBER

When you unlock your iPad, you might have to enter a passcode. To learn more about passcodes, see Chapter 18.

In the following sections, I tell you briefly about the icons preloaded on your iPad's Home screen pages, as well as the icons you find on the dock. Because the rest of the book covers most of these babies in full and loving detail, I provide only brief descriptions here.

Exploring the Home screen

As shown in Figure 1-5, the first page of the iPad Home screen is divided into three sections:

>> **Widgets:** These items appear in the top half of the screen in landscape mode and include the following default widgets: Clock, Notes, Calendar, Photos, and Weather. See Chapter 10 to learn how to customize your widgets.

>> **App icons:** These items represent (mostly) apps that you can launch with a tap of your finger.

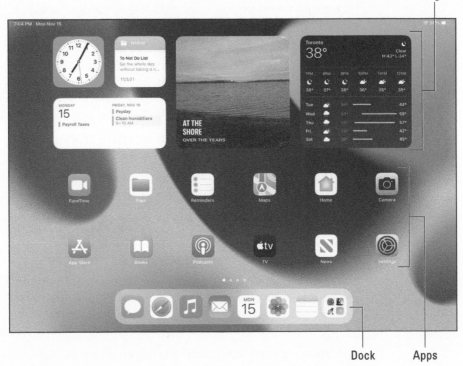

Widgets

Dock   Apps

FIGURE 1-5:
The iPad's
first Home
screen page.

>> **Dock:** This area also contains (mostly) app icons, but the dock appears on every Home screen page, so you always have quick access to these apps.

If you haven't rearranged your icons, you see the following apps on the first Home screen page, starting on the left side of the first row of apps:

>> **FaceTime:** Participate in FaceTime video chats, as you discover in Chapter 8.

>> **Files:** View and work with the files you've saved to your iCloud Drive. Apple apps as well as many third-party apps know how to use the Files app to store documents.

>> **Reminders:** Display alerts that remind you to perform some task. You can think of Reminders as a kind of fancy-schmancy to-do list. If you ask Siri to remind you, it's added as a reminder in this app, too. You can do both location- and time-based reminders, which will be synced to your other Apple devices. Learn more about reminders in Chapter 12.

>> **Maps:** View street maps, satellite imagery, transit information, and more for locations around the globe. Or ask for directions, traffic conditions, or the location of a nearby pizza joint. I show you more about Maps in Chapter 13.

>> **Home:** Access and control your HomeKit smart home devices. Almost like a sci-fi movie, you can control lights, appliances, and surveillance cameras from an app or with your voice using Siri. You'll read much more about this great app, but you have to wait until Chapter 12.

>> **Camera:** Shoot pictures or videos with your iPad's front- or rear-facing camera. You find out more in Chapters 8 (videos) and 9 (camera).

>> **App Store:** Search for iPad apps you can purchase or download for free. Chapter 10 is your guide to buying and using apps from the App Store.

>> **Books:** Read e-books, which you can buy in the Book Store. I discuss the Books app more deeply in Chapter 7.

>> **Podcasts:** Subscribe and listen to your favorite podcasts.

>> **TV:** Watch and manage your movies, TV shows, and music videos. You add videos via Finder in recent versions of macOS or iTunes on older Macs or on PCs or by purchasing them directly in the TV app or the iTunes Store app. Check out Chapter 8 to find out more.

>> **News:** Read the latest news from magazines, newspapers, and websites, and subscribe to Apple News+ for access to paid content from many mainstream sources. You read more about News in Chapter 7.

>> **Settings:** Customize your iPad and apps by modifying their settings. With so many options in the Settings app, you'll be happy to hear that Chapter 14 is dedicated exclusively to Settings.

The second Home screen page (swipe your finger left on the screen to get there) contains the following default apps:

>> **Photo Booth:** Take fun selfies with your iPad's front camera. Chapter 9 explains how.

>> **Find My:** Locate a lost iPad (or iPhone, AirPods, or Mac). I look more closely at Find My in Chapter 14.

>> **Shortcuts:** Combine two or more actions — such as taking a photo and sending it via text message to someone — into a single script that you run by tapping an icon.

>> **Clock:** Check the current time (locally as well as from anywhere in the world) and set alarms and timers. You hear more about this nifty app in Chapter 12.

>> **Contacts:** Store information about the people you know. Chapter 11 explains how to use the Contacts app.

>> **Stocks:** Track stocks. You can also get news articles about the companies you're following.

>> **Translate:** Translate a word or phrase in one language (entered by typing or speaking) into another language. See Chapter 12 for the details.

>> **Voice Memos:** Record everything you speak into your iPad's microphone. For more about the Voice Memos app, turn to Chapter 12.

>> **Measure:** Measure distances in the real world by using the iPad's back camera. Seriously, try it! Turn to Chapter 12 for more on the Measure app.

>> **iTunes Store:** Buy or rent music, movies, TV shows, audiobooks, and more. You find more info about iTunes Store in Chapter 7.

>> **Magnifier:** Using the iPad's rear camera, zoom in on real-world objects that are too small to see clearly. Chapter 12 shows you how the Magnifier app does its job.

>> **Tips:** Get tips for using your iPad.

Depending on your iPad model, the second page of the Home screen might also house a few other Apple apps, such as Pages (word processor), Keynote (presentations), Numbers (spreadsheet), Apple Store (buy Apple stuff), iMovie (create digital movies), Clips (create short video clips), and GarageBand (record and edit music).

Getting to know the dock

At the bottom of every iPad Home screen page, you see a special shelflike area called the dock. By default, the eight icons on the dock are as follows:

>> **Messages:** Exchange free, unlimited text or multimedia messages with any other device running iOS 5 or later or Mac OS X Mountain Lion or later. Find out more about Messages in Chapter 6.

>> **Safari:** Navigate sites and pages on the web. Chapter 4 shows you how to start using Safari on your iPad.

>> **Music:** Listen to music or podcasts. You discover how the Music app works in Chapter 7.

>> **Mail:** Send and receive email with most email systems. Chapter 5 helps you start emailing from your iPad everyone you know.

» **Calendar:** Create and manage appointments. You learn more about Calendar in Chapter 11.

» **Photos:** View, edit, and manage the photos in your iPad library. To get started, see Chapter 9.

» **Notes:** Type short notes while you're out and about. For help using Notes, flip to Chapter 11.

» **App Library:** Get quick access to all your apps organized by category. I explain more in Chapter 10.

Feel free to add icons to or remove icons from the dock to suit the way your work or play. To add or remove dock icons, press and hold down on any icon and tap Edit Home Screen on the menu that appears. Your app icons will begin wiggling. Tap and drag a wiggling app icon to move it to or from the dock. Tap and drag an existing dock icon to change its position. When you're satisfied, tap Done in the upper-right corner of the Home screen (or press the Home button, if your iPad has one) to exit wiggly mode and save your arrangement.

Depending on your iPad model, you have between 11 and 15 app icons on the dock. If you find you don't use App Library all that much, choose Settings ⇨ Home Screen & Dock and tap the Show App Library in Dock switch to off (that is, from a green background to a light gray background). You can now add an extra app icon to the dock.

Two last points:

» *Notifications* are messages from iPadOS and your apps that tell you about recent activity on your tablet. I wanted to mention them even though they don't have an icon of their own. You hear much more about notifications in Chapter 12. To see them now (I know you can't wait), swipe from the top of your screen to the middle to make them appear. Then swipe from the bottom to put them away again.

This gesture works anytime — even when your iPad is locked. If it's locked, you'll see your most recent notifications when you swipe down. Then swipe up to see older notifications.

» I'd be remiss not to mention the useful Control Center, with controls for Wi-Fi, Bluetooth, audio playback, and much more, all available from any screen in any app. You discover much more about Control Center in Chapter 14, but if you can't stand the suspense, put your finger in the top-right corner of your iPad screen and swipe down to open Control Center (and then tap some other part of the screen to put it away).

Chapter **2**

Basic Training

By now you know that the iPad you hold in your hands is very different from other computers.

You also know that the iPad is rewriting the rule book for mainstream computing. How so? For starters, iPads don't come with a mouse or any other kind of pointing device. They lack traditional computing ports or connectors, such as USB. And they have no physical or built-in keyboard, though Apple will sell you a Smart Keyboard accessory for recent iPad models.

iPads even differ from other so-called tablet PCs, some of which feature a pen or stylus and let you write in digital ink. As I point out (pun intended) in Chapter 1, the iPad relies on an input device that you always have with you: your finger. Okay, some iPads can use Apple Pencil and other styluses, but what makes an iPad so powerful is that a stylus is optional.

If you own an iPhone, you already have a gigantic start in figuring out how to master the iPad multitouch method of navigating the interface with your fingers. If you've been using iOS 15, you have an even bigger head start. You have my permission to skim the rest of this chapter, but I urge you to stick around anyway because some aspects of iPadOS work in subtly different ways than iOS on the iPhone. If you're a total novice, don't fret. Nothing about multitouch is painful.

Getting Started on Getting Started

You can set up your iPad with or without a Mac or PC. In Chapter 3, I show you how to set it up with a computer. But first, I show you how to set up your iPad without a computer.

Here are the two things you need to use your iPad:

>> **An Apple ID account:** You'll want an account to download content from iTunes and the App Store, and to take advantage of iCloud, including iCloud backups. Read Chapter 7 for details on how to set up an account. Like most things Apple, the process isn't difficult.

>> **Internet access:** Your iPad can connect to the internet through Wi-Fi or cellular (if you bought an iPad with cellular capabilities). With Wi-Fi you can connect your iPad to cyberspace in your home, office, school, favorite coffeehouse, bookstore, or numerous other spots. If your iPad has cellular capabilities, you can connect anywhere.

A Closer Look at Cellular Data on Your iPad

Some iPad models come with the internal hardware required to operate on a cellular network. If your iPad doesn't have cellular support, go ahead and skip to the next section.

Wireless technology is constantly evolving, but support for cellular capabilities on mobile devices is everyday stuff now. You need to pay for a cellular plan with a carrier to use your iPad's cellular capabilities. Read on to learn more about your cellular options.

TECHNICAL
STUFF

In the United States, you can choose among AT&T, Verizon Wireless, and T-Mobile. Most carriers offer some version of 4G and 5G wireless. All iPad cellular models support 4G, and as this book went to press, 5G support was built into the latest models of the iPad Pro and iPad mini (but not the iPad and iPad Air).

Figuring out how much data you need beforehand isn't always easy, but it's simple enough to adjust along the way. If you're streaming a lot of music, T-Mobile for one provides a nice benefit: the capability to stream free on most major services, including Spotify and Apple Music. A friendly warning pops up on your iPad when you get close to your limit. At that point, you can pay more to add to your data bucket or start from scratch next month.

Whichever carrier you go with, I recommend finding a (secure) Wi-Fi network when streaming movies, lest you exhaust your data allotment in a hurry.

iPads with cellular hardware may include an Apple SIM card that theoretically allows you to bounce from one carrier to another. The process isn't always simple, however, because such SIM cards are sometimes locked down, either by Apple or by the carrier from which you bought the tablet. Moreover, the type of SIM card inside your iPad varies. Some models have nano-SIM cards. Others, including most early models dating all the way back to the original iPad, have a micro-SIM card. More recent models have both an embedded Apple SIM card and a tray for a nano-SIM card.

If you can't get your iPad to work with a chosen wireless carrier, check with that carrier for advice.

Turning On and Setting Up the iPad

Unless your iPad is brand spanking new and fresh out of the box, chances are you've already performed the following steps. If you choose to use your iPad computer-free, these steps make up the entire setup process.

Apple has taken the time to fully charge your iPad, so you can set it up right away in one of two ways. I strongly encourage you to use the first method — automatic setup — because it's so easy. However, it does require you to have another iOS 11 or later device already set up and running with the same Apple ID.

If you don't have another device using iOS 11 or later, never fear! I also show you how to set up your iPad manually. In fact, you can skip straight down to the section called "Manual setup" to get started.

Automatic setup

Automatic setup enables you to transfer your settings and Apple ID-related data from one iPhone or iPad running iOS 11 or later, including iPadOS, to your iPad. As just mentioned, the device you're transferring from must be running the same Apple ID that you want to use on your new iPad. Depending on the choices you make during the setup process, some of these steps may be different for you.

1. **Begin the setup process:**

    a. *Press and hold down the top button on the upper-right edge.* You see the Apple logo, followed by the word *hello* and similar greetings in a bunch of other languages.

b. *When you see either the* Press Home to Open *message (if your iPad has a Home button) or the* Swipe Up to Open *message (in English or another language), do so.* The language screen appears.

c. *Tap to choose your language, followed by your country or region preferences.* The Quick Start screen appears, along with a blue Set Up Manually button. Resist the urge to tap that one!

2. **Pair the two devices:**

a. *Bring your other iOS or iPadOS device close to your iPad.* And by *close,* I mean a couple of inches away. Make sure this other device is unlocked and look for the Set Up New iPad pop-up notification. The automatic setup magic has begun!

TECHNICAL
STUFF

The pairing process uses the camera on your existing device to view shifting dots on your new device described in the next step. This security procedure makes it difficult for someone to hijack the pairing process and steal your Apple ID and other data.

b. *On the second device, tap the gray Continue button.* Your second device displays the instruction *Hold Your New iPad Up to the Camera,* while the iPad gets a cool screen with a rotating 3D blob of dots. (The dots are a code, similar to a QR code, generated by your iPad.)

c. *Hold your other device over the iPad you're setting up until the camera is positioned over the blob of dots, as shown in Figure 2-1.* After the camera captures the blob of dots, your other device will say *Finish on New iPad,* while your new iPad asks you to *Enter Passcode of Your Other Device.*

d. *On your new iPad, enter the passcode from your other device.* This passcode is now the one for your iPad, too. (You can change it later, as detailed in Chapter 18.) As soon as you enter the passcode successfully, your iPad automatically displays the Touch ID screen (for iPads with Touch ID) or the Face ID screen (for iPad Pro models with Face ID).

3. **Set up Touch ID or Face ID:**

To set up Touch ID on iPad models that support it:

a. *Tap Continue.*

b. *Place your finger on the top button (or the Home button, if your iPad has one) each time you're asked.* With each touch, sensors comprehensively map your fingerprint.

c. *When the Adjust Your Grip screen appears, tap Continue, and continue the process until the Complete screen appears.*

Hold Your New iPad
Up to the Camera

Position the pattern in the circle

Authenticate Manually

FIGURE 2-1:
Maneuvering an iPad to pair with an existing iOS or iPadOS device for automatic setup.

To set up Face ID on iPad Pro models that support it:

a. *Tap Continue.* The front camera activates.

b. *When asked, turn your head in different directions until your entire face is scanned.*

c. *After completing one scan, complete a second scan when asked.*

4. On the Complete screen, tap Continue.

The screen displays *Setting Up Your Apple ID* while your other device and your iPad exchange information, including Contacts, Calendar, and Keychain passwords. Your other device also copies over all your Wi-Fi settings, even passwords, so your iPad automatically joins your networks. This process could take a few minutes. When it's finished, the Make This Your New iPad screen appears.

5. Tap Continue.

The Apps & Data screen appears.

6. If you want to set up your iPad as new, skip to Step 8.

7. Choose how to set up your iPad by tapping one of the options and following the on-screen prompts.

Your five choices are Restore from iCloud Backup, Restore from Mac or PC, Transfer Directly from iPad, Move Data from Android, and Don't Transfer Apps & Data. When the process is complete, the Terms and Conditions screen appears.

8. Tap Agree to accept the terms and conditions, and then tap Agree again on the pop-up dialog that appears.

When you tap Agree the second time, the Transfer Settings from your Other iPad screen appears. If you were using an iPhone, it would be the Transfer Settings from Your iPhone screen. They both do the same things, including allowing Siri to use your personal information when handling your requests; allowing apps and Maps to use Location Services; and sharing your analytics and diagnostics with Apple.

9. Tap Continue.

The Apple Pay screen appears.

10. Confirm or set up Apple Pay.

If Apple Pay is set up on your other iOS or iPadOS device, confirm each credit card you've set up. Otherwise, you can now add credit cards one at a time or set up Apple Pay later by tapping the Set Up Later in Settings button. (Learn more about Apple Pay in Chapter 6.)

11. **Tap Continue.**

If you already have an Apple Card set up on your other iOS or iPadOS device, the Get Daily Cash Every Time screen appears.

12. **If you have an Apple Card, tap Set as Preferred Card and follow the on-screen instructions.**

You can make your Apple Card the default credit card for Apple Pay transactions. You can also set up Apple Pay cash on your iPad.

13. **Decide whether to share your analytic data with developers.**

In Step 8, you chose whether to share analytics data with Apple. Now you're asked if you want to share analytics with developers. If you agree to share with developers, you're not just trusting Apple; you're trusting all those developers, too.

14. **Tap Continue to cycle through a series of screens highlighting new features of iPadOS specific to your iPad model.**

At the end, the Get Started screen appears.

15. **Tap Get Started.**

You are taken to the Home screen! That's it! You're now ready to use your iPad.

REMEMBER

If you ever need to restore your iPad to factory condition, follow the preceding steps to set it up again.

Manual setup

If you've already gone through the automatic setup process, skip this section. If you want to know how to manually set up your iPad, however, you're in the right place. In the interest of space, I won't repeat details for instructions that are identical to what I explained in the "Automatic setup" section. Also, depending on the choices you make during the setup process, some of these steps may be different:

1. **Begin the setup process:**

a. Press and hold down the top button on the upper-right edge. You see the Apple logo, followed by the word *hello* and similar greetings in a bunch of other languages.

b. When you see either the Press Home to Open *message (if your iPad has a Home button) or the* Swipe Up to Open *message (in English or another language), do so.* The language screen appears.

c. Tap to choose your language, followed by your country or region preferences. The Quick Start screen appears, along with a blue Set Up Manually button.

2. **Tap the Set Up Manually button.**

3. **Tap to choose an available Wi-Fi network, provide a password (if necessary), tap the Join button, and then, after the connection is complete, tap the Next button.**

   Certain iPad models may allow you to choose a cellular network, if available, and set up or change your Wi-Fi network later. (See Chapter 15 for setting up Wi-Fi in Settings.) After you tap Next, your iPad automatically advances to the Data & Privacy screen.

4. **Tap Continue to acknowledge the Data & Privacy icon and its meaning.**

   Apple takes your privacy seriously, calling privacy a human right! The icon you see at the top of this screen appears whenever your iPad asks to use your personal information.

   You advance to the Set Up Touch ID or Set Up Face ID screen, depending on your iPad model.

5. **Set up Touch ID or Face ID:**

   If your iPad model supports Touch ID but you don't want to set up Touch ID now, tap Set Up Touch ID Later (see Chapter 18 for the details), tap Don't Use, and then skip to Step 7. Otherwise, follow these steps to set up Touch ID:

   a. *Tap Continue.*

   b. *Place a finger on the top button (or the Home button, if your iPad has one) each time you're asked.* With each touch, sensors comprehensively map your fingerprint.

   c. *When asked, tap Continue to adjust your grip, and continue the process until the Complete screen appears.*

   If your iPad model supports Face ID but you don't want to set up Face ID now, tap Set Up Face ID Later (see Chapter 18 for the details), tap Don't Use, and then skip to Step 7. Otherwise, follow these steps to set up Face ID:

   a. *Tap Continue.* The front camera activates.

   b. *When asked, turn your head in different directions until your entire face is scanned.*

   c. *After completing one scan, complete a second scan when asked.*

6. **Tap Continue.**

   Your iPad prompts you to create a passcode.

7. **Type a 6-digit passcode to unlock your iPad. When the Re-enter Your Passcode screen appears, type your passcode again.**

   The Apps & Data screen appears.

8. **Choose how to set up your iPad by tapping one of the options and following the on-screen prompts.**

   Your five choices are Restore from iCloud Backup, Restore from Mac or PC, Transfer Directly from iPad, Move Data from Android, and Don't Transfer Apps & Data. When the process is complete, the Apple ID screen appears.

9. **If you don't have an Apple ID or you've forgotten it:**

   a. *Tap the Forgot Password or Apple ID? button.*

   b. *Set up a new account or bypass this step until later by choosing Settings ⇨ Apple ID.*

   The Terms and Conditions screen appears.

10. **If you have an Apple ID:**

    a. *Enter your Apple ID email address, click Next, enter your Apple ID password, and click Next.*

    b. *If you have activated two-factor authentication (sometimes called 2FA), approve this login on one of your other Apple devices, and then enter the passcode displayed on that device.*

    c. *If you use a different Apple ID for iCloud than you do for iTunes, enter both by tapping the Use Different Apple IDs for iCloud & iTunes? button and entering your credentials for both.*

    When your Apple ID has been set up, the Terms and Conditions screen appears.

11. **Tap Agree to accept the terms and conditions.**

    When you tap Agree the second time, the Express Settings screen appears.

12. **Tap Continue.**

    The Siri screen appears.

13. **Tap Continue to activate Siri.**

    Siri is activated by default. Although you can turn Siri off in Settings, I strongly recommend that you keep this feature on and use it. Siri is a good voice assistant, and Apple is improving it steadily.

    Your iPad prompts you to say a few phrases to set up the Hey Siri feature.

14. **Say the phrases as each is offered to you.**

    When Hey Siri is set up, you see the Improve Siri & Dictation screen.

15. **Tap Share Audio Recordings.**

    The iPad Analytics screen appears.

SECURITY USING YOUR FINGER OR YOUR FACE

Every iPad covered in this book is equipped with either Face ID or Touch ID, which is a fingerprint scanner cleverly embedded in the top button (or the Home button, if your iPad has one).

With Touch ID and a gentle press of any designated finger, you bypass your passcode. (Setting up passcode safeguards is a good idea and is something I cover in the chapter on security, Chapter 18.)

What's more, you can use your own digit (not the numerical kind) to authenticate iTunes and App Store purchases, and to access your iCloud Keychain passwords or even third-party password keepers. (Go to Settings ⇨ Touch ID & Passcode and make sure that the iTunes & App Store switch is turned on.) You can also use Touch ID to authorize Apple Pay purchases on the web (but not in bricks-and-mortar retail stores).

Face ID is much like Touch ID in terms of how you use it, but instead of touching your finger to a fingerprint sensor you look into your camera. The camera has a special Face ID sensor that uses infrared and other camera data to carefully and securely measure your face. As of this writing, only recent iPad Pro models come with Face ID. I cover Face ID in Chapter 18.

16. **Tap Share with Apple.**

   The Welcome to iPad screen appears.

17. **Tap Get Started.**

   You are taken to the Home screen! You're now ready to use your iPad.

REMEMBER

If you ever need to restore your iPad to factory condition, follow the preceding steps to set it up again.

Locking the iPad

I can think of several sound reasons for locking your iPad:

>> You don't want to turn it on inadvertently.

>> You want to keep prying eyes at bay.

» You have a persistently inquisitive child.

» You want to spare the battery some juice.

Apple makes locking the iPad a cinch.

REMEMBER

You don't need to do anything to lock the iPad; it happens automatically as long as you don't touch the screen for a minute or two. As you find out in Chapter 18, which is all about security, you can also set the amount of time your iPad must be idle before it automatically locks.

Can't wait? To lock the iPad immediately, press the top button.

TIP

If you have an iPad with a Smart Cover (or a third-party equivalent), opening and closing the cover locks and unlocks your iPad, but the Smart Cover has the advantage of awakening your iPad without making you press the Home button (though you may still have to enter a passcode).

Unlocking the iPad is easy, too. Here's how:

1. **Press the top button, or press the Home button on the front of the screen.**

2. **Do one of the following:**

   • *If you have Touch ID, use one of your registered fingers to press the top button (or the Home button) to unlock the iPad and go to your Home screen.*

   • *If you have Face ID, just look at the camera.*

   • *If you don't have Touch ID or Face ID, or your iPad was just restarted, enter your passcode.*

   See Chapter 18 to find out how to password-protect your iPad.

Mastering the Multitouch Interface

The iPad, like the iPhone, dispenses with a physical mouse and keyboard in favor of a virtual keyboard — a step that seemed revolutionary several years ago but is just-how-it-is today.

In the following sections, you discover how to move around the multitouch interface with ease. Later, I home in on how to make the most of the keyboard.

Training your digits

Rice Krispies have *Snap! Crackle! Pop!* Apple's response for the iPad is *Tap! Flick! Pinch!*

Fortunately, tapping, flicking, and pinching are not challenging gestures, so you can master many of the iPad's features in no time:

>> **Tap:** Use any finger to lightly press on and release the iPad screen. Tapping is the single most important element of multitouch interfaces. Tap to open, tap to play, tap to select, tap to shoot (in games).

>> **Double-tap:** Tap the screen twice in rapid succession. This action usually has the effect of zooming into (or out of) what's on the screen (such as a web page, map, or email).

>> **Long-press:** Place a finger on a screen object and leave your finger there until the desired action occurs (such as a menu of options appearing). This gesture is also called *press and hold* or *tap and hold*.

>> **Flick:** Quickly swipe a finger along the screen. Flicking lets you scroll through lists of songs, emails, and picture thumbnails. Tap the screen to stop scrolling, or wait for the scrolling list to stop.

>> **Pinch/spread:** Place two fingers on the screen and pinch them together to zoom out of images, web pages, text, videos, and more. Or spread the fingers apart to zoom in on things. These gestures will quickly become second nature!

>> **Drag:** Place a finger on a screen object and then move the finger along the screen. The object moves along with your finger.

>> **Swipe downward from the top center of the screen:** This special gesture displays notifications. Place your finger at the very top of the screen and drag downward.

>> **Swipe downward from the top right of the screen:** This time, you're calling up Control Center, a handy repository for controls related to music, airplane mode (see Chapter 15), Wi-Fi, Bluetooth, do not disturb, mute, volume, orientation lock, timer (Clock app), camera, AirPlay, and brightness. Check out Figure 2-2 for one view of Control Center.

>> **Swipe downward in the middle of any screen:** Display the search feature, a discussion for later in this chapter.

>> **Swipe from left to right on the first Home screen page:** Summon the Today screen, where you see the appointments and reminders you have coming up, get app suggestions and News stories, and access the search feature. The today view is available on the lock screen and the Home screens.

>> **Swipe from right to left on the lock screen:** Summon the iPad's camera app.

>> **Swipe up from the bottom of the screen:** Open App Switcher, which enables you to quickly switch among or view running apps (see the later section, "Multitasking"). You can also use App Switcher to quit an app by dragging the app's thumbnail above the top of the screen.

Later in the chapter, you read about a couple of other ways to employ your digits: slide over and split views.

FIGURE 2-2:
I think you'll call on Control Center a lot.

Navigating beyond the main Home screen page

As I discuss in Chapter 1, by default your iPad comes with two Home screen pages, indicated by the row of two tiny dots that appear just above the dock. After you start adding apps from the App Store (see Chapter 10), that row might expand to three or more dots. Each dot denotes a Home screen page, each of which can contain up to 30 additional icons (depending on your iPad model), not counting the additional icons on your iPad's dock. You can have up to 15 Home screen pages. You can also have more or fewer icons on your dock, but I can't think of a decent reason why you'd want to ditch any of them. In any case, more on these in a moment.

Here's what you need to know about navigating among the Home screen pages:

>> To navigate between pages, flick from right to left or left to right across the middle of the screen or tap directly on the dots. The number of dots you see represents the current number of Home screen pages on your iPad. The all-white dot denotes the page you're currently viewing. Flicking from left to right from the first Home screen page brings up the aforementioned Today screen.

>> Make sure you flick and not just tap, or you'll probably open one of the apps on the current screen instead of switching pages.

>> If your iPad has a Home button, press the Home button to jump back to the Home screen. You can also swipe up from the bottom of the screen. Doing so the first time takes you back to the last-viewed Home screen page. A second time takes you to the first Home screen page.

TIP

>> You can now put as many as 15 apps and as few as none on the dock. The dock also shows the three most recently opened apps on the right side of the divider line, making for a quick return to an app. (If you don't see recent apps on the dock, launch Settings, tap Home Screen & Dock, and then tap the Show Suggested and Recent Apps in Dock switch to on.) You can access the dock from an open app by swiping up a short way from the bottom of your screen.

Select, cut, copy, and paste

You can select and copy (or cut) content from one place on the iPad and then paste it elsewhere, just like you can with a Mac or PC. You might copy text or a URL from the web and paste it into an email or a note. Or you might copy a bunch of pictures or video into an email.

Here's how you to exploit the copy-and-paste feature:

1. **Select a word by tapping and holding down on it or double-tapping it.**

   iPadOS selects the word and displays the Edit menu just above the selection. If you don't see the Edit menu, tap the selection.

2. **Drag the *grab points* (also called *grab handles*) to select a larger or smaller block of text.**

   The grab points, which are vertical lines connected to circles, appear to the left and right of the selected text, as shown in Figure 2-3. The tininess of the grab points means that dragging them may take a little practice.

   FIGURE 2-3:
   Drag the grab handles to select text.

3. **Tap Copy.**

   If you were deleting text from a document you created, instead of copying and pasting, you would tap Cut instead.

4. **Open the app into which you want to paste the copied text.**

5. **Position the cursor where you want to insert the text you just copied, and then tap the cursor.**

   Up pops the Edit menu, a version of which is shown in Figure 2-4. (The commands you see vary by app.)

6. **Tap Paste to paste the text into the document.**

FIGURE 2-4:
Tap Paste and text will appear.

TIP

If you make a mistake when you were cutting, pasting, or typing, shake the iPad. Doing so undoes the last edit (provided that you tap the Undo Paste or Undo option when it appears and keep the shake feature enabled in Settings ⇨ Accessibility ⇨ Touch ⇨ Shake to Undo).

You might also see these options:

» **Auto-Correct:** If you happen to select a word with a typo, the iPad might underline that word. If you tap the underlined word, the iPad might show you one or more words it thinks you meant to spell (or you see No Replacements Found). Tap a suggested word to accept it.

» **Predict:** A predictive word feature reveals up to three word or phrase options in buttons just above the keyboard. If one of these words or phrases is what you had in mind, tap the appropriate button.

» **Replace:** The iPad might show you possible replacement words. For example, replacement words for *test* might be *fest, rest,* or *text.* Tap the word to substitute it for the word you originally typed.

» **Indent Right or Left:** Pretty self-explanatory. With this option, you can indent highlighted text to the right or left.

» **Look Up:** Tap your selected word for a definition, courtesy of the *New Oxford American Dictionary,* the *Oxford Dictionary of English,* an Apple dictionary, or a foreign language dictionary if you've downloaded any dictionaries onto your iPad. Look Up goes well beyond definitions and includes searches that extend to the App Store, Apple Music, Twitter, the web, Wikipedia, and more.

Multitasking

Through *multitasking,* you can run two or more apps simultaneously and switch from one app to another. The following examples illustrate what multitasking enables you to do on your iPad:

>> A third-party app, such as Slacker Personal Radio, can continue to play music while you surf the web, peek at pictures, or check email. Without multitasking, Slacker would pause the moment you opened another app.

>> A navigation app can update your position while you're listening to, say, Pandora internet radio. From time to time, the navigation app will pipe in with turn-by-turn directions, lowering the volume of the music so you can hear the instructions.

>> If you're uploading images to a photo website and the process is taking longer than you want, you can switch to another app, confident that the images will continue to upload behind the scenes.

>> You can leave voice notes in the Evernote app while checking out a web page.

Double-press the Home button (if your iPad has one) or swipe up from the bottom of your screen to display App Switcher. You see thumbnail versions of your open apps. Scroll to the left to see more apps. Tap the thumbnail for the app you want to switch to; the app remembers where you left off. If you hold the tablet sideways in landscape mode, as shown in Figure 2-5, the previews for your apps appear sideways, too.

To remove an app from App Switcher, drag the app's thumbnail up and beyond the top of the screen. Poof — it's gone.

Now let's look at some other tricks that make multitasking even more powerful.

FIGURE 2-5: App Switcher shows you the apps you've recently used or are still running.

Splitting the screen

You can exploit all that gorgeous screen real estate on your iPad to make multitasking even more productive.

Split view

For starters, there's a feature called split view, which enables you to display two app windows onscreen at the same time, with each app getting half the screen.

Launch the first app you want to use and then tap the app's multitasking icon: the three dots in the top center of the app window (see Figure 2-6). This displays the multitasking menu, a version of which is pointed out in Figure 2-6. Tap the split view icon, and then tap the icon of other app you want onscreen. Now the second app is running side by side with your first app! Split view mode is shown in Figure 2-6. Drag the gray resizer bar between the two apps to resize them.

The split view feature works with Apple's own apps and some third-party apps. If you don't see the multitasking icon, it means the app doesn't support split view.

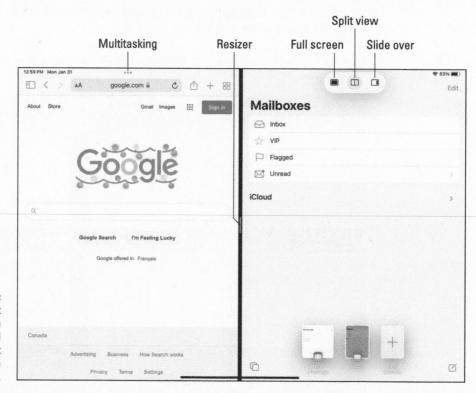

FIGURE 2-6:
iPadOS split view in action with Safari on the left and Mail on the right.

TIP

In Safari, you have two ways to open in split view. The first way is to long-press a link on a web page, which opens several options, including a preview of the link. Tap the Open in Split View command to open the linked page in split view. The second way requires you to have at least two tabs open in the Safari app. You can then drag a tab to the left or right edge of the screen and release, and a new split view is created.

I bet you can think of all sorts of reasons to run two apps at the same time. Maybe you're composing a message to a friend in the Mail app while scrolling through Safari in the smaller panel to find a place to have lunch. Or perhaps you're sketching in one app while using a photo in another as a reference point.

When you're finished with split view, tap the multitasking icon in the app you want to use and then tap the full screen icon.

Slide over

Another way to get two apps to share the screen at the same time is the slide over feature. Instead of running side by side, as in split view, with slide over one app runs full screen and a second app runs in a window that takes up about a third of the screen width. This second window is in slide over mode, which means it runs on top of the full-screen app and can be dragged to the left or right side of the screen, as needed.

To give slide over a whirl, first launch the app that you want to run in slide over mode. Tap the app's multitasking icon (labeled in Figure 2-6) to display the multitasking menu, and then tap the slide over icon (again, see Figure 2-6). iPadOS shrinks the app window and displays the Home screen. Tap the icon of the app that you want to run full screen. This second app opens normally and the slide over app remains onscreen on top of the full-screen app.

When you're finished with slide over, tap the multitasking icon in the slide over app and then tap the full screen icon.

The slide over feature works with Apple's own apps and quite a few third-party apps. If you don't see the multitasking icon, it means the app doesn't support slide over.

Picture-in-picture

There's a good possibility that your television at home has a picture-in-picture feature that enables you to watch one channel in the main portion of the TV screen while checking out a second channel in a small window on the screen. You don't really want to miss any of the action in the big game now, do you?

Your iPad has the same feature. The picture-in-picture feature on the iPad works when you're on a FaceTime video call, watching a video stored on your iPad, or streaming a video from one of the many streaming video services. These topics are reserved for Chapter 8.

 To give picture-in-picture a whirl, start a video and press the Home button (if your iPad has one) or tap the picture-in-picture icon, shown in the margin. The video picture shrinks into a small window hanging out in the upper-left corner of the display.

 You can pause the video or shut it down by tapping the controls that appear in this diminutive video window. (Tap the window if you don't see the controls.) If you want the video to take over the entire iPad screen, tap the restore icon (shown in the margin) inside the video window.

Meanwhile, if the video window is blocking a portion of the screen that you want to see, you can drag it to another space.

Organizing icons into folders

Finding the single app that you want to use among apps spread out over 15 screens may seem like a daunting task. But Apple felt your pain and added a handy organizational tool: folders. The Folders feature lets you create folder icons, each containing apps that pertain to the name that Apple assigned or you gave to that folder.

To create a folder, follow these steps:

1. **Long-press an icon until all the icons on the screen wiggle.**

2. **Decide which apps you want to move to a folder and then drag the icon for the first app on top of the second app.**

   The two apps now share living quarters inside a newly created folder. Apple names the folder according to the category of apps inside the folder.

3. **(Optional) Change the folder name by tapping the X on the bar where the folder name appears and typing a new name.**

To launch an app inside a folder, tap that folder's icon and then tap the icon for the app that you want to open.

When you drag all the apps from a folder, the folder automatically disappears.

Printing

iPadOS's AirPrint feature allows you to print wirelessly from the iPad to an AirPrint-capable printer, available from all major printer manufacturers.

AirPrint works with Mail, Photos, Safari, and Books (PDF files). You can also print from apps in Apple's iWork software suite, as well as third-party apps with built-in printing.

An AirPrint printer doesn't need any special software, but it does have to be connected to the same Wi-Fi network as the iPad.

To print, follow these steps:

1. **Tap the share icon, and then tap the Print command.**

   In the Mail app, open the message you want to print, tap the reply icon in the lower-right corner, and then tap Print.

   The icon is shown in the margin.

2. **In the Print Options dialog that appears, tap Select Printer to select a printer, which the iPad locates in short order.**

3. **Depending on the printer, specify the number of copies you want to print, the number of double-sided copies, and a range of pages to print.**

   You might even see a graphic indicating how much ink is left in the printer.

4. **When you're happy with your settings, tap Print.**

Proactive search

You can search for people and programs across your iPad and in specific apps, using a combination of the search feature and Siri. I show you how to search in apps in the various chapters dedicated to Mail, Contacts, Calendar, and Music.

The search feature can find news and trending topics, local restaurants, movie times, and content in Apple's own iTunes Store, App Store, and Book Store. Moreover, with Siri teaming up with the search feature, you'll also see circled icons representing the contacts you engage with the most, the people you are next scheduled to meet, as well as eateries, shops, and other places of possible interest nearby.

Searches are also proactive, meaning that the device gets to know you over time and makes suggestions accordingly. It attempts to read your mind. The tablet might surface the News app, for example, if it learns that you turn to it every morning (while enjoying your coffee). Or if you're in a particular area, you may see the news that's trending in your location.

Here's how the search feature works:

1. **Swipe down from the center of any Home screen page to access Search.**

   The Search dialog slides into view at the top of the screen.

2. **Tap the Search text box and use the virtual keyboard to enter your search text.**

   The iPad spits out results the moment you type a single character; the list narrows as you type additional characters.

   The results are pretty darn thorough. Say that you entered *Ring* as your search term. Contacts whose last names have *Ring* in them show up, along with friends who might have done a trapeze act in the now defunct Ringling Bros. circus. All the songs on your iPad by Ringo Starr show up too, as do such song titles as "Ring-A-Ling," from the Black-Eyed Peas if that happens to be in your library. The same goes for apps, videos, audiobooks, events, and notes with the word *Ring*. You'll see web and App Store references as well.

3. **Tap any listing to jump to the contact, ditty, or app you seek.**

TIP

At the bottom of the search results list, you see several commands for running your search query in specific apps, such as Contacts, Messages, and Maps.

You can prevent some apps and their content from appearing in the search results by choosing Settings ➪ Siri & Search. In the list of apps, tap an app and then tap the Show App in Search switch to off to prevent the app from appearing in your search results. To also prevent the app's content from appearing in your search results, tap the Show Content in Search switch to off.

Getting to Know the iPad's Virtual Keyboard

As you know by now, instead of a physical keyboard, a virtual keyboard slides up from the bottom of the iPad screen. You have a choice of several English-language or (depending upon what you chose during setup) foreign-language keyboard layouts, including variations on the alphabetical keyboard, the numeric and punctuation keyboard, the more punctuation and symbols keyboard, and the emoji keyboard.

Indeed, the beauty of a software keyboard is that you see only keys pertinent to the task at hand. The keyboards in Safari, for example, differ from the keyboards in Mail. In Mail, you'll see a Return key (and the @ symbol when typing in an address field). The similarly placed key in Safari is labeled Go, as shown in Figure 2-7.

TIP

See the little gray letters and numbers at the top of most keys in Figure 2-7? If you swipe down on one of these keys instead of tapping it, you'll get that second character instead of the main one. Try it!

FIGURE 2-7:
The keys on the Mail (top) and Safari (bottom) keyboards.

Before you consider how to *use* the keyboard, I want to share a bit of the philosophy behind its so-called *intelligence*. Knowing what makes this keyboard smart can help you make it even smarter when you use it. The keyboard

>> Has a built-in English dictionary that includes words from today's popular culture. Apple uses machine learning to quickly identify new trending words, too. Dictionaries in other languages are automatically activated when you use a given international keyboard, as described in the sidebar "A keyboard for all borders," later in this chapter.

>> Adds your contacts to its dictionary automatically.

>> Uses complex analysis algorithms to predict the word you're trying to type.

>> Suggests corrections as you type. It then offers you the suggested word just below the misspelled word. When you decline a suggestion and the word you typed is *not* in the iPad dictionary, the iPad adds that word to its dictionary and offers it as a suggestion if you mistype a similar word in the future.

TIP

If the term you typed is correct, tell your iPad to accept it as-is by tapping the term, which appears in quotation marks to the left of the suggested corrections. This helps train your intelligent keyboard.

>> Reduces the number of mistakes you make as you type by intelligently and dynamically resizing the touch zones for certain keys. The iPad increases the zones for keys it predicts might come next and decreases the zones for keys that are unlikely or impossible to come next. Cool!

A KEYBOARD FOR ALL BORDERS

Apple expanded the iPad's reach globally with international keyboard layouts for dozens of languages. To access a keyboard that isn't customized for Americanized English, tap Settings ➪ General ➪ Keyboard ➪ Keyboards ➪ Add New Keyboard. Then flick through the list to select the keyboard you want to use. Have a multilingual household? You can select as many of these international keyboards as you might need by tapping the language in the list.

When you're in an app that summons a keyboard, long-press the emoji key (the one with a smiley face) or the international key (globe icon) to display a list of keyboards, and then tap the keyboard you want to use.

To remove a keyboard that you've already added to your list, tap the Edit button in the upper-right corner of the Keyboard settings screen displaying your enabled keyboards and then tap the red circle with the white horizontal line that appears next to the language to which you want to say *adios*, and then tap Delete.

Meanwhile, your iPad keyboard is even more fluent with iPadOS. You can now type in two languages at once, without switching keyboards. You can type with any pair of the following languages: English, French, German, Italian, Portuguese, and Spanish. This multilingual typing feature is also supported for English and Chinese.

Anticipating what comes next

The keyboard takes an educated stab at the next word you mean to type and presents what it surmises to be the best possible word choices front and center. Say you're in the Messages app and the last message you received was an invitation to lunch or dinner. Above the row of keys on the iPad keyboard, you'd see buttons with three word suggestions: *Dinner, Lunch,* and *Not sure* (as shown in Figure 2-8). If one of those was the appropriate response, you could tap the button to insert its text into your reply.

If you wanted to respond with something different than the three options presented by Apple, you'd just type your response with the regular QWERTY keys. As you type additional letters and words, the three suggested word choices above the keyboard change in real time. For instance, if you start by typing *That's a* in your message, the new trio of word choice buttons that show up might be *great, good,* and *very.*

To exploit the predictive text feature, make sure the Predictive setting is turned on (as it is by default). Go to Settings ➪ General ➪ Keyboards and slide the Predictive switch to on.

Discovering the special-use keys

The iPad keyboard contains several keys that don't type a character. Here's the scoop on each of these keys:

>> **Caps Lock (iPad Pro only):** If you're using the alphabetical keyboard, press Caps Lock to lock the uppercase letters. This enables you to type a long stretch of uppercase without having to constantly press the Shift key (discussed next).

>> **Shift:** If you're using the alphabetical keyboard, the Shift key switches between uppercase and lowercase letters. You can tap the key to change the case or hold down Shift and slide to the letter you want to be capitalized. If you want to type a run of uppercase characters, double-tap Shift to enable Caps Lock; when you're done, tap Shift to disable Caps Lock.

>> **Keyboard:** Tap the key with the keyboard graphic to hide the keyboard. Alternatively, long-press the keyboard key and then tap Floating to shrink your keyboard to a smaller version that you can then drag. Tap and drag the gray bar at the bottom of the floating keyboard to drag it where you want it; if you drag to the bottom of the screen, you dock the keyboard and expand it to its full size.

>> **.?123:** Tap this key to switch to a keyboard that shows only numbers and symbols. The traditional Shift key is replaced with a key labeled #+=. Pressing that key displays a keyboard with more symbols.

>> **Emoji:** Tap the key with the smiley face and you can punctuate your words by adding smiley faces and other emojis.

>> **Delete:** Tapping this key (otherwise known as the backspace key) erases the character immediately to the left of the cursor.

>> **Return:** This key moves the cursor to the beginning of the next line. You might find this key labeled Go or Search, depending on the app you're using.

>> **Dictation:** Tap the key with the microphone icon and start talking. The iPad listens to what you have to say. You can use this dictation feature in many of the instances in which you can summon the keyboard, including the built-in Notes and Mail apps, as well as many third-party apps. See Chapter 14 for more on dictation. When you're done, tap the key again to tell your iPad to stop listening.

WARNING

When you use dictation, some of the things you say are recorded and sent to Apple, which converts your words into text. Just make sure to proofread what you've said because the process isn't foolproof. Apple also collects other information, including your first name and nickname, the names and nicknames of folks in your contacts list, song names in Music, and more. Apple says it anonymizes this information, which helps the Dictation feature perform its duties. If any of this freaks you out, however, tap Settings ⇨ General ⇨ Keyboard and slide the Enable Dictation switch to off. You can also restrict the use of dictation in Settings, as explained in Chapter 15.

On the top row of the keyboards that pop up in certain apps — Mail and Notes, for instance — tap Aa to find **B**, *I*, U, and S formatting keys. These permit you to bold, italicize, underline, or strikethrough selected text, respectively. Other formatting options, depending on the app you're using, might include paragraph alignment, ordered and unordered lists, font colors, and more.

To the left of the three alternative word suggestions on various keyboards, you'll see icons for undoing or redoing your last steps, plus a third icon that pastes the last selected word or passage that you copied or cut. These icons are visible in the top image in Figure 2-7. You might see different icons depending on the app you're using.

What you see also varies by what you do. For example, after you select text in the Mail app, a scissors icon appears on the top row of the virtual keyboard (see the bottom image in Figure 2-7); when you tap the icon, it cuts the selected text.

Choosing an alternative keyboard

Good as the keyboards that Apple supplies to your iPad are, you can choose an alternative keyboard from a third-party app developer, including SwiftKey, Swype, and Fleksy keyboards. You can fetch new keyboards in the App Store. Some are free; others require a modest sum.

After you've downloaded a keyboard, visit Settings ➪ General ➪ Keyboard ➪ Keyboards ➪ Add New Keyboard and select the keyboard of choice. Then long-press the emoji key (shown in the margin) or the globe key on the iPad's own keyboard and select your new keyboard from the list that appears.

Finger-typing on the virtual keyboards

The virtual keyboards in Apple's multitouch interface might be considered a stroke of genius. Or they might drive you nuts. If you're patient and trusting, in a week or so, you'll get the hang of finger-typing — which is vital to moving forward because you have to rely on a virtual keyboard to tap a text field, enter notes, type the names of new contacts, and so on.

Apple has built intelligence into its virtual keyboard, so it can correct typing mistakes on the fly or provide helpful word choices by predicting what you're about to type next. The keyboard isn't exactly Nostradamus, but it does an excellent job of coming up with the words you have in mind. Apple is also increasingly relying on deep neural network technology to improve accuracy even more.

TIP

As you start typing on the virtual keyboard, I think you'll find the following additional tips helpful:

>> **See what letter you're typing.** As you press your finger against a letter or number on the screen, the individual key you press darkens until you lift your finger, as shown in Figure 2-9. That way, you know that you struck the correct letter or number.

>> **Slide to the correct letter if you tap the wrong one.** No need to worry if you touched the wrong key. You can slide your finger to the correct key because the letter isn't recorded until you release your finger.

>> **Long-press to access special accent marks, alternative punctuation, or URL endings.** Sending a message to an overseas

FIGURE 2-9:
The ABCs of virtual typing.

pal? Keep your finger pressed against a letter, and a panel of keys showing variations on the character for foreign alphabets pops up, as shown in Figure 2-10. This panel lets you add the appropriate accent mark. Just slide your finger until you're pressing the key with the relevant accent mark and then lift your finger.

FIGURE 2-10:
Accenting your letters.

Meanwhile, if you long-press the .? key in Safari, it offers you the choice of .us, .org, .edu, .com, or .net with additional options if you also use international keyboards.

» **Tap the space bar to accept a suggested word, or tap the typed word (the one in quotation marks) to decline the suggestion.** Alas, mistakes are common at first. Say that you meant to type a sentence in the Mail app that reads, "I'm writing to you about an important . . ." But because of the way your fingers struck the virtual keys, you actually entered "I'm writing to you about an *impirtant* . . ." Fortunately, Apple knows that the *o* you meant to press is next to the *i* that showed up on the keyboard, just as *t* and *y* and *e* and *r* are side by side. (Note that the suspect word is highlighted.) So, the software determines that *important* was indeed the word you had in mind and, as Figure 2-11 reveals, places it front and center above the keyboard. To accept the suggested word, either tap the space bar or the suggested word. And if for some reason you actually did mean to type *impirtant* or maybe Apple's other suggestion, *importantly,* tap that instead.

If you don't appreciate these features, turn off Auto-Correction and Predictive in Settings. See Chapter 15 for details.

FIGURE 2-11:
Fixing an *important* mistake.

Because Apple knows what you're up to, the virtual keyboard is fine-tuned for the task at hand, especially when you need to enter numbers, punctuation, or symbols. The following tips help you find common special characters or special keys that I know you'll want to use:

» **Putting the @ in an email address:** If you're composing an email message (see Chapter 5), a dedicated @ key pops up on the main Mail keyboard when you're in the To field choosing whom to send a message to. That key disappears when you tap the body of the message to compose your words. You can still get to the @ by tapping the .?123 key.

» **Switching from letters to numbers:** When you're typing notes or sending email and want to type a number, symbol, or punctuation mark, tap the .?123 key to bring up an alternative virtual keyboard. Tap the ABC key to return to the first keyboard. This toggle isn't hard to get used to, but some may find it irritating. Meanwhile, after tapping the .?123 key, the Shift key shifts to a #+= key. Tap #+= to summon additional character and symbol keys.

» **Adding apostrophes and other punctuation shortcuts:** If you long-press the exclamation mark/comma key, a pop-up offers the apostrophe. If you long-press the question mark/period key, you'll see the option to type quotation marks.

If you buy any current iPad Pro model or the 10.2-inch iPad, you might want to consider purchasing one of the optional Smart Keyboard covers. Ranging from $159 to $199, these accessories are pricey, but you just might be tempted to go with a physical keyboard. You may be tempted also by the Apple Pencil (first generation costs $99 and second generation is $129). For more on iPad accessories, let me direct you to Chapter 16.

I already mentioned that iPads don't *need* a stylus, but sometimes you might want to use one anyway. If the Apple Pencil is too pricey for you, check out some of the many third-party options. Wacom sells various Bamboo Stylus models, starting around $15. It's a potentially useful tool for those with too broad, oily, or greasy fingers, or those who sketch, draw, or jot notes. You can find lower-priced styluses as well.

Editing mistakes

I think typing with abandon, without getting hung up over mistyped characters, is a good idea. The self-correcting keyboard can fix many errors (and occasionally introduce errors of its own). That said, plenty of typos are likely to turn up, especially in the beginning, and you have to correct them manually.

TIP

A neat trick for doing so is to hold your finger on the line of text you want to edit. A cursor will appear, and you can then slide your finger to the spot to the right of where you need to make the correction. An even neater trick is to tap and hold down on the space bar, which effectively turns the entire keyboard into a virtual trackpad. You can then slide you finger not only left and right but also up and down to the spot to the right of where the correction is needed. Either way, you then use the Delete key (also called the Backspace key) to delete the error and tap whatever keys you need to type the correct text.

And with that, you are hereby notified that you've survived basic training. The real fun is about to begin.

IN THIS CHAPTER

» Getting your head around iCloud

» Synchronizing contacts, calendars, bookmarks, and more

» Synchronizing music, videos, photos, and more

» Synchronizing manually

Chapter **3**

Synchronicity: Getting Stuff to and from Your iPad

have good news and . . . more good news. The good news is you can easily set up your iPad so your contacts, appointments, reminders, events, mail settings, bookmarks, books, music, movies, TV shows, podcasts, and photos are synchronized between your computer and your iPad (or other iDevices). And the more good news is that after you set up your iPad, your contacts, appointments, events, and everything else just mentioned can be kept up to date automatically on all of those devices.

This communication between your iPad and computer is called *syncing* (short for *synchronizing*). Don't worry: It's easy, and I walk you through the entire process in this chapter.

Another form of syncing is moving files to and from your iPad and other iDevices or to and from a Mac or PC. You can do so via iTunes with macOS Mojave and earlier and Windows, or you can do it using Finder in macOS Catalina and later. You can also wirelessly transfer files via AirDrop!

In this chapter, you find out how to sync all the digital data your iPad can handle, right after a short interlude about Apple's iCloud service.

TIP

The information in this chapter is based on iTunes version 12.9, Finder in macOS Monterey 12.1, and iPadOS version 15.1, the latest and greatest when these words were written. If your screens don't look exactly like mine, you probably need to upgrade to iTunes 12.9 or higher (PCs and Macs using macOS Mojave or earlier) or macOS 12.1 or higher (Macs using macOS Monterey or later).

A Brief iCloud Primer

Apple's iCloud is a complete online data synchronization and wireless storage service. In a nutshell, iCloud stores and manages your digital stuff — music, photos, contacts, events, and more — and makes it available over the internet to all your computers and iDevices automatically.

iCloud pushes information such as email, calendars, contacts, reminders, and bookmarks to and from your computer and to and from your iPad and other iDevices, and then keeps those items updated on all devices without any effort on your part. iCloud also includes nonsynchronizing options, such as Photo Stream and iCloud photo sharing (see Chapter 9) and email (see Chapter 5).

Your free iCloud account includes 5GB of storage, which is all many users will need. If you have several devices (including Macs and PCs) or like saving data in the cloud, you'll probably need more storage; 50GB, 200GB, and 2TB upgrades are available for $0.99, $2.99, and $9.99 (all prices in US dollars) a month, respectively.

A nice touch is that music, apps, periodicals, movies, and TV shows purchased from the iTunes Store, as well as your photo stream and iTunes Match content (see Chapter 7), don't count against your 5GB of free storage. E-books don't count against your 5GB either, but audiobooks do. You'll find that the things that do count — such as mail, documents, account information, settings, and other app data — don't use much space, so 5GB might last a long time.

Conversely, if you use iCloud Photos and take a lot of photos and videos with your iDevice cameras, you're going to fill up your free 5GB pretty fast.

REMEMBER

If you're not using iCloud Photos (lovingly described in Chapter 9), you might want to sync your iPad photos with a computer every so often and then delete the photos from the iPad. Otherwise, over time, those photos will take up a lot of space and eventually fill up your iPad.

If you plan to go PC-free, as described in Chapter 2, but still want to have your email, calendars, contacts, and bookmarks automatically synchronized between your computers and other iDevices (and believe me, you do), here's how to enable iCloud syncing on your iPad:

1. **On your Home screen, tap Settings.**

2. **At the top of the Settings list, tap your name.**

3. **Tap iCloud.**

   The iCloud screen appears, displaying a list of apps.

4. **Tap an app's switch on or off to enable or disable iCloud sync.**

   Your choices are Mail, Contacts, Calendars, Reminders, Notes, Safari (Bookmarks), and several other apps with on/off switches.

In the same list are several items that don't have switches, including Photos, iCloud Backup, and Keychain. Tap any of these three items to reveal more controls and options:

>> **Photos:** Enable or disable three iCloud services — iCloud Photos, My Photo Stream, and Shared Albums — with the by-now familiar on/off switches. See Chapter 9 for details.

>> **iCloud Backup:** Enable or disable this service, which backs up your iPad's photo library, accounts, documents, and settings whenever your iPad is plugged in to power, locked, and connected to Wi-Fi. Tap the Back Up Now button to initiate a backup, well, now.

>> **Keychain:** Enable Apple's Keychain password service. Keychain keeps passwords and credit card information you save up to date on all devices you approve. The info is encrypted and can't be read by Apple (or, I hope, by anyone else).

TIP

Tap Manage Storage (near the top of the iCloud screen) to open the iCloud Storage screen and manage iCloud storage or upgrade your storage plan. Tap Share with Family — or Family Usage, if you've already set up Family Sharing (both are near the top of the iCloud Storage screen) — to add or remove family members and shared payment methods from your Family Sharing plan (which you read more about in Chapter 15).

You find out much more about iCloud in the rest of this chapter and several other chapters, so let's move on to syncing your iPad.

Getting in Sync

You can sync your calendars, reminders, bookmarks, and other data and documents among your iDevices and computers via iCloud, iTunes (macOS Mojave or earlier and Windows), Finder (macOS Catalina or later), or a combination of the three.

WARNING

While I'm talking about syncing, it's important to remember that although you can back up your iPad to iCloud, you'll need to sync it with a Mac or PC to have a local backup, too. I strongly believe that a single backup is never enough. The best practice is to maintain at least two different backups: one in iCloud and another stored locally on your Mac or PC.

Sync prep 101

Synchronizing your iPad with your computer isn't difficult, as the following steps show:

1. **Start by connecting your iPad to your computer with the Lightning-to-USB or USB-C cable that came with your iPad.**

2. **If this is the first time you've introduced your iPad to iTunes or Finder:**

    a. *When an alert on your Mac or PC asks "Do you want to allow this computer to access information on this iPad?" click Continue.*

    b. *On your iPad screen, when you see an alert asking, "Trust this computer?" tap Trust. Enter your passcode if requested, put down the iPad, and go back to iTunes or Finder on your computer.*

    When you connect your iPad to your computer, iTunes (or Finder in macOS Catalina or later) should launch automatically. For Windows or macOS Mojave and earlier, if iTunes doesn't launch automatically, try launching it manually. In macOS Catalina or later, click Finder to open a Finder window.

3. **If you see an alert on your Mac or PC asking whether you want iTunes to open automatically when you connect this iPad, click Yes or No, depending on your preference.**

    You can change this setting later, so don't give it too much thought.

4. **Click the iPad icon, shown in the margin and near the top left of the iTunes window or in the left sidebar of a Finder window. If you see a message asking whether to trust this iPad, click Trust.**

If you don't see the iPad icon and you're positive it's connected to a USB port *on your computer* (not the keyboard, monitor, or hub), try restarting your computer.

If you're using a Mac running macOS Catalina or later, skip to Step 8.

5. **For Windows PCs and Macs running macOS Mojave or earlier, if you use more than one iDevice with this computer, select your iPad in the drop-down list of all your devices that appears when you click the iPad icon.**

   The Welcome to Your New iPad screen appears.

6. **Click Set Up as New iPad or select a backup from the Restore from This Backup drop-down menu, and then click Continue.**

   See Chapter 17 for the scoop on restoring from iCloud or iTunes backups. For this example, I clicked Set Up as New iPad.

   The Sync with iTunes screen appears.

7. **Click the Get Started button.**

   The iPad screen appears.

8. **If you're not using iTunes, click the General tab, as shown in Figure 3-1. If you're using iTunes, click the Summary pane.**

   This takes you to some useful basic options, which I get into next.

On the General tab, you can set any options you want from the Options area:

>> **Prefer Standard Definition Videos:** If you want high-definition videos you import to be automatically converted into smaller standard-definition video files when you transfer them to your iPad, select this check box.

Standard-definition video files are significantly smaller than high-definition video files. You'll likely notice the poorer quality when you watch the video on your iPad, but you can have more video files on your iPad because they take up less space.

The conversion from HD to standard definition takes a *long* time, so be prepared for very long sync times when you sync new HD video and have this option selected.

If you plan to use Apple's digital AV adapter (choose the Lightning or USB-C version, as appropriate) or Apple TV (starting at $149) to display movies on an HDTV, consider going with high definition. Although the files will be bigger and your iPad will hold fewer videos, the HD versions look spectacular on a big-screen TV.

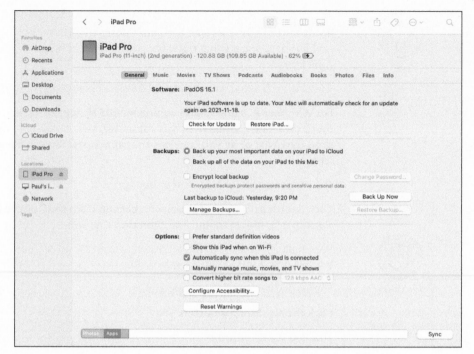

FIGURE 3-1:
The General
tab for a
connected
iPad Pro.

>> **Show This iPad When on Wi-Fi:** If you want to see your iPad in Finder when both your Mac and iPad are on the same Wi-Fi network, select this check box.

>> **Automatically sync when this iPad is connected:** Select this option if you want your iPad to sync every time you connect it to your Mac or PC. If you don't select this option, your iPad will be synced only when you back up or when you manually sync.

>> **Manually Manage Music, Movies, and TV Shows:** To turn off automatic syncing in the Music, Movies, and TV Shows tabs, select this check box.

>> **Convert Higher Bit Rate Songs to 128/192/256 Kbps AAC:** If you want songs with bit rates higher than 128, 192, or 256 Kbps converted into smaller AAC files when you transfer them to your iPad, select this check box and choose the lower bit rate from the drop-down menu.

A *higher* bit rate means the song will have better sound quality but use more storage space. Songs you buy in the iTunes Store or on Amazon, for example, have bit rates of around 256 Kbps. So a four-minute song with a 256-Kbps bit rate is around 8MB; convert it to 128-Kbps AAC, and it's roughly half that size (that is, around 4MB) while sounding almost as good.

Everyone's hearing is different: Some people can't tell the difference between higher and lower bit rate music, while others think listening to lower bit rate files is little better than fingernails down a chalkboard! Song file size has become less important as iPad storage has increased and more people listen to music through streaming services. (See Chapter 7 for more on Apple Music.) If you're picky about your music quality, don't convert it. If you aren't picky and are concerned about storage on your iPad, convert it.

Backing up your iPad

With your iPad connected to your computer, you can use Finder or iTunes to decide how you want your iPad backed up:

>> **Back Up Your Most Important Data on Your iPad to iCloud:** This is the default setting and it means that iPadOS automatically backs up all data, settings, your Home screen configuration, text messages, and purchase history. This backup doesn't include your purchased content. Note that in iTunes, this option is named iCloud.

>> **Back Up All of the Data on Your iPad to This Mac:** Select this option to perform a full backup of your iPad to your computer. Note that in iTunes, this option is named This Computer.

If anything goes wonky, or you get a new iPad, you can restore most (if not all) of your settings and files that aren't synced with iCloud or your computer. Or, if you've backed up an iPhone, an iPod touch, or another iPad, you can restore the new iPad from the older device's backup.

Regardless of whether you back up locally or to iCloud, you should encrypt your backups. Unless you enable encryption, important data such as website and Wi-Fi passwords won't be backed up. Because backups to iCloud are encrypted by default with the Apple ID password associated with the account, you don't have to do anything else if you choose iCloud backups. But if you back up to your computer, encryption is turned off by default. So, select the Encrypt Local Backup check box (refer to Figure 3-1) and type a password (and don't forget it), and you'll never have to think about it again.

TIP

One last thing: Many users maintain both types of backup — iCloud and computer — and that's what I strongly recommend. To do so, first click Back Up Now to perform a backup to iCloud. When the backup is complete, select the Back Up All of the Data on Your iPad to This Mac option (or the This Computer option in iTunes) and click the Back Up Now button. You now have a backup on your hard drive and a second backup in iCloud. Although your iCloud backups use some of your iCloud space, redundancy in backups is a good thing.

Disconnecting the iPad

If your iPad is connected and syncing, you'll see the syncing icon next to the device (as shown in Figure 3-2). At the same time, a message appears at the top of the iTunes window to inform you that your iPad is syncing, as shown at the top of Figure 3-2.

Syncing icon   Click to cancel sync

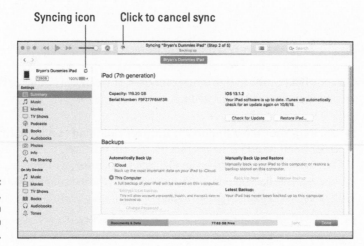

FIGURE 3-2:
During a sync, the eject icon turns into a syncing icon.

 When your iPad is connected and not syncing, you'll see the eject icon (shown in the margin) to the right of its name rather than the syncing icon.

When the sync is finished, the syncing icon in Figure 3-2 stops spinning and morphs back into an eject icon, and the message at the top of the window disappears.

WARNING If you disconnect your iPad before the sync finishes, all or part of the sync may fail. Although early termination of a sync isn't usually a problem, it's safer to cancel the sync and let it finish gracefully than to yank the cable out while a sync is in progress. So just don't do that, okay?

To cancel a sync properly and disconnect your iPad *safely* from your Mac or PC, first hover your cursor over the animated syncing icon in the left column in iTunes (see Figure 3-2) or Finder until it becomes an x-in-a-circle. Then click the x-in-a-circle and the sync will stop.

Synchronizing Your Data

Your next order of business is to tell iTunes what data you want to synchronize between your iPad and your computer.

To get started, first select your iPad by clicking the iPad icon (or the devices drop-down menu, if you have more than one iDevice) near the top left of the iTunes window. Then click the Info tab, which is the last tab in the Settings list on the left.

If you're using iCloud to sync contacts, calendars, bookmarks, or notes, you won't be able to enable these items in iTunes. Turn off iCloud syncing on your iPad (choose Settings ⇨ iCloud) for items you want to sync with your Mac or PC.

The Info pane has three sections: Sync Contacts, Sync Calendars, and Advanced, which you look at one by one. One last thing: To use your iPad with a Google or Yahoo! account, you must sign in with the appropriate account on your iPad, as described in Chapter 5. After you've added the account to your iPad, you can enable contact or calendar syncing with it in the Settings app under Mail, Contacts, and Calendars.

Contacts

In Figure 3-3, note that the section is named Sync Contacts because this image was captured on a Mac. Contacts is the Mac application that syncs with your iPad's Contacts app.

If you use a PC, you see a drop-down list that gives you the choices of Outlook, Google Contacts, Windows Address Book, or Yahoo! Address Book. Don't worry — the process works the same on either platform.

FIGURE 3-3:
Want to synchronize your contacts? This is where you set up things.

The iPad syncs with the following address book programs:

>> **Mac:** Contacts and other address books that sync with Contacts, such as Microsoft Outlook

>> **PC:** Windows Contacts (Vista, Windows 7 or later), Windows Address Book (XP), Microsoft Outlook, and Microsoft Outlook Express

>> **Mac and PC:** Yahoo! Address Book and Google Contacts

You can sync contacts with multiple apps.

The Sync Contacts section has the following options:

>> **All Groups:** One method is to synchronize all your contacts by selecting this option. This will synchronize every contact in your Mac or PC address book with your iPad's Contacts app. In iTunes, the option is All Contacts, as shown in Figure 3-3.

>> **Selected Groups:** You can synchronize any or all groups of contacts you've created in your computer's address book program. Select the Selected Groups option and then select the appropriate check boxes in the Selected Groups list, and only those groups will be synchronized.

>> **Add Contacts Created Outside of Groups on This iPad To (iTunes on macOS Mojave or earlier or Windows) or Add New Contacts from This iPad To (macOS Catalina or later):** Enable this option and you can choose a group from the pop-up menu. New contacts created on this iPad will belong to the group you select.

WARNING

If you sync with your employer's Microsoft Exchange calendar and contacts, all personal contacts and calendars already on your iPad might be wiped out.

Calendars

The Sync Calendars section of the Info pane determines how synchronization is handled for your appointments, events, and reminders. You can synchronize all your calendars, as shown in Figure 3-4. Or you can synchronize any or all individual calendars you've created in your computer's calendar program. Just select the appropriate check boxes.

FIGURE 3-4:
Set up sync for your calendar events here.

The iPad syncs with the following calendar programs:

>> **Mac:** Calendar

>> **PC:** Microsoft Exchange and Outlook 2003, 2007, 2010, and later

>> **Mac and PC:** Google Calendar and Yahoo! Calendar

Advanced syncing

Every so often, the contacts and calendars on your iPad get so messed up that the easiest way to fix things is to erase that information from your iPad and replace it with information from your computer.

If that's the case, go to the Advanced section of the Info pane and click to select the Contacts or Calendars check box (or both). (In Finder, the check boxes are Replace Contacts and Replace Calendars.) Then, the next time you sync, that information on your iPad will be replaced with the contacts or calendars from your computer.

REMEMBER

Because the Advanced section is at the bottom of the Info pane and you have to scroll down to see it, you can easily forget that the Advanced section is there.

Synchronizing Your Media

If you chose to let iTunes manage synchronizing your data automatically, welcome. This section looks at how you get your media — your music, podcasts, videos, and photos — from your computer to your iPad.

REMEMBER

Podcasts and videos from your computer are synced only one way: from your computer to your iPad. If you delete a podcast or a video that got onto your iPad via syncing, the podcast or video will not be deleted from your computer when you sync.

That said, if you buy or download any of the following items from the iTunes Store, Book Store, or App Store *on your iPad,* the item *will* be copied back to your computer automatically when you sync:

>> Songs

>> Podcasts

>> Videos

>> E-books and audiobooks from the Book Store

>> Playlists you created on your iPad

And if you save pictures from email messages, the iPad camera, web pages, or screen shots, these too can be synced.

You use the Music, Movies, TV Shows, and Photos panes to specify the media you want to copy from your computer to your iPad. The following sections explain the options you find in each pane.

To view any of these panes, make sure your iPad is still selected and then click the appropriate tab in the Settings list on the left (iTunes) or across the top of the screen (Finder).

The following sections focus only on syncing. If you need help acquiring apps, music, movies, podcasts, or anything else for your iPad, just flip to the most applicable chapter for help.

Music, music videos, and voice memos

To transfer music to your iPad, select the Sync Music check box in the Music pane. You can then select the option for Entire Music Library or Selected Playlists, Artists, Albums, and Genres. If you choose the latter, select the check boxes next to particular playlists, artists, albums, and genres you want to transfer. You also can choose to include music videos or voice memos or both by selecting the appropriate check boxes near the top of the pane (see Figure 3-5).

FIGURE 3-5: Use the Music pane to copy music, music videos, and voice memos from your computer to your iPad.

WARNING

If you choose Entire Music Library and have more songs in your iTunes library than storage space on your iPad, the sync will fail and the capacity bar at the bottom of the screen will display your overage.

HOW MUCH SPACE DID I USE?

If you're interested in knowing how much free space is available on your iPad, look near the bottom of the iTunes window while your iPad is connected. You'll see a chart that shows the contents of your iPad, color-coded for your convenience. As you can see in the figure, this iPad has 77.67GB of free space. Hover your cursor over any color to see a bubble with info on that category, as shown for Documents & Data in the figure.

You can find similar information about space used and space remaining on your iPad by tapping Settings ⇨ General ⇨ iPad Storage. You can also see how much storage each of your apps is using.

WARNING

Music, podcasts, and videos are notorious for using massive amounts of storage space on your iPad. If you try to sync too much media content, you see lots of error messages. Forewarned is forearmed. One solution is to create one or more iPad-specific playlists and sync only those. You might also listen to podcasts with the Podcasts app, which can stream episodes (in addition to letting you download them). Streamed episodes don't take up storage on your iPad!

Finally, if you select the Automatically Fill Free Space with Songs check box, iTunes fills any free space on your iPad with music. I strongly recommend against choosing this option because you can easily run out of space for pictures and videos you shoot or documents you save (to name just a few of the possible consequences of filling your iPad with songs outside your control).

Movies

To transfer movies to your iPad, select the Movies pane in the sidebar on the left (macOS Mojave or earlier or Windows) or select your iPad in the Finder sidebar (macOS Catalina or later), and then click Movies. Next, select the Sync Movies check box and then, from the pop-up menu, choose an option for movies you want to include automatically. In Figure 3-6, I am choosing to automatically include all movies using iTunes. If you choose an option other than All, you can optionally select individual movies and playlists by selecting the boxes in appropriate sections.

FIGURE 3-6:
Your choices
in the
Movies pane
determine
which movies
are copied to
your iPad.

TV shows

The procedure for syncing TV shows is almost the same as the one for syncing movies. First, select the Sync TV Shows check box to enable TV show syncing. Then select the Automatically Include check box. Next, choose how many episodes to include from the pop-up menu and whether you want all shows or only selected shows from the second pop-up menu. If you want to also include individual episodes or episodes on playlists, select the appropriate check boxes in the Shows, Episodes, and Include Episodes from Playlists sections of the TV Shows pane.

Podcasts

To transfer podcasts to your iPad, select the Sync Podcasts check box in the Podcasts pane. Then you can automatically include however many podcasts you want by making selections from the two pop-up menus, the same way you did for TV Shows.

Books and Audiobooks

By now I'm sure you know the drill: You can sync all your e-books and audiobooks as well as just sync selected titles by choosing the appropriate buttons and check boxes in the Books and Audiobooks panes. I talk more about the Books app in Chapter 7.

Photos

To sync photos between computers and iDevices via iCloud, you must enable iCloud Photos (formerly known as iCloud Photo Library).

You can also *copy* photos to your iPad from the Photos app (Mac only) or any folder on your computer that contains images (Mac or PC).

Syncing via iCloud

To enable iCloud Photos, choose one of the following:

» **On your iPad:** Choose Settings ➪ *yourname* ➪ iCloud ➪ Photos, and then turn on iCloud Photos.

» **On your Mac:** Choose System Preferences ➪ Apple ID, and then select the check box for Photos.

» **On your PC:** Download and launch iCloud for Windows. Click Options (next to Photos), select iCloud Photos, click Done, and then click Apply. Now enable iCloud Photos on all your Apple devices.

Syncing via your Mac or PC

Connect your iPad to your computer and return to iTunes (Windows PC or macOS Mojave or earlier) or Finder (macOS Catalina and later). Select the Photos tab, and then select the Sync Photos check box and the Automatically Include check box. Next, choose an application or folder from the pop-up menu.

If you choose an application that supports photo albums (such as Photoshop Elements, Aperture, or Photos), projects (Aperture), events (Photos), facial rec-ognition and places (Aperture or Photos), or any combination thereof, you can automatically include recent projects, events, or faces by making a selection from the same pop-up menu.

Note that although Photoshop Elements includes features called Places and Faces, those features are not supported by your iPad.

TIP

You can also type a word or phrase in the Search field (an oval with a magnifying glass) to search for a specific event or events.

If you choose a folder full of images, you can create subfolders inside it that will appear as albums on your iPad.

If you've taken any photos with your iPad or saved images from a web page, an email, an MMS message, or an iMessage since the last time you synced, the appropriate program launches (or the appropriate folder is selected) when you connect your iPad, and you have the option of uploading the pictures on your iPad to your computer.

Manual Syncing

This chapter has focused on automatic syncing thus far. Automatic syncing is great; it selects items to sync based on criteria you've specified, such as genre, artist, playlist, and album. But it's not efficient for transferring a few items — songs, movies, podcasts, or other files — to your iPad.

The solution? Manual syncing. With automatic syncing, iTunes updates your iPad automatically to match your criteria. With manual syncing, you merely drag individual items to your iPad.

Automatic and manual sync aren't mutually exclusive. If you've set up automatic syncing, you can still sync individual items manually.

You can manually sync music, movies, TV shows, and podcasts, but not photos and info such as contacts, calendars, and bookmarks.

Want to see which songs, movies, TV shows, and other media are already on your device? iTunes users can use the On My Device section in the sidebar (if the sidebar isn't displayed, choose View ⇨ Show Sidebar). macOS Catalina or later users should select their iPad in the sidebar, and then click the Files tab.

To configure your iPad for manual syncing:

1. **Connect your iPad to your computer via USB-to-Lightning, USB-C, or Wi-Fi.**

   If iTunes doesn't open automatically, open it manually.

2. **iTunes users should click the iPad icon to the right of the media kind drop-down menu. Finder users should click their iPad in the sidebar.**

   If you have more than one iDevice, the iPad icon becomes a drop-down menu listing all your connected iDevices. Click the icon to display the menu with your devices, and then select the device you want.

   In Finder, you see all connected iOS and iPadOS devices in the sidebar of all windows.

   If you're happy with automatic syncing and just want to get some audio or video from your computer to your iPad, feel free to skip Step 3.

3. **(Optional) If you're using iTunes, click the Summary tab and, in the Options section, select Manually Manage Music and Videos. If you're using Finder, click the General tab and, in the Options section, select Manually Manage Music, Movies, and TV Shows.**

   This step disables automatic syncing for music and videos.

TIP

You can wirelessly transfer a file, photo, movie, and anything you can share from your iPad to another Apple device by using AirDrop — and vice versa! Both devices must be on the same Wi-Fi network, nearby, unlocked, and the destination device much be set to allow AirDrop file transfers (go to Settings ⇨ General ⇨ AirDrop). To transfer a file using AirDrop, tap the share icon for a file and then the AirDrop icon that appears on the Sharing pane. Nearby, unlocked devices on the same Wi-Fi network will appear. Choose which device to send the file to and wait until the AirDrop pane says Sent. This method is great for getting a small number of files to and from your iPad quickly.

That's pretty much all you need to know to sync files automatically or manually. And if you haven't figured out how to watch movies or listen to audio on your iPad yet, it's only because you haven't read Part 3 on multimedia, where watching and listening to your iPad are made crystal clear.

2
The Internet iPad

Explore Safari, the best web browser to ever to grace a handheld device.

Set up email accounts and send and receive email messages and attachments.

Discover the amazing world of iMessage and the Messages app.

Chapter **4**

Exploring the Web with Safari

Recent years have seen the rise of a new pastime: *couch surfing*. This term refers to exploring the seemingly infinite realm of the web from the comfy and cozy confines of your couch. Sure, you might have a decent-sized screen connected to your desktop computer, but that means meandering from one site to another while sitting at your desk. Ugh. That plush sofa is much more inviting, but what device is best? Is it a laptop? Perhaps, but they can get awfully hot and lead to the ickily-named *toasted skin syndrome* (a skin rash caused by lengthy exposure to a heat source, such as laptop balanced on the thighs for an extended period). Your iPhone? Not bad, but even the most humungous iPhone screen is often too small to display many websites.

No, if you want a couch-surfing session that's both safe and satisfying, the clear winner here is your iPad. With its generous screen size, light weight, and never-hotter-than-warm temperature, it just might be the ideal web device. In this chapter, you discover the pleasures — and the few drawbacks — of navigating cyberspace on your iPad.

Introducing the Safari Web Browser

The app of choice when it comes to navigating the web on your iPad is the Safari web browser. Safari comes with every bell and every whistle you'll need to get around the web as well as a few you probably didn't know you needed.

Exploring the browser

You start your cyberexpedition with a quick tour of the Safari browser. To get Safari onscreen, tap the Safari icon (the compass) in the dock. The screen you see will look similar to the one shown in Figure 4-1, which points out the major features. Not all browser controls found on a Mac or a PC are present, but Safari on the iPad still has a familiar look and feel. I describe these controls and others throughout this chapter.

Blasting off into cyberspace

Most of the time, your web adventures begin with a web address, which you type in the Smart Search field (labeled in Figure 4-1). Why is it smart? Because you can use it to enter not only web search text but also web addresses.

TIP

When you tap inside the Smart Search field, your iPad parks its virtual keyboard at the bottom of the screen. When you're entering an address in the Smart Search field, here are a few tips for using the keyboard in Safari (see Chapter 2 for more help with using the virtual keyboard):

Safari sidebar

Previous page

Next page

Website settings

Smart Search field

Tabs

Add tab

Share

Reload

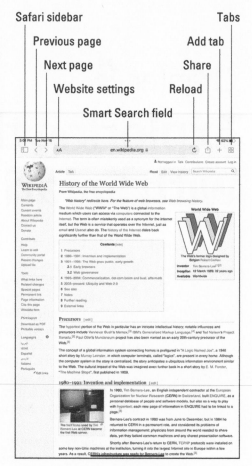

FIGURE 4-1:
The iPad's Safari browser.

» Almost all website addresses these days begin with the characters *https://*. Safari knows this and will add these to the start of the address automatically, so you don't need to type them.

» You usually don't need to type **www** to start a web address. For example, if you want to visit www.theonion.com, for example, typing **theonion.com** is sufficient to transport you to the humor site. However, some sites (thankfully, very few) work only if the address includes *www*, so if your site fails to load, try adding **www.** to the address.

» As you type, Safari displays a list of web addresses that match what you've entered so far. For example, when I typed *new* (as shown in Figure 4-2), I saw web listings for The New Yorker (newyorker.com) and CBC News (cbc.ca/news). You'll likely see other sites, but the point is that if you see the site you want, you can stop typing and just tap the site in the menu to go there directly.

» Many web addresses end with one of the following suffixes: .us, .edu, .com, .net, or .org. Instead of typing one of these suffixes manually, long-press the .? key. iPadOS displays a menu that includes these five suffixes. Slide your finger up to the suffix you need and then release your finger to add the suffix to the Smart Search field. Some options appear only if you've selected an international keyboard (as discussed in Chapter 2).

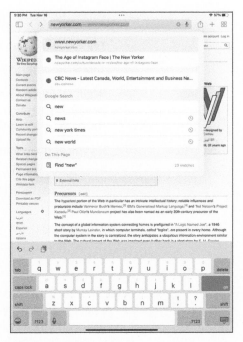

FIGURE 4-2:
Safari displays web pages that match what you've typed so far.

TIP

While you're entering a web address in the Smart Search field, the iPad uses three resources to determine which websites to suggest:

» **Bookmarks:** The iPad suggests websites you've bookmarked in Safari (or synchronized from your other devices, as described in Chapter 3). More on bookmarks later in this chapter.

>> **History:** The iPad suggests sites from the history list — those cyberdestinations where you recently hung your hat, including websites you've visited on your other Apple devices. Because history repeats itself, I tackle that topic later in this chapter.

>> **Smart Search field:** When you type an address in the Smart Search field, you see icons for sites you frequent most often. You can tap any of those icons to jump immediately to the associated site.

So, here are the steps to follow to open a web page by entering its address:

1. **Tap the Safari icon docked at the bottom of the Home screen.**

2. **Tap in the Smart Search field (refer to Figure 4-1).**

3. **Begin typing the web address, or _URL_ (which is short for _uniform resource locator_, if you must know), on the virtual keyboard that slides up from the bottom of the screen.**

4. **Do one of the following:**

    -   *To accept one of the bookmarked (or other) sites that show up in the list, tap the name.* Safari automatically fills in the URL in the Smart Search field and takes you where you want to go.

    -   *Keep tapping the required keyboard characters until you enter the complete web address for the page you have in mind, and then tap the Go key on the right side of the keyboard.*

TECHNICAL
STUFF

Safari in iPadOS is a desktop browser first — even more so than it was when iPad ran Apple's iOS. When you pull up a website on your iPad, it no longer defaults to the mobile version, because Apple takes steps behind the scenes to make sure your iPad is requesting the full desktop version of every website.

TIP

You can still pull up the mobile version of a website, though I can't imagine why you'd want to. Tap the ᴀA icon in the Smart Search field and then tap Request Mobile Website in the menu that appears. This action affects only the current site. To return to the desktop version, tap the ᴀA icon in the Smart Search field and then tap Request Desktop Website in the menu.

Zooming in and out of a page

Most web pages are easily read on your iPad, but every now and then you come across a page where the type or images or both are too small to decipher. No problem: You can zoom in on the page to read and see the page content without ruining your eyesight.

Here are the techniques you can use:

» **Rotate the iPad to its side.** This action reorients your tablet from portrait view to a widescreen landscape view. That wider screen often results in in an increased size of the screen content, which might get the job done for you.

» **Increase the text size.** Tap the ᴀA icon in the Smart Search field and then tap the A button to the right of the percentage value. As you tap, Safari increases the web page text, first to 115%, then 125%, and so on. Figure 4-3 shows a page with the text size set to 175%.

» **Zoom the entire page.** Placing two fingers (usually your thumb and either your index finger or middle finger) on the screen and then spreading them apart zooms in on the page and makes the page's content bigger. Not all the content will fit on the screen, so you'll need to flick left and right and up and down to see more of the page. When you're done, you zoom back out to normal size by placing two fingers on the screen and pinching them together.

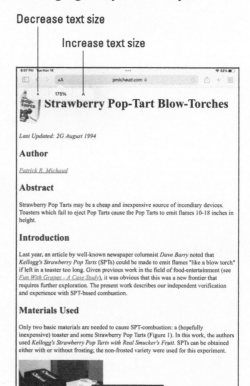

FIGURE 4-3:
Set the text percentage to a value that makes the web page readable.

Reading clutter-free web pages with reader view

It's all too easy to get distracted reading web pages, what with ads, videos, and other clutter surrounding the stuff you want to take in. Reader view (shown in Figure 4-4, right) can remove most of those distractions, but you need to activate it first.

When you first pull up a new web page that has reader view available, the Smart Search field briefly displays *Reader Available*. To activate reader view, tap the Smart Search field's ᴀA icon and then tap Show Reader. If Show Reader appears dimmed, reader view is not available on this page.

FIGURE 4-4:
Reducing
web page
clutter thanks
to reader view.

Finding Your Way around the Web

In this section, I discuss ways to navigate the web on your iPad by using links and tabs.

Looking at links

Because Safari functions on the iPad in the same way browsers work on your Mac or PC, text links that transport you from one site to another typically are under-lined, are shown in blue, red, or bold type, or appear as images or items in a list. Tap the link to go directly to the site or page.

Other types of links lead to different outcomes:

>> **Map location link:** Tap a real-world address and the iPad usually launches the Maps app and displays the location.

>> **Email address link:** Tap an email address and the iPad opens the Mail app (see Chapter 5), starts a new message, and populates the To field with that address. The virtual keyboard is also summoned so you can add other email addresses and compose a subject line and message. For this feature to work, your Mail app must be set up (see Chapter 5).

TIP

To see the URL for a link, long-press the link until a preview of the linked web page pops up, along with a list of options (see Figure 4-5). You can use this method also to preview where a linked image will take you. (If you don't see the preview, tap the Tap to Show Preview text.)

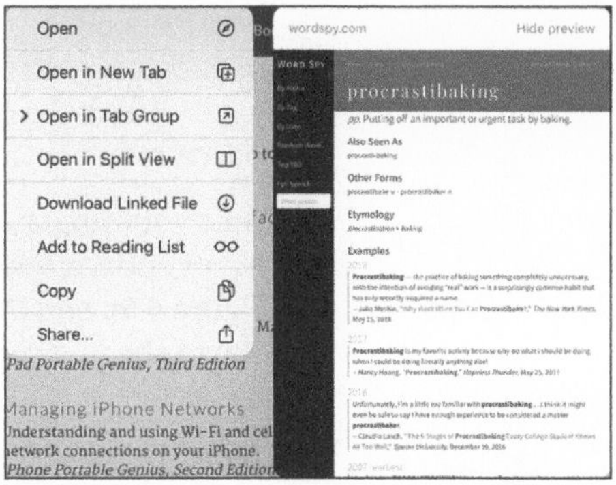

As for the link options shown in Figure 4-5, here's what six of them do:

FIGURE 4-5:
Long-press a link to see a preview and other options.

>> **Open:** Opens the link in the current tab

>> **Open in New Tab:** Opens the link in a new tab (see "Tabbed browsing," next)

>> **Open in Tab Group:** Opens the link in a new or existing tab group (see "Wrangling tabs into tab groups," later in this chapter)

>> **Open in Split View:** Opens the link in a separate Split View window (see Chapter 2)

>> **Copy:** Copies the link URL to your iPad's clipboard so you can paste it elsewhere

>> **Share:** Opens the same sharing options presented when you tap the share icon

Tabbed browsing

When I surf the web on a Mac or PC, I rarely go to a single web page and call it a day. In fact, I often have multiple web pages open at the same time. Sometimes I choose to hop around the web without closing the pages I visit. Sometimes a link automatically opens a new page without closing the old one, whether I want it to or not.

Safari on the iPad, like the desktop version of Safari (and other browsers), lets you open multiple pages, and each page is displayed in a separate browser area called a *tab*. After you have one page open, you have two ways to open additional web pages in Safari so they appear on the tab bar at the top of the screen (rather than replace the page you're currently viewing):

>> **Tap + (add tab) near the top-right corner of the Safari screen.** A tab named Start Page appears, as shown in Figure 4-6. Now type a URL, tap a

bookmark or an icon for a favorite or frequently visited site, or initiate a search, and the result will appear on this tab.

>> **Hold your finger on a link until a list of options appears (refer to Figure 4-5), and then tap Open in New Tab.**

FIGURE 4-6:
A new tab, ready to display any page you choose.

To switch tabs, tap the tab you want to view. To close a tab, switch to that tab and then tap the gray x-in-a-square that appears near the left edge of the tab.

You can manage tabs in one other way. Tap the tabs icon in the top-right corner of the browser (labeled in Figure 4-1 and shown in the margin) to summon thumbnail views of your open web pages, as shown in Figure 4-7. (Alternatively, place three fingers on the iPad screen and pinch them together.) With the tab thumbnails displayed, you can perform any of the following tasks:

Tab Groups

>> Tap a thumbnail to switch to that tab.

>> Tap + (add tab) to create a fresh tab.

>> Tap the X on any thumbnail to close the tab.

FIGURE 4-7:
A thumbnail view of all your open tabs.

>> Go into private browsing mode (discussed later in this chapter).

>> Work with tab groups, the topic you dive into in the next section.

>> Tap Done to close the thumbnails and return to the tab you were viewing.

Wrangling tabs into tab groups

Most of the time, the tabs you have open in Safari will be unrelated to each other. However, sometimes you find yourself working with two or more tabs that are connected in some way. For example, if you're working on a special project for work, you might have a fistful of tabs open for web pages related to that project. If you then get a second project and also have a personal hobby you're researching, your tabs can get messy in a hurry.

The solution is to organize your related tabs into separate tab groups: one for each project, interest, or obsession that you currently have in your life. Safari gives you two methods to create and populate a tab group:

» Open a tab for each page you want in your tab group and close any tabs you don't want in your group. Tap the tabs icon (shown in the margin), tap Tab Groups (labeled in Figure 4-7), and then tap New Tab Group from *X* Tabs, where *X* is the number of tabs you have open. In the New Tab Group dialog, type the tab group name and then tap Save.

» Tap the tabs icon, tap Tab Groups, and then tap New Empty Tab Group. In the New Tab Group dialog, type the tab group name and then tap Save. Safari creates a new tab for the group, which you can populate with a page. For subsequent pages, display each page in a new tab.

If you want to move a tab from one group to another, long-press the tab, tap Move to Tab Group, and then tap the group in the list that appears.

To switch from one tab group to another, tap the name of the current tab group in the upper-left corner of the Safari screen (just beside the Safari sidebar icon). Alternatively, tap the Sidebar icon (shown in the margin) to display the sidebar, which includes a list of your tab groups. Tap the name of the tab group you want to use.

Doing the splits

You can use the split view mode (discussed in Chapter 2) to display two web pages onscreen at the same time. This feature is helpful, for instance, if you're trying to decide between two cars or exploring different places to go on vacation.

In typical Apple fashion, you can arrive at this split view in more than one way:

» Tap the multitasking icon (three dots at the top center of the Safari window) and then tap the split view icon.

» Long-press a link and then tap Open in Split View.

» Drag a tab to the left or right edge of the screen and release.

» Tap and drag any link in a web page to the left or right edge of the screen and release.

To exit split view, tap the multitasking icon and then tap the full screen icon. Alternatively, drag the vertical gray bar in the middle of the Safari screen to the left or right edge of the screen and release. If you drag to the right, the window on the left side takes over the entire screen. If you drag to the left, the window on the right side takes over your screen.

Revisiting Web Pages

Surfing the web would be a lot less fun if you had to enter a URL every time you wanted to navigate from one page to another. To find those favorite websites in the future, the iPad provides bookmarks, web clips, the reading list, and the history list.

Bookmarking your favorite sites

In the same way that a bookmark helps you find a specific page in a physical book, a *bookmark* in Safari help you return to a specific page on the web. Follow these steps to create a bookmark for a web page that you want to save or visit often:

1. **Make sure the page you want to bookmark is open, and then tap the share icon (shown in the margin) at the top of the screen.**

   You have many options beyond bookmarking when you tap the share icon, as you discover later in this chapter.

2. **Tap Add Bookmark.**

   The Add Bookmark dialog opens with a default name for the bookmark, its web address, maybe a logo, and its folder location.

3. **To change the default bookmark name, tap the *x*-in-a-circle next to the name and then type the new title.**

4. **To change the location where the bookmark is saved, tap the Location field, which likely shows Favorites, and then tap the folder where you want the bookmark to be kept.**

   A check mark appears beside the folder.

5. **Tap Save.**

To open a bookmarked page after you set it up, tap the Safari sidebar icon (shown in the margin) to open the Safari sidebar, and then tap Bookmarks. If the bookmark you have in mind is buried inside a folder, tap the folder name first and then tap the bookmark you want.

Managing bookmarks

Once you have a bunch of bookmarks stuffed into Safari, you might need to make changes or even get rid of a bookmarked site that's no longer meaningful. Here are some techniques you can use:

>> **To display the Bookmarks list,** tap the Safari sidebar icon and then tap Bookmarks.

>> **To remove a bookmark (or folder),** display the bookmarks list and then tap Edit. Tap the red circle next to the bookmark (or custom folder) you want to toss off the list, and then tap Delete.

To remove a single bookmark or folder, you can also swipe its name from right to left and then tap the red Delete button.

TIP

>> **To change a bookmark name or location,** display the bookmarks list and then tap Edit at the bottom-right corner of the list. Tap the bookmark to open the Edit Bookmark pane with the name, URL, and location of the bookmark already filled in. Tap the fields you want to change. In the Name field, tap the gray *x*-in-a-circle and then use the keyboard to enter a new title. In the Location field, tap the location name and scroll up or down the list until you find a new home for your bookmark.

>> **To create a new folder for your bookmarks,** display the bookmarks list, tap Edit, and then tap New Folder. Enter the name of the new folder and then use the Location field to choose where to put the new folder.

>> **To move a bookmark up or down in a list,** display the bookmarks list, tap Edit, and then drag the three bars that appear to the right of the bookmark's name up or down to the bookmark's new resting place.

Saving a page to your reading list

When you visit a web page you'd like to read, but just not now, the reading list feature is sure to come in handy, including when you're offline. Here's how it works:

>> **Saving a page for later:** Tap the share icon and then tap Add to Reading List. Or, if you see a link to a page you'd like to read later, long-press the link until a list of options appears (refer to Figure 4-5) and then tap Add to Reading List. The first time you add an article to your reading list, you may be asked if you would like to automatically save reading list articles for offline viewing. Tap Save Automatically or Don't Save Automatically, as you want.

» **Viewing your reading list:** Tap the Safari sidebar icon and then tap Reading List. Safari displays your saved pages, as shown in Figure 4-8.

» **Reading a page on your reading list:** Open the reading list and then tap the page.

» **Keeping track of what you've read:** Open the reading list and then tap Show Unread to display only those items you haven't read yet. Tap Show All to show all the items in the reading list.

» **Marking an item as read or unread:** Open the reading list, swipe the item from left to right, and then tap its blue Mark Read or Mark Unread button.

» **Removing an item from the Reading List:** Open the reading list, swipe the item from right to left, and then tap its red Delete button.

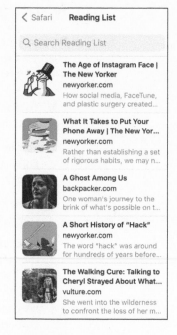

FIGURE 4-8:
Tap a page in the reading list to read it.

Finally, don't forget you can share your reading list (and bookmarks) among your computers and iDevices with iCloud.

Clipping a web page to the Home screen

You frequent lots of websites, some way more than others. For example, perhaps you consult the train schedule several times during the day. Your iPad lets you bestow special privileges on frequently visited sites, not just by bookmarking pages but also by affording them unique Home screen icons. To create one of these so-called web clips, follow these steps:

1. **Open the web page in question and tap the share icon.**

2. **Tap Add to Home Screen.**

   Apple creates an icon out of the area of the page that was displayed when you saved the clip, unless the page has its own custom icon.

3. **Type a new name for your web clip or leave the one Apple suggests.**

4. **Tap Add.**

   The icon appears on your Home screen.

TIP

As with any icon, you can remove a web clip by tapping and holding down on its icon until it starts to wiggle. Tap the X in the corner of the icon, and then tap Delete. You can also move the wiggling web clip to a more preferred location on one of your Home screen pages or to the dock.

Letting history repeat itself

Sometimes you want to revisit a site you failed to bookmark, but you can't remember the darn destination or what led you there in the first place. Good thing you can study the history books.

Safari records the pages you visit and keeps the logs on hand for several weeks. Here's how to access your history:

1. **Tap the Safari sidebar icon (shown in the margin) to open the Safari sidebar, and then tap History.**

   The history list appears.

2. **Scroll down to the day you think you hung out at the site.**

   Sites are listed under such headings as This Morning, Thursday Evening, or Thursday Morning, or segregated by a specific date.

   If you're not sure when you visited the site, you can also use the Search History text box to type a word or two that describes the site.

3. **When you find the page, tap it.**

   You're about to make your triumphant return.

TIP

To clear your history so no one can trace your steps, tap Clear in the bottom-right corner of the history list and then tap what you want to clear: All Time, Today and Yesterday, Today, or The Last Hour. Alternatively, starting on the Home screen, tap Settings ⇨ Safari ⇨ Clear History and Website Data, and then tap Clear when Settings asks you to confirm.

WARNING

When you clear your history from settings, your history, cookies, and browsing data will be removed from all the devices signed into iCloud. If that was not your intention, tap Cancel.

Saving web pictures

You can capture most pictures you come across on a website — but be mindful of any potential copyright violations, depending on what you plan to do with the images. To copy an image from a website, follow these steps:

1. **Long-press the image.**

   A preview of the image you have selected appears, along with a pop-up menu offering the following options: Share, Add to Photos, and Copy.

2. **Tap Add to Photos.**

   Saved images end up in your Photos, where they can be synced back to a computer.

TIP

Tap Copy instead, and you can paste the image into an email or as a link in a program such as Notes. Tap Share to display the regular Sharing pane.

Sharing Your Web Experiences

When you find a great website you just must share, tap the share icon (shown in the margin) or tap Share after tapping and holding down on a link, and you find these sharing options:

>> **One Tap Suggestions:** Tap an icon in the top row of the Sharing pane, which contains people and places iPadOS thinks you're most likely to want to share with, such as nearby AirDrop devices, as described next, as well as a combination of your most-used and recent Messages contacts.

>> **AirDrop:** Share the page with other people who have compatible devices and AirDrop. You'll need to turn on AirDrop in Control Center (swipe down from the top-right corner of the screen). Then choose whether to make your iPad discoverable to everyone or only people in your contacts.

>> **Messages:** Send a link to the web page in a text or an iMessage.

>> **Mail:** Open the Mail program, with a new message containing a link for the page and the name of the site or page in the Subject line.

>> **News:** Go to the Apple News version on the article you're viewing.

>> **Reminders:** Add to a new reminder a link to the web page you're viewing so you don't forget! If you tap Details, you can be reminded on a given day or location.

- **»** **Notes:** Open a pane that allows you to save the web page as an attachment in an existing or a new note. Tap Save to finish the process and return to Safari.

- **»** **Books:** Convert the web page you're viewing into a PDF that is then added to your Books library.

- **»** **More:** Display other recent apps — including social networking apps such as Twitter, Facebook, Tencent Weibo, and others.

TIP

Your list may not look exactly like the list just described, which was based on a clean iPad set up just for this book. If you've been using your iPad for a while, you'll see your frequently used apps.

- **»** **Copy:** Copy the page in question.

- **»** **Add Bookmark:** Bookmark the web page.

- **»** **Add to Favorites:** Add the web page you're viewing to this most-favored-nation-status grouping (which appears when you tap + to add a new tab).

- **»** **Find on Page:** Type a word you want to find. Matching words are highlighted; use the up and down arrows that appear to cycle through each mention. Tap Done when you're finished.

- **»** **Add to Home Screen:** This feature is described in the "Clipping a web page to the Home screen" section.

- **»** **Add to reading list:** See the "Saving a page to your reading list" section for details.

- **»** **Markup:** Convert the web page to a PDF you can then draw on! Use the brush palette that appears at the bottom of the screen to choose a color, a type of pen, and other markup controls. Tap Done to either save or delete the PDF.

- **»** **Print:** Print to an AirPrint printer. You can choose the number of copies you want. Tap Print to complete the job.

Launching a Mobile Search Mission

Most of us spend a lot of time using search engines. And the ones we summon most often are Google, Yahoo!, and Microsoft's Bing, at least in the United States. All these search options are available on the iPad, along with DuckDuckGo, a search engine that doesn't track your web footsteps.

Apple combines the address bar and Search fields into a single, convenient, unified strip called the Smart Search field, following the path taken on most popular web browsers for PCs and Macs. Although you can certainly use the virtual keyboard to type *google.com, yahoo.com, bing.com,* or other search engines in this field, Apple doesn't require that tedious effort. Instead, just type your search query directly in the box.

To conduct a web search on the iPad, tap the Smart Search field. You immediately see icons for your favorite web destinations. But when you start typing in the Smart Search field, a Google (or other) search mission commences, with live guesses shown at the top.

You see other search suggestions as you start tapping additional letters. In Figure 4-9, for example, typing the letters **app** yields some suggested sites and Google searches (your results will no doubt be different). Tap any search result that looks promising or tap Go on the keyboard to immediately land on the top hit. Or keep tapping out letters until you generate the search result you want.

FIGURE 4-9:
Running a search on the iPad.

TIP

You can also find your search word or phrase on the web page you have on-screen. If there's a match, you'll see an On This Page entry at the bottom of the Smart Search results. If you tap that result, the Smart Search pane vanishes, and the Find on Page pane comes up from the bottom of your screen.

TIP

To switch the search field from the current search engine to another search engine on your iPad, check out the "Smart Safari Settings" section, later in this chapter.

Through the search engine suggestions and Safari suggestions features, you can get potentially useful information even if you don't explicitly search for it. If you search the name of a movie, for example, Safari will also provide showtimes at nearby theaters without being asked. If you're not comfortable with this feature, you can turn it off in Settings.

Private Browsing

Don't want to leave any tracks while you surf? Turn on private browsing for a "what happens in Safari stays in Safari" tool. Those truly bent on staying private will also want to tap Clear History, as mentioned earlier in this chapter.

To go incognito, you have two choices:

» Tap the tabs icon (labeled in Figure 4-1 and shown in the margin), tap Tab Groups (labeled in Figure 4-7), and then tap Private.

» Tap the Safari Sidebar icon (labeled in Figure 4-1 and shown in the margin) to display the Safari sidebar, and then tap Private.

After private browsing is on, any traces of your visit to shhhh.com (or wherever) are nowhere to be found. Your history is wiped clean, open tabs don't appear in iCloud tabs, and your autofill information is not stored anywhere. To remind you that you're browsing privately, the Smart Search field now shows white text on a dark gray background.

To come out of hiding, tap the tabs icon again or display the Safari sidebar and then tap a tab group.

TIP

The history of pages you've visited can be useful and a huge timesaver, so don't forget to disable private browsing when you're finished.

TIP

Be mindful of your settings on other machines. If you run Safari on both an iPad and a Mac, but choose to go private only on Apple's tablet, your Mac browsing history will still show up in your history list on the iPad. Safari browsers marked private on the iPad will still bring in sites from iPhones or Macs via iCloud. Mark things private across all devices to keep things really private.

Smart Safari Settings

Safari works well in its default setup, but the app comes with a ton of settings that you can use to customize your Safari experience. To get started, tap the Settings icon on the Home screen and then tap Safari. The following settings enable you to create a bespoke version of Safari to suit your surfing style:

» **Siri & Search:** Tap this setting to specify what Safari content you want accessible via Siri and the iPadOS search feature.

- **Search Engine:** Tap the search engine you desire — just as long as that search engine happens to be Google, Yahoo!, Bing, DuckDuckGo, Ecosia, or if you've enabled a Chinese keyboard, Baidu. Other settings found here let you determine whether the iPad can make search engine suggestions and Safari suggestions, features touched on earlier in this chapter.

- **Quick Website Search:** When this setting is on, you can use website shortcuts when you're searching in a website. For example, you can type **wiki FDR** to show Wikipedia entries for Franklin Roosevelt.

- **Preload Top Hit:** When this setting is on, Safari preloads the top search result in the background for speedier surfing.

- **AutoFill:** Safari can automatically fill out web forms by using your personal contact information, usernames, and passwords, or information from your other contacts. Tap AutoFill and then use the following settings to customize AutoFill.

  - Tap the Use Contact Info switch to on if you're comfortable using the information found about your contacts.

  - Tap My Info to select yourself in your contacts so that Safari knows which address, phone number, email address, and other information to use when it fills in a form.

  - Tap the Credit Cards switch to on if you're okay with allowing AutoFill to use your saved credit-card information. Tap Saved Credit Cards to view the cards you've saved on your tablet or to add others.

WARNING

Turning on AutoFill can compromise your security if someone gets hold of your iPad. It can also affect security across all your iCloud-enabled devices. If you use AutoFill, be sure to protect your iPad as described in Chapter 18.

- **Favorites:** Apple lets you quickly access favorite bookmarks when you enter an address, search, or create a tab. Tap the category of sites for which you'd like to see icons (News, Business, Technology, whatever). A check mark appears next to your selection. Or leave the default category setting as Favorites.

- **Show Favorites Bar:** If you enable this option, you'll see Safari's Favorites bar between the Smart Search field and tab bar.

- **Block Pop-Ups:** *Pop-ups* are web pages that appear whether or not you want them to. Often, they're annoying advertisements. But on some sites, you welcome the appearance of pop-ups, so remember to turn off blocking under such circumstances.

- **Extensions:** Enables you to manage any Safari extensions you've installed. An *extension* is a mini-program that extends the functionality of Safari is some small (but, I hope, useful) way.

>> **Downloads:** Tap through to decide where the files you download to your iPad will reside, in iCloud drive or directly on your iPad. If you choose the iCloud Drive option, the files will be available on all of your Apple devices signed into iCloud drive.

>> **Tabs:** You can choose either Separate Tab Bar (which appears under the Smart Search field) or Compact Tab Bar (which appears near the top-left corner of the Safari display).

>> **Open New Tabs in Background:** If you enable this setting, new tabs that you open in Safari will load in a new tab, but you stay in the current tab.

>> **Close Tabs:** Tap through to decide whether you want to close tabs manually — which I recommend — or have them closed automatically after one day, one week, or one month.

>> **Prevent Cross-Site Tracking:** Apple is the tech leader in protecting your privacy, and no close second exists. The Prevent Cross-Site Tracking feature makes it difficult for Google, Facebook, and the myriad of advertising trackers on the internet to track you as you go from site to site. This feature is enabled by default, and I recommend you keep it enabled.

>> **Hide IP Address:** When you set this option to From Trackers, Safari doesn't share your IP address with sites that are trying to track you across the web.

>> **Block All Cookies:** *Cookies* are tiny bits of information a website places on the iPad when you visit so that the site recognizes you when you return. You need not assume the worst; most cookies are benign.

If this concept wigs you out, take action and block cookies from third parties and advertisers by tapping the Block All Cookies switch to on.

REMEMBER

If you set the iPad so that it doesn't accept cookies, certain web pages won't load properly, and other sites such as Amazon won't recognize you or make any of your preferred settings or recommendations available.

>> **Fraudulent Website Warning:** Safari can warn you when you land on a site whose producers have sinister intentions. The protection is better than nothing, but don't let down your guard because this feature isn't foolproof. The setting is on by default.

>> **Privacy Preserving Ad Measurement:** When this setting is on, Safari prevents websites from accessing your personal info to serve ads targeted at you.

>> **Check for Apple Pay:** If you come to a website that accepts Apple Pay (Apple's mobile payments service), the site can check whether you have Apple Pay enabled on your tablet. If you're not comfortable with this idea, make sure this switch is off.

>> **Clear History and Website Data:** You met this option earlier. Tap it to erase everything in Safari's history, leaving nary a trace of the pages you've visited.

>> **Page Zoom:** Apple offers several settings for controlling what happens on every website, starting with Page Zoom. Tap Page Zoom to change the default setting for every website. You have options ranging from 50% to 300%, which is useful if you find yourself constantly adjusting the zoom level for new web pages.

>> **Request Desktop Website:** Earlier in this chapter, I talk about how Safari for iPadOS requests the desktop version of every website, rather than the mobile version. If you want to turn off this feature for some reason, tap Request Desktop Website and toggle the All Websites switch from green to white. Turning off this feature allows the server to decide whether you get the website's mobile version or desktop version.

>> **Reader:** Tap the Reader category, and then tap the All Websites toggle to green if you want to view in reader mode every website you visit (or, at least, every website that supports reader mode).

>> **Camera, Microphone, or Location:** You set up all three features in the same way. Tap through Camera, Microphone, or Location to control how websites request access to these features on your iPad. By default, they're all set to Ask, which means a website must ask for your permission before accessing one of these features.

>> **Show Color in Compact Tab Bar:** When this setting is on, Safari changes the background color of the compact version of the tab bar to match the background color of the current web page.

>> **Automatically Save Offline:** Tap the toggle for this setting to have your iPad automatically save to your iPad any web page you added to your reading list so you can read the page offline, without an internet connection.

>> **Advanced:** The Advanced category has several settings most iPad users will never need to worry about. But because I love you, dear reader, I'm going to explain just in case! Tap Advanced to access the following additional settings.

- Tap *Website Date* to view and manage the data cached by websites you've visited. They're listed in order by how much data they've saved, showing only the top ten by default. Tap Show All Sites to see the rest. If you tap and slide to the left on an individual website, you reveal a red Delete button. Tap Delete to remove that site's data. Tap and slide back to the left to hide the Delete button after you're finished with the site. Tap the Remove All Website Data to remove all cached data from every site at once.

- Tap to toggle *JavaScript* on or off. Be careful when turning off JavaScript, however, because it adds advanced functionality to websites.

- Tap the *Web Inspector* toggle to enable the capability to inspect different elements of a website. This feature is typically used by developers and isn't something the rest of us will ever need to think about. Similarly, the *Remote Automation* feature is a developer feature, and I do not recommend that you enable it.

- Tap the *Experimental Features* category to unveil a wealth of different things Apple is experimenting with in WebKit, the engine that powers Safari. I strongly recommend that you leave this entire section alone, unless you're a developer who needs to access these features to develop a website.

Chapter **5**

The Email Must Get Through

On any computing device, emails come and go with a variety of emotions. Messages may be amusing or sad, frivolous or serious. Electronic missives on the iPad are almost always touching. Because, you know, you're touching the display to compose and read messages.

Okay, so I'm having a little fun, but the truth is that Apple's Mail on the iPad is a modern app designed to send and receive plain-text emails, as well as rich HTML email messages formatted with font and type styles and embedded graphics.

Furthermore, your iPad can read several types of file attachments, including (but not limited to) PDFs, JPG images, Microsoft Word documents, PowerPoint slides, and Excel spreadsheets, as well as stuff produced through Apple's own productivity software, notably Pages, Keynote, and Numbers. Better still, all this sending and receiving of text, graphics, and documents happens in the background, so you can surf the web or play a game while your iPad quietly and efficiently handles your email behind the scenes. Apple even lets you grant VIP status to important senders so there's almost no chance you'll miss mail from the people who matter most.

In this chapter, you learn the ins and outs of the Mail app: sending and viewing emails, working with attachments, setting up and managing email accounts, and more.

Prep Work: Setting Up Your Accounts

First things first. To use Mail, you need an email address. You can get a free email account (for example, `yourname@icloud.com`) from Apple as part of iCloud. If you need to create a new iCloud account, go to Settings ⇨ Mail ⇨ Accounts ⇨ Add Account ⇨ iCloud. Then tap Create a New Apple ID and follow the onscreen directions.

If you have broadband internet access (that is, a cable modem, FiOS, or DSL), you may have received one or more email addresses when you signed up. If you're one of the handful of readers who doesn't already have an email account, you can get one for free from Google Gmail (`https://gmail.com`), Microsoft Outlook (`https://outlook.live.com/`), or numerous other service providers.

You can add as many accounts as you want to your mail or just stick with the one that comes with your iCloud account.

TIP

Many so-called free email providers add a bit of advertising to the end of your outgoing messages, or they sift through your email to add to their profile of you, which they then use to sell advertising. If you'd rather not be a billboard for your email provider, use an iCloud email, use the address that came with your broadband internet access (`yourname@comcast.net` or `yourname@att.net`, for example), or pay a few dollars a month for a premium email account.

Finally, while the rest of the chapter focuses on the Mail app, you can also use Safari to access most email systems, if that's your preference. You can also install separate Gmail, Outlook, and other dedicated email apps from the App Store.

Getting started

If you're ready to roll with setting up an email account on your iPad, here's how you get started:

>> **If you don't have an email account on your iPad:** The first time you launch Mail, you see the Welcome to Mail screen. Your choices are iCloud, Microsoft Exchange (business email), Google (Gmail), Yahoo!, AOL, Outlook.com, and Other.

Tap the account type you want to add to the iPad and follow the steps in the upcoming "Setting up an account with another provider" or "Setting up corporate email" section.

» **If you have one or more email accounts on your iPad and want to add a new account manually:** Tap Settings on the Home screen and then tap Mail ⇨ Accounts ⇨ Add Account.

You see an Add Account screen, shown in Figure 5-1, with the same account options that appear on the Welcome to Mail screen. Proceed to one of the next three sections, depending on the type of email account you selected.

FIGURE 5-1:
Tap a button to set up an account.

Setting up an email account with iCloud, Gmail, Yahoo!, AOL, or Microsoft Outlook

If the account you want to create is with iCloud, Gmail (Google), Yahoo!, AOL, or Outlook, follow these steps:

1. **Tap the appropriate button on the Welcome to Mail screen (refer to Figure 5-1).**

2. **Tap Create Account, as shown in Figure 5-2.**

   Each service is different and wants different information from you. Most will ask for your name and other identifying information. Follow the onscreen instructions until the process is finished.

   That's all there is to setting up your account. You can now proceed to "See Me, Read Me, File Me, Delete Me: Working with Messages."

FIGURE 5-2:
The Create Account button is below the login option offered for people who already have accounts.

Setting up an account with another provider

If your email account is with a provider other than iCloud, Microsoft Outlook, Gmail (Google), Yahoo!, or AOL, you have a bit more work ahead of you. You need a bunch of information about your email account you may not know or have handy.

I suggest you scan the following instructions, note the items you don't know, and go find the answers before you continue. To find the answers, look at the documentation you received when you signed up for your email account or visit the account provider's website and search there.

Here's how you set up an account:

1. **Starting at the Home screen, tap Settings ⇨ Mail ⇨ Accounts ⇨ Add Account ⇨ Other.**

2. **Tap Add Mail Account.**

3. **Fill in the name, address, password, and description in the appropriate fields, and then tap Next.**

   With any luck, that's all you'll have to do. The iPad will look up and retrieve your account settings. If that doesn't happen, continue with Step 4.

4. **Tap the button at the top of the screen that denotes the type of email server this account uses, IMAP or POP, as shown in Figure 5-3.**

5. **Fill in the internet hostname for your incoming mail server, which looks something like mail.*providername*.com.**

6. **Fill in your username and password.**

7. **Enter the internet hostname for your outgoing mail server, which looks something like smtp.*providername*.com.**

8. **Enter your username and password in the appropriate fields.**

FIGURE 5-3:
If you set up an IMAP or a POP email account, you may have a few more fields to fill in before you can rock.

9. **Tap the Next button in the upper-right corner to create the account.**

You're now ready to begin using your account. See the section "See Me, Read Me, File Me, Delete Me: Working with Messages."

TIP

Rarely, outgoing mail servers don't need your username and password. The fields for these items on your iPad note they're optional. Still, I suggest you fill them in anyway. Doing so saves you from having to add them later if your outgoing mail server does require an account name and a password, which almost all do these days.

Setting up corporate email

The iPad makes nice with the Microsoft Exchange servers that are a staple in large enterprises, as well as many smaller businesses.

What's more, if your company supports Microsoft Exchange ActiveSync, you can exploit push email so messages arrive pronto on the iPad, just as they do on your other computers. (To keep everything up to date, the iPad also supports push calendars and push contacts.) For push to work with Exchange Server, your company must support one of the last several iterations of Microsoft Exchange ActiveSync (most companies are). If you run into a problem, ask your company's IT or tech department.

Setting up Exchange email isn't particularly taxing, but you might have to consult your employer's techie-types for certain settings.

Start setting up your corporate email on your iPad by following these steps:

1. **Tap the Microsoft Exchange listing on the Welcome to Mail or Add Account screen.**

Refer to Figure 5-1.

2. **Fill in your name and the description you want for your account. Then tap Next.**

3. **On the next screen, enter your name, email address, password, server, and domain, assuming the Microsoft Autodiscover service didn't already find it. Then tap Next.**

You might need to contact your company's IT support to fill in any information you don't know.

4. **Choose which information you want to synchronize through Exchange by tapping each item you want.**

You can choose Mail, Contacts, Calendars, Reminders, and Notes. When one of these switches is turned on, it turns green, as in Figure 5-4; otherwise, what you see appears dimmed.

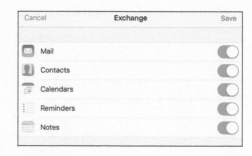

FIGURE 5-4:
Keeping your mail, contacts, calendars, and reminders in sync.

5. **Tap Save.**

WARNING

The company you work for doesn't want just anybody having access to your email — heaven forbid your iPad is lost or stolen — so your bosses may insist you change the passcode lock in Settings on your iPad. (The passcode lock is different than your email account password.) Now if your iPad ends up in the wrong hands, your company can wipe the contents clean remotely.

If you're moonlighting at a second job, you can configure more than one Exchange ActiveSync account on your iPad; there used to be a limit of just one such account per device.

See Me, Read Me, File Me, Delete Me: Working with Messages

Now that your email accounts are all set up, it's time to figure out how to receive and read the stuff. Fortunately, you did most of the heavy lifting when you set up your email accounts. Getting and reading your mail is a piece of cake.

You can tell when you have unread mail by looking at the Mail icon in the dock at the bottom of your Home screen. The cumulative number of unread messages across all your email inboxes appears in a little red badge in the upper right of the icon.

TIP

The badge display is the default behavior. If you don't care for it, turn it off by opening Settings ➪ Notifications ➪ Mail and tapping the Badges switch to off.

In the following sections, you find out how to read messages and attached files and then send messages to the trash, or maybe a folder, when you've read them. Or, if you can't find a message, check out the section on searching your email messages. Reading email on an iPad versus a desktop or notebook computer is similar, except you have the advantage of the iPad's touchscreen.

Reading messages

To read your mail, tap the Mail icon on the Home screen. Remember that what appears onscreen depends on whether you're holding the iPad in landscape or portrait mode, as well as what was on the screen the last time you opened the Mail app:

>> **Landscape:** With the iPad in landscape mode, you see the Mailboxes section (see Figure 5-5), which, as its name suggests, is a repository for all the messages across all your accounts. The number to the right of Inbox (2 in Figure 5-5) matches the number on the Mail icon on your Home screen. Again, it's the cumulative tally of *unread* messages across all your accounts. If you have more than one email account set up, Inbox will instead say All Inboxes.

Below the Inbox or All Inboxes listing are the inboxes for your individual accounts. On the test device shown in Figure 5-5, I had just set up a new account, so it looks all clean and pretty. Depending on how you use email, yours might look considerably busier. Each individual inbox you have displays the number of unread messages for that one account.

See all emails

Emails from your VIPs

Compose new message

Move message

Delete or archive message

FIGURE 5-5: When you're holding the iPad sideways, Mail looks something like this.

In this view, you can also see the available subfolders for your accounts (Drafts, Sent, Junk, Trash, and so on). If you have multiple accounts, tap through to each account to see its subfolders.

Check out the VIP mailbox, too. The VIP mailbox lists all messages from senders you deem most important. I tell you how to give someone VIP status in the later section, "More things you can do with messages."

Depending on the last time the Mail app was open, you may see previews of the messages in your inbox. Previews display the name of the sender, the time the message arrived, the subject header, and the first two lines of the message. (In Settings ⇨ Mail ⇨ Preview, you can change the number of lines shown in the preview from one line to five, or even to no preview lines.)

FIGURE 5-6:
When you're holding the iPad in portrait mode, the message fills the screen.

» **Portrait:** When you hold the iPad in portrait mode, as shown in Figure 5-6, the last incoming message fills the entire screen. You have to tap < (back icon), in the upper-left corner of the screen, to summon a panel that displays other accounts or message previews. You can display the panel also by swiping right from the left edge of the screen. The panel overlays the message that otherwise fills the screen.

Messages are displayed in *threads*, or conversations, making them easy to follow, but you can still view messages individually. To read your email:

1. **If the email mailbox you want to see isn't front and center, tap < (back icon) in the upper-left corner of the screen to display the Mailboxes list, then tap the mailbox you want. To view the unified inbox, tap All Inboxes instead.**

2. **(Optional) To check for new messages, drag down the left panel that lists your accounts or mailboxes and immediately release.**

    If you see a spinning gear, the iPad is searching for new mail. If a blue dot appears next to a message, the message hasn't been read.

3. **Tap a message to read it.**

4. **To read the next message in the current mailbox, use one of the following techniques:**

   - *In portrait mode:* Tap Next (the downward-pointing arrow near the upper-left corner of the screen).

   - *In landscape mode:* In the list of messages on the left side of the screen, tap the next message.

5. **To read the preceding message in the current mailbox, use one of the following techniques:**

   - *In portrait* mode*:* Tap the upward-pointing arrow near the upper-left corner of the screen.

   - *In landscape mode:* In the list of messages on the left side of the screen, tap the preceding message.

6. **When you've finished reading, tap < in the upper-left corner of the message.**

Threading messages

Apple lets you display related messages as *threads*. The beauty of this arrangement is you can easily trace an email conversation. When you organize messages by thread, the related messages appear as a single entry in the preview pane mailbox, with a right-pointing arrow in a circle to indicate that the message is indeed part of a larger ongoing exchange. When you tap that listing, all messages that make up the threaded conversation appear in the larger pane on the right, though you may have to scroll up or down to see them all.

Figure 5-7 (left) shows Bryan and Bryan (it's a thing!) hanging together by a thread. If you tap an individual message from the thread in the pane on the right, you can swipe to quickly reply to the message, forward it, or mark it unread. These are the same options you see when you swipe a preview in the message list.

When you look at a message that's part of a thread, the number at the top of the screen tells you how many individual messages make up the entire conversation.

To turn on threading, go to the Home screen and tap Settings ⇨ Mail, and then tap on Organize by Thread so the toggle turns green. You can also choose whether to display the most recent message in a thread on top, and whether to complete the thread so all messages in the conversation are shown, even if you subsequently moved some messages to other mailboxes.

Unread message indicator

Threaded message indicator

FIGURE 5-7:
Your emails
are hanging
together by a
thread.

Managing messages

Managing messages typically involves either moving the messages to a folder or deleting them. To herd your messages into folders, you have the following options:

>> **To create a folder to organize messages you want to keep:** Open the Mail app and tap Edit in the Mailboxes column. If you're in portrait mode, you may have to first tap the blue < in the upper-left corner of your screen to reveal the Mailboxes pane. In the list of mailboxes on the left side of the screen, tap Edit. Then tap New Mailbox at the bottom. Type a name for the mailbox and choose a location for it.

>> **To file a message in another folder:** Tap the move message icon (refer to Figure 5-5). When the list of mailboxes appears, tap the folder where you want to file the message. Watching the message fly and land in the designated new folder is cool.

- » **To read a message you've filed:** Tap the folder where the message now resides and then tap the header or preview for the message in question.

- » **To delete, move, or mark multiple messages:** Tap Edit. In both portrait and landscape views, Edit appears at the top of your inbox or another mailbox when its mail folder is selected. Tap Edit, and it becomes a Cancel button, and Mark, Move, and Trash buttons appear at the bottom of the list. Tap each message you want to select so that a check mark appears, or tap Select All to work with every message. You manage the selected messages as follows:

  - *Tap Trash* to delete all selected messages.

  - *Tap Move* to move all selected messages to another folder in the same or another Mail account, and then tap the new folder or mailbox (or both) in which you want those messages to hang out.

  - *Tap Mark* to mark all selected messages read (or unread) or flagged (or unflagged), or to move messages to the Junk folder.

- » **To delete a single message:** Tap the delete message (trash can) icon in that open message. If you tap the delete message icon by mistake, you have a chance to cancel, provided the Ask Before Deleting switch is turned on in Settings ⇨ Mail.

- » **To delete a single message without opening it:** Swipe left across the message in the mailbox list, and then tap the red Trash button that appears to the right of the message. You'll also see a Flag option and a More button. Tapping More gives you, well, more options: reply, forward, mark it as unread, move it to junk or elsewhere, or have the iPad send a notification when someone replies to the message or thread.

TIP

In certain Mail accounts, Gmail being one, the Trash option may be replaced by an Archive option, depending on your preference. That means you're not getting rid of a message but stashing it or, to be precise, saving the message in your All Mail folder. If the Archive option does present itself, you can turn the feature on or off in Settings ⇨ Mail.

Searching emails

With the search feature, you can quickly and easily search through a bunch of messages to find the one you want to read — such as that can't-miss stock tip from your broker. In the Search box at the top of a mailbox preview pane, type whichever search term seems relevant. You'll notice a couple of things right off the bat. You can confine your search to just the current mailbox or widen the search to include all your mailboxes, as in Figure 5-8. What's more, Apple has helpfully organized the search results, so senders who have *dummies* as part of their name are separated from the subject headings of email messages that include the search term.

FIGURE 5-8:
Searching your
email is easy.

Search in the Mail app is powerful. For example, you can search by time frame by typing something along the lines of *March meetings.* You can also search to find just flagged messages from your VIPs (*flag unread VIP*).

TIP

Siri can also find emails on your behalf. For example, ask Siri to find all the emails from a particular person in a particular month, or have Siri run a text search.

If you're using Exchange, iCloud, or certain IMAP-type email accounts, you may even be able to search messages stored on the server.

Dealing with attachments

Your iPad can receive email messages with attachments in a wide variety of popular file formats. Which file formats does the iPad support? Glad you asked:

>> **Images:** .jpg, .tiff, .gif, .png

>> **Microsoft Word:** .doc, .docx

- **»** **Microsoft PowerPoint:** .ppt, .pptx
- **»** **Microsoft Excel:** .xls, .xlsx
- **»** **Web pages:** .htm, .html
- **»** **Apple Keynote:** .key
- **»** **Apple Numbers:** .numbers
- **»** **Apple Pages:** .pages
- **»** **Preview and Adobe Acrobat:** .pdf
- **»** **Rich Text:** .rtf
- **»** **Text:** .txt
- **»** **Contact information:** .vcf

WARNING

If the attachment is a file format the iPad doesn't support (for example, an Adobe Photoshop .psd file), you see the name of the file in your email, but you can't open it on your iPad, at least not without an assist from a third-party app you may have installed.

Here's how to read a supported attachment:

1. **Open the email that contains the attachment, which you can identify by a little paper clip icon.**

   Another option is to conduct a search for *Messages with Attachments.*

2. **Tap the attachment.**

   The attachment typically appears at the bottom of the message, so you might need to scroll down to see it.

   In some cases, the attachment downloads to your iPad and opens automatically. In other instances, you may have to tap the button representing the attachment to download it.

3. **Read or (in the case of a picture) eyeball the attachment.**

   Tap the attachment (in the case of a document), and you can likely read it immediately. Tap Done to return to the message text.

TIP

Alternatively, long-press the attachment in the email and then tap the app from the presented options. Among the possible choices: Tap Quick Look for a quick peek at the attachment or tap Markup and Reply to add your comments to a document before whisking it back to the sender. You can also add the attachment to iCloud Drive or Notes or import it to Apple's Pages word processor should that app resides on your tablet. Third-party apps you added to your iPad may also become available as a destination for said attachment.

More things you can do with messages

Wait! You can do even more with your incoming email messages:

>> **To see all recipients of a message:** Assuming you can't see all the names of the people receiving the message, tap the triangle to the right of the recipient. That name expands to show everyone to whom the email was sent or cc'd as a recipient.

>> **To add an email recipient or sender to your contacts:** Tap the name or email address at the top of the message and then tap Create New Contact or Add to Existing Contact.

>> **To make a sender a VIP:** Tap the name or email address at the top of the message and then tap Add to VIP. You may want to give VIP status to important people in your life, such as your significant other, family members, boss, or doctor. A star appears next to any incoming message from a VIP. You can summon mail from all your VIPs by tapping the VIP folder in the list of Mailboxes. To demote a VIP to an NVIP (not very important person), tap the name or email at the top of the message and then tap Remove from VIP.

>> **To mark a message as read or unread:** Swipe left on the message in the message list to reveal three buttons: More, Flag, and Trash. Tap More and then tap either Mark as Read or Mark as Unread.

Choose Mark as Unread for messages you may want to revisit at some point. The message is again included in the unread message count on the Mail icon on your Home screen, and its mailbox again has a blue dot next to it in the message list for that mailbox.

>> **To flag, reply to, or delete a message:** Swipe left on the message in the message list to reveal the More, Flag, and Trash buttons. Tap More and then tap Reply, Reply All, and Forward. Tap Flag to flag the message so it will turn up in any search for flagged messages. Tap Trash to quickly delete the message.

>> **To access other controls for your open email message:** Tap the Reply button at the bottom of the screen to reveal another way to access the options already mentioned, as well as Archive Message (for Gmail and other services that support this feature), Move to Junk, Move Message, Notify Me, and Print. The options you see may differ, depending on the features supported by your email service.

>> **To zoom in on and out of a message:** Use the pinch and spread gestures, at which I suspect you now excel. See Chapter 2 if you need help with your touchscreen moves.

>> **To follow a link in a message:** Tap the link. Links are typically displayed in blue but sometimes appear in other colors, or underlined, or both. If the link is a URL, Safari opens and displays the web page. If the link is a phone number, the iPad gives you the chance to add it to your contacts, copy it, call it using FaceTime Audio or your iPhone (through the Handoff feature), or send a message. If the link is an address, the Maps app opens and displays the location. If you tap a date, you can create an event on that date or display it in Calendar. And last but not least, if the link is an email address, a new pread-dressed blank email message is created.

Sending Email

Sending email on your iPad is a breeze. You'll encounter several subspecies of messages: pure text, text with a photo, a partially finished message (a *draft*) you want to save and complete later, or a reply to an incoming message. You can also forward an incoming message to someone else — and in some instances print messages. The following sections examine these message types one at a time.

Sending an all-text message

To compose a new email message, tap Mail on the Home screen. As before, what you see next depends on how you're holding your iPad. In landscape mode, your email accounts or email folders are listed in a panel along the left side of the screen, with the message filling the larger window on the right. In portrait mode, your view will depend on what you were viewing the last time you opened the Mail app. If you don't see the Mailboxes folder, tap the blue < (back icon) in the upper-left corner.

Now, to create a message, follow these steps:

1. **Tap the compose new message icon (labeled in Figure 5-5).**

   The New Message screen appears, like the one shown in Figure 5-9.

2. **Type the names or email addresses of the recipients in the To field, or tap the + symbol to the right of the To field to choose one or more contacts from your iPad's contacts list.**

TIP

   If you start typing an email address, email addresses that match what you typed appear in a list below the To or Cc field. If the correct one is in the list, tap it to use it.

As part of the intelligent and proactive iPadOS, your iPad may suggest people you typically include when you start to address a message.

3. **(Optional) Tap Cc/Bcc, From to display Cc, Bcc, and From as separate fields.**

   The Cc label stands for *courtesy copy* (some folks still insist on calling it a *carbon copy* — a throwback term from another era). A courtesy copy is kind of an FYI to a recipient. It's like saying, "We figure you'd appreciate knowing this, but you don't need to respond."

   The Bcc label stands for *blind courtesy copy*. When using Bcc, you can include a recipient on the message, but other recipients can't see that this recipient has been included. Bcc is great for those secret agent emails!

   Tap the respective Cc or Bcc field to type names. Or tap the + symbol that appears in those fields to add a contact.

4. **(Optional) If you tap From, you can choose any of your email accounts on the fly — assuming you have more than one account set up on the iPad.**

5. **In the Subject field, type a subject.**

   The subject is optional, but it's considered poor form to send an email without one.

6. **In the message area, type your message.**

   The message area is immediately below the Subject field. You have ample space to get your message across.

7. **Tap the Send button in the upper-right corner of the screen.**

   Your message wings its way to its recipients almost immediately. If you aren't in range of a Wi-Fi network or a cellular network when you tap Send, the message is sent the next time you're in range of one of these networks.

Formatting text in an email

One of the goodies in Mail is the capability to format email text by underlining, bolding, or italicizing it. First you select the text by long-pressing a word until you see the options to select some or all text. You can also double-tap a single word to select it. You then expand the selection by dragging the selection handles to include more words.

After making your selection, you'll have various other options: Cut, Copy, Paste, Replace, BIU, Look Up, Translate, Share, Quote Level, Insert Photo or Video, Attach File, Scan Document, and Insert Drawing. (Note that to see all of these options, you need to tap the right arrow in the context menu.) To format text, tap the BIU button. Then apply whichever style (bold, italics, underline) suits your fancy.

FIGURE 5-9:
The New
Message
screen is ready
for you to
start typing.

If you tap Quote Level (if you don't see it, tap the right-pointing arrow after selecting a word), you can quote a portion of a message you're responding to. *Note:* Increase Quote Level must be turned on in Mail Settings (Settings ⇨ Mail ⇨ Increase Quote Level). You can also increase or decrease the indentation in your outgoing message.

If you tap Replace, you're provided with alternative word choices to the word you selected. Tap one of the alternative options to select it.

If you tap Look Up, you can summon a definition from the *New Oxford Dictionary* or another available dictionary, as well as see suggestions, if appropriate, from iTunes, the App Store, nearby locations, movie showtimes, and more.

Sending a photo or video with an email message

Sometimes a picture is worth a thousand words, and a video can be priceless. When that's the case, follow these steps to send an email message with a photo or video attached:

1. **Tap the Photos icon on the Home screen.**

2. **Find the photo or video you want to send.**

3. **Tap the share icon at the top of the screen (and shown in the margin).**

4. **Tap the Mail button.**

   An email message appears on-screen with the photo or video already attached. The image is embedded in the body of the message because that's how your recipient receives it (that is, not as a regular email attachment).

   On the Cc/Bcc line of your outgoing message, you see the size of the attached photo. If you tap the size of the image shown, a new line appears, giving you the option to choose an alternative size among Small, Medium, Large, or Actual Size. Your choice affects both the visible dimensions and file size of the photo (with the actual size of the file measured in kilobytes or megabytes reported for each possible choice). You don't have the option of modifying your video size.

5. **Choose what size photo you want to send.**

6. **Address the message and type whatever text you like, as you did for an all-text message previously, and then tap the Send button.**

You have an alternative way of inserting pictures (or videos) in your outgoing mail messages. When you're in the composition window of a new email and your cursor is in the body of that new email, you see the insert photo or video icon just above the keyboard. Tap the icon to reveal a menu that allows you to go to your Photo library, where you can choose from your existing photos and videos, or to Take Photo or Video. Tap Take Photo or Video to open the camera interface, where you can take a new photo or video.

When you 're finished, tap Retake for a do-over or tap Use Photo (or Video) to attach the image you just took to your email.

Adding an attachment to an email message

Besides attaching photos and videos to an email, you can attach documents. When you're in the composition window of a new email with the keyboard displayed and the cursor in the body field, long-press an empty spot in the message body and then tap Attach File in the options that appear. (You have to tap the right-pointing arrow to see the Attach File command.)

Mail opens a files-based interface for navigating the files on your device, on iCloud Drive, or on any third-party file-hosting service you may have added to your iPad. Navigate to and tap the document you want to send, and Mail will attach it automatically to your email.

Alternatively, long-press the message body and then tap the Scan Document command to turn your iPad into a mobile scanner! The iPad is just accessing your camera so you can take a picture of the document you want to send. But it offers some additional controls, such as adjusting which portion of the image is included in your attachment. Tap the camera button to take the image. You can then drag the corners of the selection area to adjust your image. When you're satisfied, tap the Keep Scan button at the bottom right of your screen and the Mail app will automatically attach it to your email. If you aren't satisfied, tap the Retake button to make a new scan.

Marking up an attachment

If you're attaching a photo or a PDF document, you can take advantage of iPadOS's Markup feature. With a picture attachment or PDF embedded in your outgoing message, double-tap the attachment and then tap Markup from the menu that appears.

You can summon the Markup feature also when you receive a PDF or picture attachment. Long-press the attachment and then tap Markup and Reply in the context menu that appears.

Now that you're in markup mode, you can draw on that image or PDF, tapping the simple annotation tools just below. (If you don't see the tools, tap the markup icon, which appears to the left of the share icon in the upper-right corner.) The tools, which are represented by icons, include several pens (your finger will be that pen unless you use an Apple Pencil or another optional stylus), a highlighter, and a pencil. You even have a ruler you can use to draw perfectly straight lines. Come on, how cool is that? To use the ruler, tap to select it from the palette of tools at the bottom of the Markup screen and drag it to where you want to draw your straight line. Then tap to choose the pen you want to use. Use your finger or a stylus to draw along the edge. Now, just pull your finger down the edge of the ruler and you'll have a perfectly straight line. It's great.

Tap + in the palette menu to access the text tool, a magnifier, or the signature tool, which lets you draw your signature. You'll also find an arrow tool for placing perfect arrows in your photo or document, and some other basic shape tools.

In markup mode, you have the option to change the color and thickness of the lines and symbols you draw and change the font and size of text.

Saving an email to send later

Sometimes you start an email message but don't have time to finish it. When that happens, you can save it as a draft and finish it some other time. Here's how:

1. **Start an email message, as described in one of the previous sections.**

2. **When you're ready to save the message as a draft, tap the Cancel button in the upper-left corner of the screen.**

3. **Tap the Save Draft button if you want to save this message as a draft and complete it another time.**

   If you tap the Delete Draft button, the message disappears immediately without a second chance. Don't tap Delete Draft unless you mean it!

To work on the message again, tap the Drafts mailbox or long-press the compose new message icon. A list of all messages you saved as drafts appears. Tap the draft you want to work on, and it reappears on the screen. When you're finished, you can tap Send to send it or tap Cancel to save it as a draft again.

REMEMBER

The number of drafts appears to the right of the Drafts folder, the same way the number of unread messages appears to the right of other mail folders, such as your inbox.

Replying to, forwarding, or printing an email message

When you receive a message and want to reply to it, forward it, or print it, open the message and then tap the reply icon (the curved arrow at the lower-right corner of the screen, as shown in Figure 5-10). Then tap Reply, Reply All, Forward, or Print, as described next:

>> **Reply and Reply All:** The Reply button creates an email message addressed to the sender of the original message, with the content of the original message embedded in your reply. The Reply All button creates an email message addressed to the sender and to everyone who was listed in the To and Cc lines of the original message. (The Reply All option appears only if more than one recipient was on the original email.) In both cases, the subject is retained with a *Re:* prefix added. So if the original subject were *iPad Tips,* the reply's subject would be *Re: iPad Tips.*

>> **Forward:** Tapping the Forward button creates an unaddressed email message that contains the text of the original message. Add the email address(es) of the person or people you want to forward the message to, and then tap Send. In this case, rather than a *Re:* prefix, the subject is preceded by *Fwd:.* So this time, the subject would be *Fwd: iPad Tips.* If the email you're forwarding has an attachment, you'll be given the option to forward the attachment along with the message.

>> **Print:** Tap Print if you want to print using an AirPrint-capable printer.

TIP

It's considered good form to leave the subject lines alone (with the *Re:* or *Fwd:* prefix intact), but you may want to change them sometimes. You can edit the subject line of a reply or a forwarded message or edit the body text of a forwarded message the same way you'd edit any other text. Worth noting: When the *Re:* is modified, a new email thread is created and the modified message won't be included in the old thread listing.

FIGURE 5-10:
Reading and managing an email message.

To send your reply or forwarded message, tap the Send button as usual.

Settings for sending email

You can customize the mail you send and receive in lots of ways. In this section, you explore settings for sending email. Later in this chapter, I show you settings that affect the way you receive and read messages.

You can customize your mail in the following ways:

>> **To hear an alert when you successfully send a message:** Tap Settings ➪ Sounds. Make sure the Sent Mail setting is turned on. You'll know because you'll see a sound type listed (among alert sounds and ringtones), Swoosh by default. Tap Sent Mail to select a different sound or choose None if going silent is your preference.

>> **To add a signature line, phrase, or block of text to every email message you send:** Tap Settings ➪ Mail ➪ Signature. The default signature is *Sent from my iPad.* You can add text before or after it or delete it and type something else. Your signature will be affixed to the end of all your outgoing email. You

can choose a signature that is the same across all your accounts or select different signatures for each account.

>> **To set the default email account for initiating email from outside the Mail application:** Go to Settings ➪ Mail ➪ Default Account. Note that if you have only one email account set up on your iPad, the Default Account setting will not be visible. If you have more than one email account on your iPad, tap the account you want to use as the default. The designated email account is the one that's used when you want to email a picture directly from the Photos app, for example. Also, if you choose one default account, you can dispatch mail from another account when you send your message.

Setting Your Message and Account Settings

The final discussion of Mail involves more settings that deal with your various email accounts.

Checking and viewing email settings

Several settings affect the way you can check and view email. You might want to modify one or more, so I describe what they do and where to find them:

>> **To specify how often the iPad checks for new messages:** Tap Settings ➪ Mail ➪ Accounts ➪ Fetch New Data. You're entering the world of *fetching* or *pushing.* Check out Figure 5-11 to glance at your options. If your email account supports push and the Push setting is enabled on your iPad, fresh messages are sent to your iPad automatically as soon as they hit the server. If you turned off push or your email account doesn't support it, the iPad periodically fetches data instead. Choices for fetching are Every 15 Minutes, Every 30 Minutes, Hourly, Manually, and Automatically. Tap the one you prefer. With push email, messages can show up on the lock screen and in Notification Center.

>> **To set the number of lines of each message to be displayed in the message list:** Go to Settings ➪ Mail ➪ Preview, and then choose a number. Your choices are 1, 2, 3, 4, and 5 lines of text or None. The more lines of text you display in the list, the fewer messages you can see at a time without scrolling, so think before you choose 4 or 5.

FIGURE 5-11:
Fetch or push?
It's your call.

» **To specify whether the iPad shows the To and Cc labels in message lists:** Tap Settings ➪ Mail and then turn on or off the Show To/Cc Label setting.

» **To turn on or off the Ask before Deleting warning:** Go to Settings ➪ Mail. Next, turn on or off the Ask before Deleting setting. If this setting is turned on, every time you want to delete an email, you must tap the trash (or archive) icon at the top of your email and then tap the red Delete button. When the setting is turned off, tapping the trash icon deletes the message, and you never see a red Delete button.

» **To change swipe options:** Go to Settings ➪ Mail ➪ Swipe Options. You can choose whether swiping left (on the preview pane) flags messages and whether swiping right marks messages as unread.

» **To flag email addresses that are outside one or more designated domain names:** Tap Settings ➪ Mail ➪ Mark Addresses. Type @ followed by the domain name (say, of your company) that you do *not* want marked. If you want to designate multiple domains, separate each with a comma. From then on, when you're composing a message, all email addresses sent to or from the specified domain(s) will appear in blue, while all other mail addresses will be shaded red. Why do this? The idea is that you can more easily identify mail dispatched to or from addresses outside your organization, alerting you to a potential security risk if you're exchanging, say, sensitive information.

>> **To specify whether the iPad will automatically display images embedded in an email:** Tap Settings ⇨ Mail and then tap Load Remote Images in the right pane so the switch is on. If it's off, you can still manually load remote images. Security risks are associated with loading remote images, and they can also hog bandwidth.

>> **To organize your mail by thread:** Tap Settings ⇨ Mail ⇨ Organize by Thread so that the setting is on. Then, as mentioned, you can choose whether to show the most recent message on top and whether to show all messages in a thread, even those since moved to other mailboxes.

Altering account settings

The last group of email settings you explore in this chapter deals with your email accounts. You most likely will never need most of these settings, but I'd be remiss if I didn't at least mention them briefly. So here they are, whether you need 'em or not:

>> **To stop using an email account:** Tap Settings ⇨ Mail ⇨ Accounts ⇨ *account name,* and then flip the switch for Mail to off (gray).

This setting doesn't delete the account; it only hides it from view and stops it from sending or checking email until you turn it on again. (You can repeat this step to turn off calendars, contacts, reminders, and notes in a given account.)

TIP

>> **To delete an email account:** Tap Settings ⇨ Mail ⇨ Accounts ⇨ *account name* ⇨ Delete Account ⇨ Delete. Tap Cancel if you change your mind and don't want your account blown away, or tap Delete to proceed.

Deleting an email account also removes calendar entries, contact names, and notes from the given account.

WARNING

You can find still more advanced Mail settings, reached the same way: Tap Settings ⇨ Mail ⇨ Accounts ⇨ *account name.* From here, your exact path may be different depending on the kind of account you're working with. For example, Gmail requires you to tap Account ⇨ Advanced and iCloud requires you to tap Account ⇨ iCloud ⇨ Mail ⇨ Advanced.

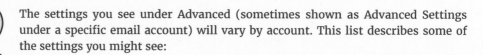

REMEMBER

The settings you see under Advanced (sometimes shown as Advanced Settings under a specific email account) will vary by account. This list describes some of the settings you might see:

>> **Specify how long until deleted messages are removed permanently from your iPad:** In iCloud Mail, your choices are Never, After One Day, After One Week, and After One Month. Tap the choice you prefer. Other mail accounts may give you different time frame options or not present this setting.

>> **Choose whether drafts, sent messages, archived messages, and deleted messages are stored on your iPad or on your mail server:** Tap Advanced and then choose the setting under Mailbox Behaviors. You can decide for drafts, sent messages, and trash. If you choose to store any or all of them on the server, you can't see them unless you have an internet connection (Wi-Fi or cellular). If you choose to store them on your iPad, they're always available, even if you don't have internet access. In certain circumstances, you also get to determine whether to delete or archive discarded messages.

WARNING

I strongly recommend that you don't change the next two items unless you know exactly what you're doing and why. If you're having problems with sending or receiving mail, start by contacting your ISP (internet service provider), email provider, or corporate IT person or tech department. Then change these settings only if they tell you to. Again, these settings and exactly where and how they appear vary by account.

>> **Reconfigure mail server settings:** In the Incoming Mail Server or Outgoing Mail Server section of the account settings screen, tap Host Name, User Name, or Password and make your changes.

>> **Adjust SSL, authentication, or IMAP path settings, or the server port:** Tap Advanced and then tap the appropriate item and make the necessary changes.

And that, as they say in baseball, retires the side. You're now fully qualified to set up email accounts and send and receive email on your iPad.

IN THIS CHAPTER

» **iMessages compared with their SMS and MMS sisters**

» **Sending text messages**

» **Shipping messages with photos, videos, and other media**

» **Reading and managing text messages**

» **Using the Messages app**

» **Jazzing up iMessages**

Chapter **6**
Text Messaging

M essages is your one-stop shop for communicating with your friends, colleagues, and anyone who sends you a text message. You can communicate with individuals or groups. You can share images, Maps directions, and files. You can customize your messages with stickers and memoji, a feature that lets you create a cartoon version of yourself. Apple even has apps for Messages that add all kinds of features, such as stickers, song lyrics, and games you can play with your friends. In addition, Messages uses end-to-end encryption, which keeps prying eyes out of your conversations. I show you how to use all these great features in this chapter, so read on!

iMessage versus SMS/MMS: What's the Difference?

One point of confusion that I need to clear up right off the bat is that the Messages app can deal with two types of messages:

» **iMessages:** These messages can include not only text but also a wide variety of other media, such as photos, videos, maps, voice recordings, stickers, and animated GIFs. You can also get read receipts, see when the other person is typing a reply, and use Apple Pay. You can send iMessages only to folks who have an iPad, an iPhone, an iPod touch, or a Mac.

>> **SMS/MMS:** SMS (short messaging service) messages are text-only affairs, while MMS (multimedia messaging service) can include photos, videos, and audio. If you're exchanging messages with someone who doesn't have an iPad, an iPhone, an iPod touch, or a Mac, those messages will be SMS or MMS messages.

REMEMBER

You can communicate with people who don't have an Apple device, but messages will be exchanged through SMS text messages or MMS multimedia-type missives. If you're involved in an SMS schmooze-fest, your message bubbles will be green. If you're exchanging iMessages with others, your bubbles will be blue. The distinction is important because most of the fancy multimedia tricks I tell you about in this chapter won't work unless you're exchanging iMessages.

TIP

The Messages app used to be called iMessage. But individual messages sent through the Messages app are still called iMessages. Confused? Don't be, because no one is going to call the tech police on you if you use either word when talking about Apple's messaging system.

REMEMBER

In this chapter, I refer to all the missives you send or receive with the Messages app as *text messages*. Unless I specify otherwise, this umbrella term refers to both iMessages and SMS or MMS messages and includes those missives that contain media, not just text.

Sending Text Messages

The next few sections show you various ways to ship out text messages to friends, family, colleagues, and perhaps even a stranger or two.

Sending a text message to one person

To start a new text message, tap the Messages icon on the Home screen to launch the Messages app and then tap the little pencil-and-paper (compose) icon in the left pane of the screen (shown in the margin).

At this point, with the To field active and awaiting your input, you can do three things:

>> **If the recipient is in your contacts list, type the first few letters of the name.** A list of matching contacts appears. Scroll through the list if necessary and tap the name of the contact. The more letters you type, the shorter the list becomes.

>> **Tap the blue circled + icon on the right side of the To field to select a name from your contacts list.**

>> **If the recipient isn't in your contacts list, type the person's phone number or email address.**

Now tap inside the message box that appears near the bottom of the New Message window. Type your text message. Note that you can start a new line in your text message by tapping the Return key.

 When your text message is ready to go, tap the send icon, shown in the margin.

Sending group text messages

You aren't limited to sending text messages to a single person. Group chats in Messages allow multiple people to carry on a conversation, including sharing images, directions, files, and all the other goodies in Messages (assuming that each person is using an iPad, an iPhone, an iPod touch, or a Mac).

REMEMBER

If even one member of a group chat is not using Messages — for instance, that cousin who insists on using an Android device — all messages in the group chat are sent as SMS or MMS messages. You can tell because your outgoing chat bubbles will be green.

To initiate a group message, open Messages, tap the compose icon (a pencil writing on a sheet of paper), and then type in the To field the names or phone numbers of everyone you want to include. When you've finished addressing and composing, tap the send icon to send your message on its merry way. To name the group, tap the group chat in the list of ongoing chats on the left side of the Messages screen. Then, at the top of the message history for the group chat, tap the bar containing the group chat's members to open a dialog that shows the group chat's details. Tap Change Name and Photo, tap the Enter a Group Name field, and then enter the name you want.

You can see all participants in a group chat by tapping the group chat in your list of chats, and then at the top of the message history for the group chat, tapping the bar containing the group chat's members. If any group members are sharing their location with you, you'll also see a Maps interface with their location in the details dialog. Scroll down to the bottom of the details dialog to see the images and links shared in the group chat and the files sent. To leave a group, tap Leave This Conversation in the details dialog.

To add someone to the group, tap the X People button in the details dialog (where X is the number of people currently in the group chat), and then tap the Add Contact button.

Adding voice to an iMessage

You can record an audio message and send it to a recipient. Apple calls this feature Tap to Talk, and here's how to take advantage of it.

Start a new text message or open an existing conversation. Tap and hold down on the sound wave icon to the right of the text-entry field. (Note that the sound wave icon appears only if you haven't typed text in the message field.) Start speaking, keeping your finger on the icon the entire time. Your voice appears as a waveform at the bottom of the screen, as shown in Figure 6-1.

To send your recording immediately, keep your finger pressed down when you've finished recording and then drag your finger up to the Send button. When you release your finger, Messages sends the voice message.

FIGURE 6-1:
Lending your voice to an iMessage.

Alternatively, to listen to your recording before you send it, lift your finger from the sound wave icon to stop recording. Then tap the play icon that appears. If you're not thrilled with what you've just recorded, swipe left to cancel or tap the X to the left of the recorded message. Once the recording is the way you want it, tap Send.

WARNING

Listen right away because by default the iMessage expires in two minutes. You can choose Settings ➪ Messages ➪ Expire ➪ Never to have audio messages never expire.

TIP

Sometimes hearing someone's voice just makes a message easier to understand or more meaningful. Sending voice recordings through Messages can be a powerful way to communicate, and I encourage you to try it!

The recipient of your recorded iMessage will be able to tap a play icon to listen to what you have to say.

Keep in mind that the sound wave icon that lets you record your voice is enabled only if you're sending a Message to a chat partner who's using the iPad, iPhone, iPod touch, or Mac. It won't be available if you're chatting with someone in SMS or MMS mode, which is when your chat bubbles are green.

Massive multimedia effects

iPadOS is chock-full of wonderful Messages effects, including the capability to draw and write using your finger, send Digital Touch effects, react to Messages, and use screen effects. You can also replace words with emojis lightning fast and use the tapback feature to offer a quick reaction to the sender.

The Messages app in iPadOS also includes a built-in App Store for third-party stickers and emojis and full-blown apps that run in Messages.

Let's plunge right in. Follow the previous instructions in the "Sending Text Messages" section and choose a recipient or group you want to engage with, and then tap the gray App Store button, between the camera icon and the iMessage text box. A new row of recent apps appears below the iMessage field, as shown in Figure 6-2.

The first icon is for Photos, which you can tap to cherry-pick images and videos from your Photos library.

The blue App Store icon accesses the Messages App Store for stickers and apps that run right inside Messages. Figure 6-3 shows the Messages App Store opened to a sampling of seasonal stickers. Tap the magnifying glass icon to browse other kinds of apps or to search for a specific Messages app.

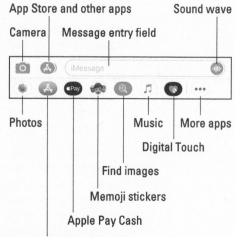

FIGURE 6-2:
When sending an iMessage, you can add a picture or a sketch, visit the App Store, choose a sticker pack, or add memoji.

Stickers are fun and a great way to convey simple or complex thoughts and feelings. Try them out. I think you'll like them, too.

TIP

With Bitmoji, one of my favorite Messages apps, you can build a cartoon representation of yourself, kind of like Apple's memoji feature (described later in the chapter). Bitmoji provides hundreds of funny, silly, and sometimes poignant stickers that you can add to your cartoon. It seems like whatever you're trying to say, Bitmoji has a sticker for it. And it's free!

The other icons in the row are for Apple Pay, memoji, find images, Music, Digital Touch, and more apps, which displays other recent apps you've opened in Messages. Keep reading to learn more about these features and other aspects of Messages.

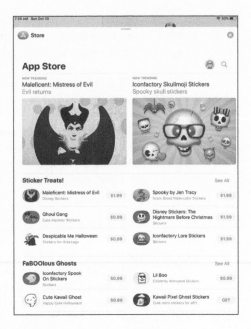

FIGURE 6-3:
The Messages App Store gives you fast access to stickers and apps just for Messages.

Let's start with some of the features that allow you to personalize and add to your Messages conversations:

>> **To comment on a message with a tapback:**
Long-press the message until the tapback bubble appears, as shown in Figure 6-4, and then tap the appropriate icon.

If you change your mind and want to dismiss the tapback bubble without adding a tapback icon to the message, just tap the screen anywhere *outside* the tapback bubble. Tapback is a great way to emphasize a message, to show your agreement or disagreement with a message, or to indicate that you like that message.

WARNING

Tapback works only with other devices running iPadOS, iOS 10 and above, or macOS Sierra and above. If the recipients are using any other operating system, they won't see any cute balloons, just plain old text that reads, "*Your*

FIGURE 6-4:
Tap a tapback icon to send a quick reaction to the sender.

name here Loved/Liked/Disliked/Laughed At/Emphasized/Questioned *item name here.*"

» **To replace text with an emoji:** You can add emoji to a message any time by tapping the emoji key on your keyboard.

iPadOS will also make quick (and usually great) recommendations for substituting written words with emojis; simply check the space between the iMessage input field and your keyboard. These recommendations shift and change depending on what you're typing. If more than one emoji is associated with the word, as shown in Figure 6-5, you'll see multiple emojis suggested; tap the emoji you want and it will replace the word you're typing. How convenient!

FIGURE 6-5:
Choose from the suggested emojis to replace a word with an emoji.

» **To add bubble or screen effects:** Prepare your message as usual, but rather than tapping the Send icon, long-press it until the Send with Effect screen appears. Tap the Bubble tab at the top and then tap Slam, Loud, Gentle, or Invisible Ink as the bubble effect for your message. The Invisible Ink effect means your iMessage recipient will have to swipe across the message or tap the message bubble to read it. Alternatively, tap the Screen tab and swipe left (or right to go back) to select Echo, Spotlight, Balloons, Confetti, Send with Love, Lasers, Fireworks, or Celebration as the screen effect for this message. Try it because you need to see it to believe it!

If you change your mind and don't want to add an effect, tap the *x*-in-a-circle to dismiss the Bubble and Screen Effects screen.

» **To send a handwritten message:** Sometimes nothing but a handwritten note will do. Tap the handwriting icon in the lower-right corner of the keyboard (and shown in the margin). You'll be whisked off to a white area where you can write your message using your finger, an Apple Pencil accessory (for iPad Pro models), or a third-party stylus. Tap > if you need more space.

If you prefer a premade message or one you previously created, tap the tiny clock icon at the bottom-left corner of the white writing area to display a list to choose from. Figure 6-6 shows premade messages saying Congratulations, I'm Sorry, Thinking of You, and more.

FIGURE 6-6:
Choosing a handwritten preset.

TIP

You can use the handwriting icon to draw images, too, so let your imagination run when using this fun feature.

» **To send Digital Touch effects:** Digital Touch effects first appeared on Apple Watch but are now found also in iPadOS. They allow you to send customized animations designed to convey emotions and other abstract thoughts. Tap the gray App Store icon to reveal the row of iMessage apps available to you. Tap the Digital Touch icon (the heart with two fingers laying across it) to reveal the Digital Touch interface shown in Figure 6-7.

Here's how Digital Touch works:

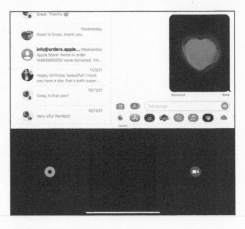

FIGURE 6-7:
I just sent a heartbeat through the Digital Touch interface.

- **To expand the Digital Touch interface to full screen:** Drag the short gray bar at the top of the Digital Touch interface towards the top of the screen.

- **To sketch:** Draw with one finger.

- **To send a pulsing circle:** Tap with one finger.

- **To send a fireball:** Tap and hold down with one finger.

- **To send a kiss:** Tap with two fingers.

- **To send a heartbeat:** Long-press with two fingers.

- **To send a broken heart:** Long-press with two fingers, and then drag down.

- **To switch ink colors:** Tap one of the circles on the left. If you see only one hue option, tap the colored circle to reveal other choices.

- **To add a picture or video to your Digital Touch effect:** Tap the camera icon on the right.

WARNING

Fireball, kiss, and heartbeat Digital Touch messages are sent automatically as soon as you lift your finger. Don't tap or press the screen in Digital Touch mode unless you really mean it.

Next, let's look at the built-in App Store I mentioned, where you can buy (or download for free) sticker packs, new effects, lyric quoting apps, games you can play with your friends, apps for professional sports, and more. To get free stickers and see what other third-party apps are available, tap the gray App Store icon to the left of the text field, and then tap the blue App Store icon that appears below (refer to Figure 6-2).

After you've acquired apps, this is also where you access them. So, for example, to send a sticker from a sticker pack you've downloaded, you'd tap the gray App Store icon to display the row of installed and available apps. Then tap the icon for the sticker packs or app you want to use (or just browse) and use the sticker pack or app as desired. When you're finished, tap another app icon to open a different app, or tap the iMessage input field to close the app interface.

Memoji, a mouthful, but worth it

Memojis are so much fun! You can use them to create a cartoon version of yourself to send in your iMessages as a sticker. Figure 6-8 shows some example memojis, including some of Apple's stock characters. Below the different memoji characters are stickers Apple created using these memojis. Every memoji you make will have these sticker options.

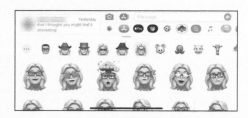

FIGURE 6-8:
Memojis give you personalized stickers for your iMessages.

Here's how to create your own memoji:

1. **Tap the gray App Store icon to the left of the iMessage input field, and then tap the memoji stickers icon (refer to Figure 6-2).**

2. **Tap New Memoji (+).**

3. **Tap Get Started.**

   Messages displays the memoji creator dialog.

4. **Customize your memoji.**

   Tap to choose the skin color, hairstyle, brows, eyes, head, nose, mouth, ears, facial hair, eyewear, and headwear. Each of these categories of features has multiple options to choose from. Spend as much or as little time as you want to create the perfect memoji for you.

5. **Tap Done on the memoji creator dialog.**

   That's it! Your new memoji is now available in the list of available memojis and, as noted, will also have stickers based on what you created, premade and ready to go.

If you want to edit, duplicate, or delete a memoji, tap the memoji and then tap the circle with three dots on the left side of the memoji pane. A list of options appears: New Memoji, Edit, Duplicate, and Delete. Then do one of the following:

» Tap Edit to make changes to the memoji you already created.

» Tap Duplicate to use what you already created as the starting-off point for a new memoji. This option is useful if you want to change a hat, glasses, or some other minor feature.

» Tap Delete to permanently delete the memoji you created. You'll be asked to tap Delete again to confirm the deletion. When you do so, the deleted memoji disappears, and the next memoji in your list takes its place.

Tap Done to go back to Messages.

Now that you've created a memoji and have a list of stickers, it's time to insert a memoji sticker in an iMessage. Tap the memoji sticker you want to use to add it to your iMessage input field. Then tap the blue send arrow on the right side of the iMessage input field to send your memoji to your recipient. Or, if you change your mind and want to delete the memoji from your iMessage input field before sending, tap the small gray x-in-a-circle.

Animoji, too!

Animojis are at least as much fun as memojis, but you'll need an iPad Pro with Face ID to use them. You can record an audio message and map it to an animoji or memoji character. That character will then move to match what your face did when you recorded the message. Here's how it works.

If you have an iPad Pro with Face ID, the row of available apps that appears below your iMessage input field when you tap the gray App Store icon will include an icon of a monkey with an open mouth. Tap the monkey icon to open the Animoji app in Messages, as shown in Figure 6-9.

FIGURE 6-9:
Animoji lets you send an animated message based on your emoji or Apple's premade characters.

Here's how to create and use an animoji:

1. **Choose an animoji character.**

   Tap one of the memojis you created, follow the steps in the preceding section to create one, or choose from Apple's premade characters. Your iPad Pro is now ready to map your facial movements and record a message.

2. **Position your iPad for recording by holding it so that it's upright and in front of your face.**

   The Face ID camera in your iPad Pro is now mapping your facial movements. If you look at your animoji, you'll see that it moves as you move. It opens its eyes with you, and its mouth moves like yours. Even your head tilts are captured. Now you're ready to record!

3. **Record your animoji:**

   a. *Tap and hold down on the red record button that appears in the bottom-right corner of your iPad's screen.*

   b. *Say (or sing!) what you want.* You have up to 30 seconds to record whatever you want.

   c. *When you're finished, simply lift your finger from the red record button.* Your animoji will immediately play back, allowing you to preview what you recorded.

   d. *Tap the blue replay button on the left side of your screen as many times as you want to preview it.*

4. **When you're ready to send your animoji, tap the blue up-arrow-in-a-circle on the right side of your screen.**

   And with that, it's sent! Now all you have to do is wait for your chat recipient to send you the LOLs and heart tapbacks.

Apple Pay Cash, right in Messages

Did you know you can send and receive money in your Messages app? It's part of Apple Pay Cash, which itself is part of Apple Pay. Although Apple limits the Wallet app to iPhone, Apple Pay is still part of iPadOS.

Outside Messages, you can use Apple Pay on your iPad on sites that have enabled support for Apple Pay. In Messages, you can both send and receive money that comes from or goes to your Apple Pay balance. You can then use that balance to pay for things or to send money to someone using Apple Pay Cash. If you want to send more money to someone than you have in your Apple Pay Cash balance, Apple Pay Cash will pull from the bank account you've added to Apple Pay Cash.

If you're paying for something that costs more than your Apple Pay Cash balance, you can do so using any of the credit cards attached to your Apple Pay account.

Here's how to send or request money via Apple Pay Cash:

1. **Tap the Apple Pay Cash icon (refer to Figure 6-2).**

   The Apple Pay Cash interface opens, as shown in Figure 6-10.

2. **Tap to choose how much money you want to send (or request).**

   Use the + and – button, or tap the $1 text to open a keypad where you can tap exactly how much money you want to send (or request).

FIGURE 6-10:
Sending money through Apple Pay Cash is easy and fast.

3. **Tap Pay or Request, depending on what you want to do:**

   - *Tap Pay to have the money taken from your Apple Pay balance or your bank account and sent to your iMessage recipient.*

   - *Tap Request to ask that person for money.*

   The amount you're sending or requesting will be added to a new message waiting to be sent.

4. **Complete the transaction by tapping the up-arrow-in-a-circle in the iMessage input field.**

To cancel an unsent Apple Pay Cash transaction, tap the gray x-in-a-circle in the upper-right corner of the transaction. After you have sent a transaction, it cannot be unsent.

To view the details of an Apple Pay Cash transaction, tap the black Apple Pay square in your Messages chat. You see who sent the money, when it was sent, the status of the transaction, how much was received, and a transaction ID.

Being a Golden Receiver: Receiving iMessages

Text messaging is very much a two-way street. In the last section, you learned the ins and outs of sending text messages. Here, you discover how to receive them, as well.

Changing some receive settings

When determining your settings for receiving iMessages, first things first. Decide whether you want to hear an alert when you receive a message:

REMEMBER

>> **If you want to hear an alert sound when you receive a message:** Go to Settings ⇨ Sounds ⇨ Text Tone, and then tap an available sound. You can audition the sounds by tapping them. You can also create your own tones in GarageBand for iPad.

  You hear the sounds when you audition them in the Settings app, even if the ring/silent switch is set to silent. After you exit the Settings app, however, you *won't* hear a sound when a message arrives if the ring/silent switch is set to silent.

>> **If you *don't* want to hear an alert when a message arrives:** Instead of tapping one of the listed sounds, tap None, which is the first item in the list of alert tones. You can also turn off alerts for individual chats and group chats. To do so, tap the iMessage you want to silence, tap the bar above that chat with the name of the person you're chatting with, tap the *i*-in-a-circle icon to reveal the Details tab, and scroll down and tap the Hide Alerts button. When that button is green, you won't hear alerts or receive notifications just for that chat!

>> **If you don't want any iMessages:** Turn off iMessage by going to Settings ⇨ Messages ⇨ and tapping the iMessage switch to off. You'll still get SMS messages when you turn off iMessages, so if you don't want any text message notifications, consider the do not disturb feature. It lives up to its name. Go to Settings ⇨ Focus ⇨ Do Not Disturb and activate this feature by tapping its switch on. You'll see a moon icon in the status bar. Even easier, turn on Do Not Disturb in Control Center (swipe down from the top-right corner of the screen, tap Focus, and then tap Do Not Disturb).

Working with received text messages

The following pointers explain what you can do with iMessages you receive:

>> **When your iPad is asleep:** All or part of the text and the name of the sender appear on the unlock screen. Slide to the right to reply to a specific message (you'll have to get past any passcodes first).

>> **When your iPad is awake and unlocked:** All or part of the message and the name of the sender appear at the top of the screen in front of whatever's already there.

These notifications are on by default; turn them off in the Settings app's Notifications pane if you don't care for them. You'll also see any notifications for messages you've received in Notification Center.

>> **Reading or replying to a message:** You can read a message or reply to a notification in three ways. Tap the Messages icon on your Home screen to simply go to the chat you want. You can also swipe downward from the middle-top of the screen to display Notification Center and choose a specific Messages notification or tap the live notification when it appears if you can be quick (the notification fades away in a few seconds).

>> **Following the conversation:** When viewing an individual chat or group chat, your messages appear on the right side of the screen in blue bubbles (green bubbles for SMS or MMS messages with someone not using iMessage) and the other person's messages appear in light gray bubbles, whether it's an iMessage, SMS message, or MMS message. When your message has been delivered, that fact will be noted just below the last bubble in your exchange. If there was a problem delivering the message, you'll see Not Delivered instead. If at first you don't succeed, try again.

>> **Forwarding a conversation:** If you want to forward all or part of a conversation to another iMessage user, long-press a text bubble in that chat and tap the More button, which shows up at the bottom of the contextual menu along with a Copy option. (You'll also see the aforementioned tapback icons.) Tap additional text, photo, or video bubbles you want to forward (the one you pressed to summon the More button is already selected) so that a check mark appears in a circle to the left of each. Then tap the forward (curved arrow) icon at the lower right of the screen. The contents of the selected text bubbles are copied to a new text message; specify a recipient and then tap Send.

>> **Deleting part of a single conversation thread:** Long-press a text bubble and tap More. Tap each text bubble you want to delete; a check mark appears in the circle next to each one. Then tap the trash can icon at the bottom of the pane, and tap Delete Message(s).

>> **Deleting an entire conversation thread:** Tap the Edit button at the upper left of the Messages list, tap Select Messages, tap the circle that appears to the left of the person's name, and then tap the Delete button at the bottom of the pane. Or swipe from right to left on the conversation in the Messages pane and then tap the red Delete button.

If you receive a picture or video in a message, it appears in a bubble just like text. You can view a still image or live photo inline, or tap the image to have it go full screen. In the case of a live photo, you can tap and hold down on it to play the short recording. (See Chapter 9 for more info on live photos.) If someone sends you a video, you can tap the play icon on the video to play it right in Messages. To have the video take over the full screen, tap the video first and then tap play.

Sharing received photos and videos

 In full-screen mode, tap the share icon (shown in the margin) in the upper-right corner of a received video or picture for additional options, such as sharing the image on Facebook or Twitter, and assigning it to a contact. If you don't see the icon, tap the picture or video once, and the icon will magically appear.

Smart Messaging Tricks

Here are some more things you can do with messages:

>> **Search your messages for a word or phrase.** Type the word or phrase in the search field at the top left of the Messages listing pane.

>> **Send read receipts to allow others to be notified when you have read their missives.** Tap Settings ⇨ Messages and tap the Send Read Receipts switch on.

TIP

In iMessages, you can see when your own message has been delivered and read, and when the other person is readying a response. You can also tap the person's name at the top of the conversation pane to reveal the details dialog and then tap Send Read Receipts. Read Receipts is turned on, but only for the person with whom you are chatting.

>> **Use a Bluetooth keyboard instead of the on-screen keyboard.** See Chapter 15 for more on Bluetooth.

>> **Dictate a message.** Tap the microphone key on your keyboard and start talking. Tap the microphone key again when you're finished. Dictating text isn't as quick or as much fun as Tap to Talk, but it works.

>> **Open a URL included in an iMessage.** Tap the URL to open that web page in Safari.

>> **From iMessages, call or FaceTime the person you're texting with.** Tap the circled picture or initials representing the person you're communicating with, and then tap the audio call icon or FaceTime icon to call the person directly. If you tap the person's name at the top of the conversation window to open the details dialog, and then tap the person's Info button, you'll open up the person's full Contacts pane, where you can initiate an email or use other contact information.

>> **See an address included in an iMessage.** Tap the address to see it on a map in Maps.

» **Choose how you can be reached via iMessage.** Tap Settings ⇨ Messages ⇨ Send & Receive. Then add another email address or remove existing addresses. You can also select the email address (or phone number) from which to start new conversations.

» **Show the Subject field.** Tap Settings ⇨ Messages and then tap the Show Subject Field switch on to show a Subject field with your messages.

» **Filter unknown senders.** Tap Settings ⇨ Messages and then tap Filter Unknown Senders on to turn off notifications for iMessages from folks who are not among your contacts. You can sort such unknown senders into a separate list. Specifically, after you activate Filter Unknown Senders, the initial Messages screen will display three lists: Known Senders, Unknown Senders, and All Messages (which includes both known and unknown senders).

» **Block a sender.** Block someone who is harassing you or has left your good graces. Tap the person's name at the top of the conversation pane to reveal the details dialog, tap Info, and then tap Block This Caller. You will no longer receive messages or FaceTime calls from this person.

» **Share your location.** Meeting a recipient in an unfamiliar place? In the middle of your conversation, you can share your location on a map. Tap the person's name at the top of the conversation pane to reveal the details dialog and then tap either Send My Current Location or Share My Location. Choosing the latter gives you the option to share your whereabouts indefinitely, until the end of the day, or for one hour. You can monitor how much time is left before your location will no longer be shared.

» **See all message attachments at once.** Tap the person's name at the top of the conversation pane to reveal the details dialog, where you can browse all the photos and videos from your conversation.

» **Keep your Messages history.** You can keep your entire Messages history on the iPad permanently, for one year, or for 30 days. Tap Settings ⇨ Messages ⇨ Keep Messages and make your choice.

You are now a certified iMessage maven.

3

Banish Boredom with the Multimedia iPad

Explore the world of Apple Music, Books, News, and TV, including Apple's many content subscription services.

Capture good video, watch video, and share video with others.

Shoot photos, store them, sync them, and more.

Chapter **7**

Apple Music, Books, News, and TV+

I f you believe that all work and no play make Jill a dull girl, prepare to shine. Why? Because your iPad is loaded with apps that fall on the "play" side of the ledger. These apps enable you to have loads of fun by turning your iPad into a multifaceted multimedia device.

If you're into music, for example, you can get your fill of everyone from Adele to ZZ Top by using the Music app, which gives you access to not only your own music library but also the seemingly infinite supply of tunes offered by the Apple Music subscription service. E-book nerds, too, have a home on the iPad: the Books app, which enables you to read almost any available book from the comfort of your tablet. If you get your jollies from knowing the latest happenings in the worlds of politics, sports, entertainment, and the like, check out the News app. Finally, if TV and movies are your thing, you can watch some great new shows with Apple TV+ using the Apple TV app. You explore all these apps and their corresponding services in this chapter.

Introducing Your iPad's Music Player

The Music app is the musical hub inside your iPad. You can not only manage your music library and listen to songs in the Music app but also tap into a library of nearly 100 million songs through the Apple Music subscription service. Read on to learn more!

The Music app sidebar is home to four icons at the top: Listen Now, Browse, Radio, and Search. You also see a Library section and a Playlists section. To view the sidebar, either swipe right from the left edge of the screen if your iPad is in portrait mode or rotate your iPad to landscape mode.

This layout is a lot like the App Store, which you read more about in Chapter 10. In the following sections, you take a closer look at these sections.

Listen Now: The Apple Music section of the Music app

You start with the Listen Now icon. Why not the Library icon? Because Listen Now is where you find Apple Music, Apple's premium music subscription service. These days, the vast majority of music is being consumed by streaming through services such as Apple Music, Spotify, and Pandora. This trend is a significant shift from the early days of the iPad, when everyone bought their music from the iTunes Store and managed it from their Macs and PCs in the iTunes app. Let's dig deeper into Apple Music so you can see what the fuss is about.

Apple Music gives you access to nearly 100 million songs. That's right, 100 million songs, plus curated playlists, song recommendations, and Beats Radio, Apple's streaming music channel with human DJs, sort of like a legacy radio station. You get all this for $9.99 per month or $99 per year, $4.99 per month for college students, or $14.99 per month for a family sharing plan for up to six people. Your first three months are free, giving you plenty of time to get hooked on Apple Music before automatic billing kicks in.

REMEMBER

You'll be married to that subscription price for as long as you want to listen to Apple Music. If you ever stop subscribing, you'll lose access to music you used to stream and any music you downloaded to your devices through your Apple Music subscription.

If you haven't already subscribed to Apple Music, you'll be asked to subscribe the first time you open the Music app. You'll be asked also when you open the Listen Now section because it's full of the curated content from Apple Music mentioned earlier. In Figure 7-1, you see the subscription options offered to new Apple Music subscribers.

To subscribe on your iPad, choose the option you want, confirm or sign in with your iCloud account, and you're done! If you're already subscribed and are signed into iCloud in Settings ➪ Apple ID, you'll find Apple Music content in the Listen Now section. In Figure 7-2, you see the Listen Now section with music suggestions from Apple Music.

After you subscribe to Apple Music, you can tap the Listen Now or Browse icons, which are discussed in more detail later, and then tap to hear any artist, genre, playlist, or song. It's that simple! You can tap the iCloud download icon next to a song or album to download that music to your device for offline listening, or stream anything you want when you have a connection to the internet, be it Wi-Fi or cellular. Note that streaming music counts against most cellular data plans; check with your provider if you're unsure.

FIGURE 7-1:
Subscribe to Apple Music for access to nearly 100 million songs.

FIGURE 7-2:
Listen Now offers recently played music and Apple Music suggestions.

Finding new music in Browse

The Browse icon in the Music app is all about finding new music, looking at music by genre, and viewing other recommended content from the Apple music team. While Listen Now is centered on what Apple Music thinks you're interested in, Browse offers a more general look at music, especially new releases and other new additions to the Apple Music catalog. Just like with Listen Now, when you have a subscription to Apple Music, you can tap any artist, playlist, genre, song, or other listing and play that music whenever you want.

But unlike Listen Now, Browse also lets you see content whether or not you have a subscription to Apple Music, allowing you to preview songs and see new releases. If you try to play a song, however, you'll be asked to sign in with an Apple ID that has subscribed to Apple Music.

Listening to human DJs in the age of streaming music

Tap the Radio icon to see the Radio section of Apple Music. You'll find several stations algorithmically designed around your music, as shown in Figure 7-3.

But the crown jewel in Apple Music's radio collection, and a feature unique to Apple Music, is Apple Music 1, an internet radio station created by humans and with human DJs. Much of the content is created hands-on by Apple's talented staff, with other content created by big and small artists. You can listen to individual shows with distinct flavors helmed by named DJs. You can tap See Full Schedule to view a schedule of shows; you also see some flagship shows promoted in the large banner at the top of the screen.

To listen to Apple Music 1 or any other radio stations, tap the show or station you want to enjoy. You can view content in the Radio section at any time, but you need an active subscription to Apple Music to listen to those shows.

FIGURE 7-3:
The Radio section features radio stations built around your music.

Managing music in the library

Now let's move on to your music, which you'll find in the Library section of the Music app sidebar. The library is dedicated to songs you've ripped from CDs, downloaded from the iTunes Store or other online music stores, or downloaded from Apple Music for offline listening. You also find songs you've synced to your iPad from your Mac or PC.

If you have multiple Apple devices and want to keep your music library synced between all of them, open Settings ➪ Music and then tap the Sync Library switch on. With Sync Library, changes to the music library on one device are synced automatically to your other Apple devices.

TIP

For more information on syncing music to your iPad from your Mac or PC, please see Chapter 3.

Figure 7-4 shows an example of the Albums section of the library, where the albums are sorted alphabetically by artist. Each album shows the album cover, the name of the album, and the artist. Tap Sort in the upper-right corner of the screen to sort your library by Recently Added, Title, or Artist.

Working with playlists

As with individual songs, you can create and listen to playlists on your iPad, or manage playlists synced to your library through the Sync Library feature. To see your playlists, display the Music sidebar and then tap Playlists. You see a list of any playlists you've created. You can tap any playlist to view its contents, and then tap the play icon on the Playlist page to listen to it.

FIGURE 7-4:
The library shows all the music on your iPad.

To create a playlist, tap All Playlists in the sidebar, and then tap New in the upper-right corner to bring up the New Playlist dialog. Tap Playlist Name and enter a name for your playlist, and then tap the Add Music button to add new songs. You can choose from your library or the Listen Now content, or you can browse for content. Add as many songs as you like. When you're finished, tap the Done button in the upper-right corner of the Add Songs to New Playlist dialog. You can tap Description to add an optional description and tap the camera icon on the left side to add cover art. Finally, tap the Done button in the upper-right corner. Your new playlist will be listed in the main playlist view, where you can tap and play it whenever you want.

To edit your playlist, tap the three dots (. . .) in the upper-right corner of your playlist screen and then tap Edit. In edit mode, you can change the name of your playlist and add cover art. If it's a playlist you created, you can also rearrange the order of the songs by dragging the three lines next to a song. If the playlist is one of Apple's Smart playlists, such as My Top Rated, you can't change the order of the songs.

Managing your own music with iTunes Match

iTunes Match is another music-related subscription service from Apple. Unlike Apple Music, however, iTunes Match helps you manage the song files in your own music library. It does so by taking the music in your iTunes (macOS Yosemite and earlier or Windows) or Music (macOS Mojave or later) library and uploading it to iCloud. You can then stream that music on your Apple devices or through iTunes on Windows, without having to sync or otherwise transfer the files. For offline listening on your other devices, you can download those uploaded files from iCloud.

Here's how it works: When you subscribe to iTunes Match, Apple goes through your music library and identifies every song. If Apple has one of these songs in its own massive library, it matches your file to its file and gives you access to that song in iCloud. If Apple doesn't have a song in your library — say a bootleg, a live recording, or something else obscure — it uploads the unknown song to your iCloud so you can access it.

TECHNICAL STUFF

As a bonus, all the music iTunes matches plays back from iCloud at 256-Kbps AAC quality even if your original copy was lower quality. You can even replace your lower bit-rate copies by downloading higher-quality versions after the matching process completes. On the other hand, if your original song file is higher quality than 256-Kbps AAC, you will be able to stream or download it from iCloud only at 256-Kbps AAC quality. Few people can hear a difference in quality at 256-Kbps or higher, but if you're an audiophile who can — and whose song files are of higher quality than Apple's 256-Kbps — think about this tradeoff before subscribing to iTunes Match.

TIP

If you don't have a bunch of obscure songs not found in Apple's extensive Music catalog, you probably don't need iTunes Match. On the other hand, if you're interested only in the music you own that's already in your library, iTunes Match is a less expensive way to stream your music from iCloud on all your devices than an Apple Music subscription.

You can store up to 100,000 songs in iCloud, and songs you purchased from the iTunes Store don't count against that limit. Only tracks or albums you specify are stored locally on your devices, saving gigabytes of precious storage space.

All this comes at a cost, $24.99 per year to be precise. To enable iTunes Match, go to iTunes (macOS Yosemite or earlier and Windows) or the Music app (macOS Catalina or later), and click iTunes Store in the sidebar or click Store at the top of iTunes in Windows. If you don't see iTunes Store in the sidebar of iTunes or the Music app on your Mac, go to iTunes ⇨ Preferences ⇨ General and enable iTunes Store. After you've clicked iTunes Store, scroll to the bottom of the screen on your Mac or Windows PC and click iTunes Match, and then click the Subscribe button. You'll be asked to sign in with your iCloud account and confirm your billing information.

Searching for music in the Music App

Search may be one of the most impor-tant parts of the Music app for many users because that's where you search both your own library and Apple Music for specific artists, songs, albums, and even lyrics. To go to the search screen, tap the Search icon above the Library heading in the. To search Apple Music (as I did in Figure 7-5), tap Apple Music if it's not already selected and then type your search term. To search your library,

FIGURE 7-5:
Search Apple Music or your own library in the Search section of the Music app.

tap Your Library and then enter the search term. When searching either Apple Music or your own library, your iPad will display live results that change the more characters you type.

What about the iTunes Store?

All this talk about Apple Music may have you wondering about Apple's venerable iTunes Store. Never fear, dear reader, because the iTunes Store is still on your iPad, but now it's a separate app from the Music app. If you prefer to own your music, you can use the iTunes Store to buy songs and download them to your iPad when-ever you want. (You can also buy movies and TV shows in the iTunes Store app.)

Tap the iTunes Store icon on your Home screen. Figure 7-6 shows the home page of the iTunes Store, which defaults to the Music section. Tap an artist, an album, or a song to view more information, including price. Note that links to Apple Music content in the iTunes Store may take you back to the Music app. That may be a little confusing at first — at least I think it is — but it's not surprising considering how hard Apple is pushing its subscription service.

If you buy a song or an album in the iTunes Store, it will be added to your music library, which is also back in the Music app. To play your newly purchased music, tap the Music app on your Home screen and then tap the Library icon at the bottom of the screen. If you don't immediately see your new music, tap Library in the upper-left corner and then tap Recently Added. Your new purchase will be at the top when it has finished downloading.

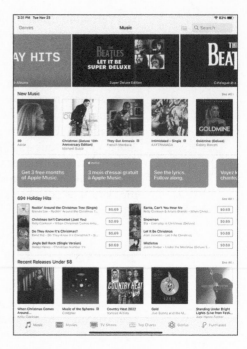

FIGURE 7-6:
Buy music from the iTunes Store.

Songs in the iTunes Store tend to be priced at $0.99 or $1.29, with most albums starting at $7.99. Purchased songs will be charged to your iCloud account, and you'll be asked to sign into your iCloud account if necessary when purchasing from the iTunes Store.

Reading Just about Anything You Want on the iPad

I love reading books on my iPad and two big reasons are the Books app and the Book Store in the Books app. With clear text, the ability to control fonts, accurate page numbers, and great page curling and turning effects that (almost) make it feel like you're reading a real book, Books offers a terrific reading experience.

Amazon's popular Kindle platform is available also on the iPad through the Kindle app in the App Store. I prefer Books, though. And even if you're already a Kindle user, I recommend checking out Books.

Open Books by tapping the Books icon on your Home screen. The first time you open the Books app, you'll see the Get Started screen. The Books app has five icons at the bottom of the screen: Reading Now, Library, Book Store, Audiobooks, and Search. You walk through all five icons in this section.

The default file format for Apple Books is EPUB (.epub), an open format for e-books. You can add EPUB files to Books through file transfers or even by emailing them to yourself and using the Open With feature to send them to Books. I discuss syncing files to your iPad in more depth in Chapter 3. Books also supports Apple's own multitouch format for e-books created with the iBooks Author app on the Mac. Most of the books available through the Book Store are EPUB files, but you'll be happy to know that you don't need to understand or care about the format of these books.

The Reading Now section offers quick access to the books you've most recently opened, as well as books Apple is promoting. As shown in Figure 7-7, the book you're currently reading is at the top of the screen, signified by the image of a physical open book. Other recent books can be viewed by swiping left to right in the Current section of the screen.

Below the list of Current books are books recommended to you based on what you've already read.

Your personal library

Tap the Library icon to view all the books you have in your Books iCloud library, whether or not they've been downloaded to your iPad. Books that haven't been downloaded have an

FIGURE 7-7:
The Reading Now section offers recent book titles and recommendations for new books.

iCloud icon below the cover art for the book. Tap that icon to download the book from iCloud to your iPad. Tap a book's cover art to open the book to the last page you had open. If you haven't previously opened a particular book, tapping it will take you to the book's designated starting page.

To view the table of contents for a book, tap to open the book, and then tap the menu icon in the upper-left of the screen. If you don't see the menu icon, tap anywhere on the page to bring up hidden controls and buttons, including the menu icon. Tap Resume to leave the table of contents and go back to the page you were on.

As you're reading, you can turn the page in two ways. One way, which turns the page quickly, is to tap the page's right margin. The second way is more fun, and some will find it more natural. If you tap and drag the right margin, you slowly turn the page, just as if you were turning a real page on a real book. You'll even see the text of the page you're turning reversed and dimmed, as if you were seeing through a piece of paper. I love this effect not for its gee-whiz awesomeness but rather because it can make the reading experience more immersive, especially for those who grew up reading printed books. Indeed, the effect will disappear into the background and you'll cease to notice it because it feels so natural. To turn back a page, tap the left margin or tap and drag the left margin to the right.

There's a third way to turn pages, too. Quickly tap and flick any page to the left (to advance it) or the right (to go back a page). For me, this technique quickly became second nature.

Let's take a second to jump to Settings ⇨ Books, where tapping the Both Margins Advance switch on allows you to advance the page by tapping either margin. You can still go back a page by tapping and dragging the left margin when this setting is active. Other settings allow you to toggle on and off full justification and auto-hyphenating. I recommend leaving those settings on, which is the way your iPad ships.

Font and layout controls in Books

Tap AA at the top of any page in a book to reveal the font control panel for Books, as shown in Figure 7-8. In this control panel, tap the small A to make the font smaller or tap the large A to make the font larger. Any changes you make will carry over to your other books in the Books app. Above the font size control buttons is a screen brightness slider. Tap and drag this slider to adjust your screen brightness as you see fit.

Tap Fonts below the font size controls to change the font of your books. Some, but not all, books will list Original as the font, probably at the top of the list. If Original is listed and selected, you're reading your book in the font chosen by the publisher. You can also choose Athelas, Charter, Georgia, Iowan, Palatino, San Francisco, New York, Seravek, or Times New Roman, all standard publishing fonts. Fonts are subjective, so feel free to choose the one you like the best or just leave it set to Original.

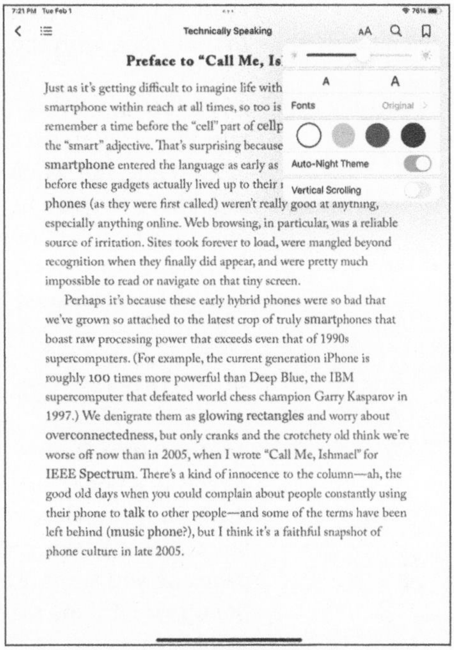

Next in the control panel are four circles that graduate from white to dark. These circles control the background color of the pages in your books, as well as the color of the text, which is optimized for each background color. Tap any circle to see how it affects your reading experience. The default is the white circle with the black outline, which gives you a white page with black text. The darkest circle is the night theme, with black pages and a very light gray (almost white) text. This mode can help reduce eye strain at night.

FIGURE 7-8:
Control the look and feel of your e-books with the font control panel in Books.

Below the circles is a toggle for Auto-Night Theme. Tap this toggle on (green), and the iPad's sensors will determine when you're in a low-light environment and switch to Night Theme (and switch back when you're in a brighter environment). I read at night a lot and find that this setting does reduce eye strain.

The last control is Vertical Scrolling, which is off by default. To activate it, tap the toggle on (green) and your book will now scroll up and down. Some people think scrolling up and down makes more sense on an iPad than flipping pages right to left. Try it. You might like it!

Searchable books

Next, let's look at the search feature, another reason that makes e-books great. Tap the magnifying glass icon at the upper right of a Books page to pull down a Search field. Type a word or page number in this field and you'll get results for every instance of your search term in the book. Tap a result and you jump straight to that page, with the word or phrase that matches your search highlighted.

At the bottom left of the screen, you'll also see a Back to Page xx button that will take you straight back to where you were. To be sure, this isn't a feature you'll use all the time, but when you need it, it's priceless. Imagine wanting to revisit a passage that has stuck in your mind or a character or event that you're sure has more meaning. Or if you're reading non-fiction, imagine wanting to find an instruction or a quote. As I've said, when you need this feature, you won't be able to imagine going back to printed books!

Bookmarks that don't fall out

Another great feature of Books is the bookmark feature. In the upper right of your screen is a bookmark icon. Tap this icon to bookmark the current page, turning the icon from white to red. It's kind of like dog-earing a page in a printed book, but without making the book lover in you cringe. You can bookmark as many pages as you want. To revisit your bookmarks, tap the table of contents icon in the upper left. You see three buttons at the top of the page: Contents, Bookmarks, and Notes.

Tap the Bookmarks button to see any bookmarks you've made in your current book. The Books app will list them, along with the chapter title and the date you made the bookmark. Bookmarks are a great way to revisit favorite passages or important bits. When you've finished looking at your bookmarks, tap Resume to go back to the page you were reading. To remove a bookmark, tap the bookmark icon on the bookmarked page to turn it from red to white.

Highlights and notes

Another great reason to embrace e-books and the Books app is the ability to highlight text and even attach a note to that highlight. To learn more about how this works, first turn to any page in any e-book. Now, tap and hold down on a word, which brings up the text selector tool. Drag the selector handles until the word or passage you want to highlight is selected.

In Figure 7-9, I selected the passage *savior come from across the sea* and then tapped Highlight, which added the yellow highlight mark, and then tapped the Note icon, which opened the yellow Note field. The highlighted text stands out if you flip through the pages, and you can tap the note icon in the margin to review your note. All notes are listed in the Notes section in the table of contents, allowing you to tap through to any of them. Not everyone needs this feature, but those who do will find it invaluable.

Buying books in the Book Store

If you're looking at a book now, tap the back arrow in the upper left to return to your library, because now it's time to go shopping in the Book Store. Tap the Book Store icon at the bottom of the page. Apple does a great job of presenting new releases, top charts (Apple's version of best sellers), and staff picks, and you can browse and read about books all you want.

At the top of Figure 7-10, you see staff picks for 2021 and a promo for books priced at $4.99 or less. You can swipe left in that section to see other promos. Below the promo section is the For You section, which are books recommended for you based on the books you've already purchased and read. Not shown in the screenshot are New & Trending books, Top Charts, Coming Soon, Books We Love (by Apple staff), special offers, and links to browsing by genre. These promotional areas are customized for you and may appear differently in your Book Store.

Tap any book to get a full-screen page of information about that book. Figure 7-11 shows *The Philip K. Dick Anthology*, with a button for buying it for $0.99, a button for marking it Want to Read, and a button for downloading a free sample. Almost every book in the Book Store will allow you to download a free sample. You can also read the publisher's description of the book, and the preview section gives you an idea of what the book's pages look like.

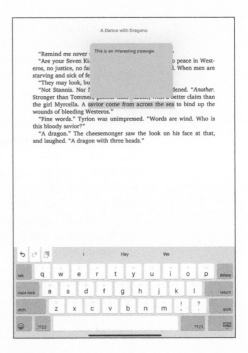

FIGURE 7-9:
Highlight passages and add Notes.

FIGURE 7-10:
Buy e-books in the Book Store.

Not shown in the screenshot are lists of More Books Like This, More Books by Philip K. Dick, More Audiobooks by Philip K. Dick, other books Customers Also Bought, and Top Books in Short Stories, and then a version history of this book along with any requirements the title might have. Tap the Buy button to purchase and download the book. Tap the x-in-a-gray-circle to close the book's promo page and go back to the Book Store. You can also swipe left and right to see other books the Books app thinks you might be interested in.

After you purchase a book, you can view it in your library. Tap the book in your library to open it, and then read it as described earlier in the chapter.

FIGURE 7-11:
Lots of information is available on the details pane.

Read books with your ears in the Audiobooks section

The Book Store also has a section for *audiobooks*, recorded books that have been read by a human narrator. Audiobooks can be listened to right in the Books app and are listed in your library along with your e-books. You can view just your audiobooks by tapping Collections in your library at the top left and choosing Audiobooks in the menu that opens. Audiobooks in your iCloud library that haven't been downloaded to your iPad will have an iCloud icon below them. Tap the iCloud icon to download the audiobook.

TIP

The Book Store has fewer audiobooks than e-books. That said, Apple has been adding more and more audiobooks to the Book Store in recent years, and many popular titles are available.

REMEMBER

Audiobooks tend to be more expensive than e-books.

Tap the cover art for the audiobook to open it, as shown in Figure 7-12. Tap the play icon to play the audiobook and tap the pause icon to stop. Tap the 15 icon with an arrow going counterclockwise to back up the recording by 15 seconds, something that's useful if you missed something or were interrupted. You can tap that icon as many times as you want. Tap the 15 icon with an arrow going clockwise to advance the audiobook by 15 seconds.

Tap and drag the timeline below the cover art to advance or rewind the audiobook to a specific point in the recording. Tap and drag the volume button to change the volume.

At the bottom of the screen are four icons: 1x, a quarter moon, the AirPlay icon, and the share icon. The 1x button is a playback speed button. Tap 1x to cycle through different playback speeds. Your options are 1x, 1¼x,

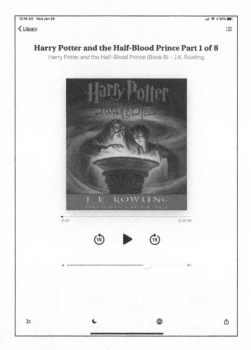

FIGURE 7-12:
Audiobook playback controls are intuitive and easy to use.

1½x, 1¾x, 2x, down to ¾x, and back to 1x. What speed works for you is subjective, so feel free to try different options to find the speed you like.

The quarter moon icon is a way of playing your audiobook for a certain number of minutes before it automatically stops, a great tool for listening yourself to sleep. Tap the quarter moon icon and choose to end the playing at a time between 5 minutes and 1 hour, when the current track ends, or after a custom number of hours or minutes or both.

The AirPlay icon at the bottom of the screen allows you to choose your audio source. Tap the AirPlay icon to pick between any connected headphones, nearby HomePods, nearby Apple TVs, connected Bluetooth speakers, or any nearby AirPlay-capable speakers.

Tap the share icon to share information about your audiobook through the standard share sheet. Tap Library in the upper-left corner to return to your library view.

Searching the Book Store

The fifth icon at the bottom of the Books app is the Search icon (magnifying glass). Tap the Search icon to open the search page for the Books app. In addition to the Search field, you'll see a list of your recent searches, if you've made any, as well as a list of trending searches that other Books customers have performed.

To perform a search, tap the Search field and enter an author, a title, or even a genre. Tap any of the results to get more information. Search results include any relevant books in your library as well as in the Book Store.

I love the Books app and the Book Store, and I think you will, too. If you're already a fan of e-books, give the Books app a spin. If you're curious about e-books but haven't tried one, dive right into the Books app, where you can download a sample for free.

Knowing What's Happening with Apple News and Apple News+

Apple got serious about its News app a few years ago, and it got even more serious with the release of iPadOS. The key to Apple's approach to presenting third-party news is human curation, a theme you may have noticed throughout this chapter. Apple uses human curation for many of its news selections, rather than relying solely on computer algorithms to make those decisions. In addition, Apple has focused on layout and presentation to make reading news stories in the News app pleasant and enjoyable. Some of the larger publications use tools that Apple provides to make News app versions of their stories visually stunning.

Tap the News app on your Home screen to open it. You'll be taken to the today view, as shown in Figure 7-13. The today view includes

FIGURE 7-13:
Today in Apple News.

Top Stories and Trending Stories sections, with stories gaining momentum in the News app. Not shown in Figure 7-13 are other curated sections, such as a For You section based on what you tend to read, Reader Favorites, multiple articles from the publications you read the most, and Business.

Tap the sidebar icon in the upper-left corner of the News app (or rotate the iPad to landscape orientation) to find links to the home pages for specific publications, as shown in Figure 7-14. Near the top of this menu is News+, which is discussed next, as well as links to Today, Shared with You, Saved Stories, and History, which contains a list of articles you've already read. You'll also see publications you're subscribed to and publications you've chosen to follow for free. Not shown in Figure 7-14 is a link to Discover Channels, where you can choose additional publications and topics to follow.

FIGURE 7-14:
The sidebar in the News app.

To edit the publications you follow, tap the Edit button in the upper-right corner of the sidebar. You can remove publications from your follow list by tapping the red circle with a – sign, and then tapping the Unfollow button that is revealed. You can move an item by tapping its icon with three lines and dragging it to the new location.

You can access a systemwide today view in iPadOS by swiping from the left side of any Home screen. One of the widgets in the iPadOS today view is the News widget, which includes headlines from the News app. What you read in the News app will help inform what the News widget shows you in the iPadOS today view.

When reading an article in the News app, you can tap the back arrow in the upper-left corner to return to the page that brought you to where you are now. You can also tap the navigation icon (shown in the margin) to jump to Today or another section of the News app, such as News+, which I describe next.

Apple News+ is yet another optional subscription service from Apple, and it gives you access to articles from top magazines and newspapers. Apple News+ is $9.99 per month, and your first month is free.

Tap the Navigation icon and tap News+ to go to the News+ section of the News app, as shown in Figure 7-15. If you haven't already subscribed, you'll be presented with a large advertisement for subscribing to the service. Below that advertisement are buttons that allow you to navigate the different publications that are part of your subscription.

Tap the Browse the Catalog button to see a list of every magazine and newspaper — there are hundreds. The other buttons break down that catalog into specific genres, such as Business & Finance, Cars, and Entertainment. If you haven't subscribed, you can tap through to individual articles, but you'll be able to read only the publication, title, author, date, and any sort of title image the article may have.

FIGURE 7-15:
 News+ in the News app.

Tap the navigation icon and then tap another section to leave Apple News+.

Tuning In to Apple TV+

Apple TV+ is Apple's new original content subscription service. Apple TV+ offers subscribers TV shows and movies developed for and available exclusively through Apple TV+. As of this writing, Apple TV+ is just $4.99 per month, with a one-week free trial when you first subscribe. For a limited time — Apple hasn't said when it will end — people who buy a new iPhone, iPad, iPod touch, Apple TV, or Mac get three months of Apple TV+ free.

I don't expect Apple to offer that free year forever, but it makes sense to do it now, while the service is new. That's because Apple is rolling out new shows as they go, and while I think many of those shows are great, there's not yet a deep catalog to justify the price. This is especially true when you consider Apple TV+'s competition is Disney+, Amazon Prime, Hulu, Netflix, and other services with more extensive catalogs of original and sometimes third-party legacy content.

As of this writing, Apple TV+ has launched shows and movies such as *Foundation, The Morning Show, Finch, The Problem with Jon Stewart, Ted Lasso,* and *Invasion,* as well as documentary movies such as *The Elephant Queen* and kids shows such as *Ghost Writer* and *Helpsters.* I know of dozens of other shows that have been signed by Apple and are in development, and Apple adds new shows every few weeks.

To watch Apple TV+ shows, tap the Apple TV app on your Home screen, and then tap the Watch Now icon at the bottom of the screen. Scroll down and tap one of the Apple TV+ buttons. You can also tap the Apple TV+ Originals button to see a landing page dedicated to Apple TV+ content, as shown in Figure 7-16.

If you haven't already subscribed to Apple TV+, you'll be able to browse the content with frequent opportunities to start a 7-day free trial. During that trial, you can watch as many shows or movies as you want. If you don't cancel your subscription before the 7 days is up, you'll be automatically billed $4.99 per month. If you have three free months because you purchased one of the devices mentioned earlier, you won't start paying until that time is up.

FIGURE 7-16:
Apple Originals on Apple TV+ in the TV app.

To view a movie or episodes of a show, tap the cover art for that movie or show. Then tap the Play First Episode button to start a new show or Play Next Episode for a show you've already started. Scroll down on the show's information page to see a list of seasons and episodes. You can download any show to your iPad by tapping the iCloud download icon below the episode. By downloading, you can watch shows offline, say on an airplane, a long car ride, or anywhere else you may not have internet access. You will, of course, need a Wi-Fi or cellular data connection to stream shows. As I say throughout the book, streaming video can use a lot of bandwidth, so be mindful of your cellular data caps if you're watching a show over your cellular connection.

To leave the Apple TV+ section of the TV app, tap the Watch Now button in the upper-left corner, or tap one of the icons at the bottom of the TV app screen.

And that concludes your look at Apple's content delivery apps and services. All these apps and services are great experiences on the iPad, and I think you're going to like them.

Chapter **8**

iPad Videography

First came the notion of the *third place*: somewhere other than home or work where a person could go to relax and gather informally with others (think coffee shop, community center, beauty parlor). These days we have the idea of the *third screen*: a video screen that a person uses almost as often as their TV and computer screens. You might nominate your smartphone as your third screen (heck, it might even be most people's *first* screen), but what if we restrict the screen to watching video? Ah, that's a different story and I think it's much more likely that your iPad with its relatively big screen and sharp image is your go-to third screen for watching video.

But your iPad is also equipped with a fancy-schmancy rear camera that you can use to shoot your own videos. Even better, you can edit those videos right on your iPad and distribute your filmic masterpieces to friends and family at the tap of an icon.

And with your iPad's front camera, you can take advantage of another useful video feature: face-to-face video chatting with old pals and far-flung family members.

In this chapter, you investigate these iPad video features courtesy of the TV app, the Camera app's video mode, and the FaceTime app. It's a veritable feast for the eyes and ears!

Finding Stuff to Watch

With iPadOS, Apple has brought all its video offerings, even shows you're watching through third-party services, under the umbrella of the TV app. In the TV app, you can find almost all the streaming content available on your iPad, as well as movies and TV shows from the iTunes Store and anything shared from iTunes on your Mac or PC. (If you haven't done so yet, now is as good a time as any to read Chapter 3 for all the details on syncing.)

You can still go to dedicated apps from third party-services, too. For example, if Netflix is the only subscription service you have, want, or need, get the Netflix app and you're covered.

Watching shows with the TV app

When you first launch the TV app, it opens on the Watch Now tab, alongside tabs named Originals, Library, and Search. These tabs are designed for content from iTunes, third-party services, and videos you've loaded onto your iPad through iTunes (or shared from iTunes). Videos you've made on your iPad are in the Photos app, which I get to later.

From the Watch Now tab, you can find TV shows and movies, no matter where they are. It's almost like having an Apple TV set-top box inside your iPad.

For instance, as of this writing, Seth McFarland's comedy *The Orville* is being offered under the What to Watch section of the TV app. Tap that show, and you get a new page with a description, an episode list, and an Open In button. Tap the Open In button, and an overlay pane appears with all the places where you can watch *The Orville*, specifically, Hulu, Fox Now, and AT&T TV, as shown in Figure 8-1. You can tap whichever app you want. If the app you tapped is not installed, you'll get a new screen inviting you to download it. A quick download later, and you have your new show!

FIGURE 8-1:
Want to watch *The Orville?*

And that's the secret of the TV app. You don't need to know which network or service a given TV show is on to find it. The TV app acts as a centralized location for finding shows available in your region, be they on Netflix, ABC, NBC, CBS, Fox, HBO, iTunes, and many other services, including streaming services in other markets. When a show is available in two places, say iTunes and Netflix, you can choose which source you want to get it from.

REMEMBER

Some streaming services, such as Netflix and HBO NOW, require subscriptions. Others, such as the ABC app, show commercials during streams. Still others, such as HBO GO, are part of a cable or satellite subscription.

You can browse the TV app by genre, hits, trending movies, trending TV shows, and a list of recently watched shows.

If you just want to check out original Apple TV+ programming, that's the job of the Originals tab at the bottom of the TV app screen. Tap Originals to see the latest releases and to browse Apple TV+ shows by genre.

Tap the Library tab at the bottom of the app and you find all the shows you've purchased or rented from iTunes as well as other videos. On the left side of the screen are organizational tabs, such as Recent Purchases, TV Shows, Movies, and Genres, as shown in Figure 8-2.

FIGURE 8-2:
The Library tab in the TV app is the home for movies, TV shows, and downloaded videos.

If you can't find what you want by browsing through the Watch Now, Originals, and Library tabs, fear not: Tap the Search tab and run a search. Search also includes tiles for video genres such as Action, Comedy, Documentary, and Sports. Tap one of those tiles and you'll see a screen full of the available titles in that genre.

Apple's TV app is a one-stop shop for all your streaming needs. You can still choose to use any given streaming app on its own — you don't have to go through the TV app — but the TV app can be a great way of finding shows you're looking for and discovering new shows you didn't even know you wanted to watch.

Renting and buying at the iTunes Store

Although you can use the TV app to find all movies and TV shows on iTunes, you can also browse in iTunes itself. iTunes features dedicated sections for purchasing or renting episodes of TV shows and for buying or renting movies, as shown in Figure 8-3.

Pricing varies, but it's not atypical (as of this writing) to fork over $1.99 to pick up an episode of a popular TV show in standard definition or $2.99 for a high-def version. And a few shows are free. You can also purchase a complete season of a favorite show — prices are usually about $24.99 for standard-def and $29.99 to $39.99 for high-def or 4K, when available.

A new release feature film typically costs $19.99 in high definition or $14.99 in standard def, but you'll see prices higher and lower.

FIGURE 8-3:
Bone up on a movie before buying or renting it.

You can also rent many movies, typically for $2.99, $3.99, or $4.99, though Apple sometimes serves up a juicy 99-cent rental as well, and I've seen rentals as high as $6.99. Not all movies can be rented, and I'm not wild about current rental restrictions — you have 30 days to begin watching a rented flick and 48 hours to finish watching after you've started.

In some instances, *Rocketman* is one example, purchasing a movie in HD also gets you iTunes Extras, featuring the kind of bonus content sometimes reserved for DVDs or Blu-rays.

Tap a movie listing in iTunes, and you can generally preview a trailer before buying (or renting) and check out additional tidbits: the plot summary, credits, reviews, and customer ratings, as well as other movies that appealed to people who bought the movie you're looking at. And you can search films by genre or top charts (the ones other people are buying or renting) or rely on the Apple Genius feature for recommendations based on stuff you've already watched. (Genius works for movies and TV much the way it works for music, as explained in Chapter 7.) Apple also groups movies by various themes — Kids Movies and Notable Indies are two examples.

Watching your own videos

You can find videos you've created in your Photos library, whether they're raw videos you filmed with your iPad or edited videos you created in iMovie. Check out the "Shooting Your Own Videos" section, later in this chapter, for directions on creating movies with the iPad.

Are we compatible?

The iPad works with many popular video standards, such as H.264, MPEG-4, M-JPEG, MP4, M4V, MOV, and HTML5 in Safari. (Note that the iPad does not support Flash.) You may run into a snag if you're trying to watch AVI, DivX, MKV, or other videos formats.

TIP

For a somewhat technical work-around for video formats not supported on iPad — without potential conversion hassles — try the $5.99 Air Video HD app from Bit Cave Ltd. Air Video HD can deliver AVI, DivX, MKV, and other videos stored on your Mac or PC that wouldn't ordinarily play on your iPad. You have to download the free Air Video Server software to your Mac or PC to stream content to your iPad. Or, for converting from a broader range of formats, try the excellent (and free) HandBrake app at `http://handbrake.fr/`.

A moment for HEVC

One of iPadOS's big under-the-hood features is the High-Efficiency Video Codec (HEVC; also known by the equally unlovely moniker H.265) for storing video. HEVC's claim to fame is smaller video files with the same or higher quality as before.

So far, the file format is used only internally by the Photos app on your Mac and the Camera and Photos apps on your iPhone or iPad running iPadOS. You can't currently export files in the HEVC format, and iPadOS intelligently exports using more common file formats. In other words, you don't need to worry about HEVC; it's just something Apple is using to make videos take up less space. I expect this to change over time, because HEVC is an industry standard like its predecessor, H.264.

Playing Video

Now that you know what you want to watch, it's time to find out how to watch it. For these steps, I walk you through watching a movie, but the steps for TV shows and downloaded videos are similar:

1. **On the Home screen, tap the TV icon.**

    You see a tabbed interface for Watch Now, Library, and Search.

2. **Tap the Library tab.**

    You see poster thumbnails for any movies you previously purchased through iTunes — even for those movies you haven't downloaded yet (refer to Figure 8-2).

3. **Tap the poster that represents the movie or other video you want to watch.**

    You're taken to a movie summary page that reveals a larger movie poster, a description, the genre, the run time, and a play icon, as shown in Figure 8-4.

FIGURE 8-4:
The movie info screen.

4. **To start playing a movie (or resume playing from where you left off), tap the play icon. Or to download the movie to your iPad for later playback, tap the iCloud icon.**

5. **(Optional) Rotate your iPad to landscape mode to maximize the video's view.**

Finding and working the video controls

While a video is playing, tap the screen to display the controls shown in Figure 8-5. Here's how to work the controls:

» **Play or pause the video:** Tap the play/pause icon.

» **Adjust the volume:** Drag the volume slider to the right to raise the volume and to the left to lower it.

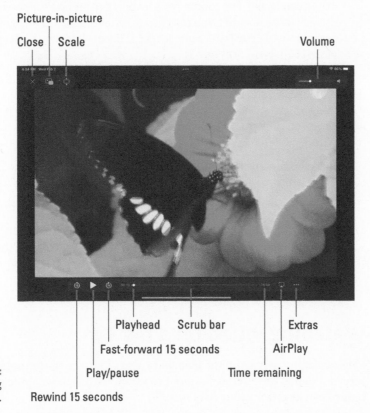

FIGURE 8-5: Controlling video.

» **Restart, skip back, or skip forward:** Tap and drag the playhead to where you want the video to start. You can use the rewind 15 seconds icon to go back 15 seconds, or the fast-forward 15 seconds icon to move ahead 15 seconds.

- >> **Set how the video fills the screen:** Tap the scale icon, which toggles between filling the entire screen with video and fitting the video to the screen. Alternatively, you can double-tap the video to go back and forth between fitting and filling the screen.

   Fitting the video to the screen displays the film in its theatrical aspect ratio. *Filling* the entire screen with the video may crop or trim the sides or top of the picture, so you don't see the complete scene the director shot.

- >> **Select subtitle settings:** Tap the audio and subtitles icon. You see options to select a different language, turn on or hide subtitles, and turn on or hide closed captioning. The control appears only if the movie supports one or more of these features. You can change certain subtitle styles by choosing Settings ⇨ Accessibility ⇨ Subtitles & Captioning and then turning on the Closed Captions + SDH switch.

- >> **Use picture-in-picture:** Tap the picture-in-picture icon to continue to watch the video in a small window, which you can drag around the screen while using a separate app on your tablet. Alternately, if you're watching a video when you close the TV app, the movie will automatically go into picture-in-picture mode.

- >> **Hide the controls:** Tap the screen again (or just wait for them to go away on their own).

- >> **Access bonus features:** Tap the Extras button. You won't see this button in every movie.

- >> **Tell your iPad you've finished watching a video:** Tap the X in the top-left corner. You return to the last video screen that was visible before you started watching the movie.

Watching video on a big TV

I love watching movies on the iPad, but I also recognize the limitations of a smaller screen. Friends won't crowd around to watch with you, so Apple offers two ways to display video from your iPad to a TV:

- >> **AirPlay:** Through AirPlay, you can wirelessly stream videos as well as photos and music from the iPad to an Apple TV set-top box connected to an HDTV or a 4K TV. Start watching the movie on the iPad, display Control Center by swiping down from the upper-right corner of the screen, and then tap the Screen Mirroring button. Apple TVs on the same Wi-Fi network will be listed as options. Tap the Apple TV you want, and your iPad's screen will be shown on that Apple TV. When you're finished, open Control Center on your iPad and tap Stop Mirroring.

You can multitask while streaming a video. Therefore, while the kids are watching a flick on the TV, you can surf the web or catch up on email.

Although you can stream from an iPad to an Apple TV and switch screens between the two, you can't stream to the iPad a rented movie that you started watching on Apple TV.

» **AV adapter cables:** Apple and others sell a variety of adapters and cables for connecting the iPad to a TV. For instance, Apple sells a Lightning-to-digital AV adapter for $49 that lets you connect an HDMI cable (which you'll have to supply) from the tablet to the TV. If you have an iPad Pro with a USB-C port, you can use a similar adapter from Apple called the USB-C Digital AV Multiport Adapter for $69. Both adapters also let you *mirror* the iPad screen on the connected TV or projector. So you can not only watch a movie or video but also view anything else that's on the iPad's screen: your Home screen, web pages, games, other apps, you name it. You can also mirror what's on the screen through AirPlay.

Restricting video usage

If you've given an iPad to your kid or someone who works for you, you may not want that person spending time watching movies or television. You might want them to do something more productive, such as homework or the quarterly budget. That's where parental restrictions come in. Please note that the use of this iron-fist tool can make you unpopular.

Tap Settings ⇨ Screen Time ⇨ Turn On Screen Time and then tap Continue. The first time you open this setting, you'll be asked whether the iPad is yours or your child's. Tap either This Is My iPad or This Is My Child's iPad, as appropriate, then tap Use Screen Time Passcode, and set up a four-digit passcode that will be required to make changes to Screen Time settings. Next, tap Content & Privacy Restrictions, and then tap the toggle next to Content & Privacy Restrictions so that it turns green. Tap Content Restrictions to view all the different ways you can limit content, including movies and TV shows.

Tap Movies to restrict movie ratings (G, PG, PG-13, and so on), or choose Don't Allow Movies to block movies altogether. Tap Content Restrictions at the top of the screen to go back to the previous screen and tap TV Shows to block based on rating or Don't Allow TV Shows to block all TV shows. For more on restrictions, flip to Chapter 15, where I explain the settings for controlling (and loosening) access to iPad features.

Deleting video from your iPad

REMEMBER

Video takes up space — lots of space. After the closing credits roll and you no longer want to keep a video on your iPad, here's what you need to know about deleting it.

To remove a downloaded video you purchased from Apple in the iTunes Store — the flick remains in iCloud — open up the TV app, tap the Library tab at the bottom of the screen, and then tap the Downloaded tab. The Library tab displays the TV shows and movies you've downloaded to your iPad. Tap Edit in the upper-right corner of the screen, and a circle will appear next to each movie or TV show in your list. Select the show you want to delete by tapping its circle, then tap the Delete button that is now in the upper-right corner of your screen. When your iPad asks if you're sure you want to delete the video, tap Delete Download. (If you change your mind, tap outside the Delete button.) You can also swipe left on any given title and tap the red Delete button that appears.

Shooting Your Own Videos

Your iPad has a great camera on the back, plus the FaceTime camera in the front. Let's take a look at the resolutions you can shoot with the camera on the back of your iPad:

>> **To 1080p:** Every iPad that can run iPadOS can shoot 1080p — or HD — video with the back camera. They all have video stabilization, too.

>> **4K video at 24fps (frames per second), 25fps, 30fps, or 60fps:** iPad Pro 10.5-inch, iPad Pro 2nd generation 12.9-inch (2017), iPad mini 6th generation, iPad Air 4th generation.

TIP

4K video image quality is astounding but is also a memory hog that claims roughly 350MB for just one minute of video, and that's at 30fps.

You can shoot video with the front-facing FaceTime camera as well, which includes a sensor that permits *HDR*, or *high dynamic range*, video.

Now that I've dispensed with that little piece of business, here's how to shoot video on the iPad:

1. **On the Home screen, tap the Camera icon.**

2. **Scroll through the list of shooting modes (Photo, Square, Pano, and so on) until Video is selected.**

   When *Video* appears in yellow instead of white, it's selected. On some models you can also choose Time Lapse or Slo-Mo.

TIP

   You can't switch from the front to the rear camera (or vice versa) while you're capturing a scene. So before shooting anything, think about which camera you want to use, and then tap the front/rear camera icon in the top-right corner of the screen when you've made your choice.

3. **Tap the red record button (labeled in Figure 8-6) to begin shooting a scene.**

   When you choose a non-video shooting format — Photo or Square — the round shutter button is white. In any case, while you're shooting a scene, the counter will tick off the seconds.

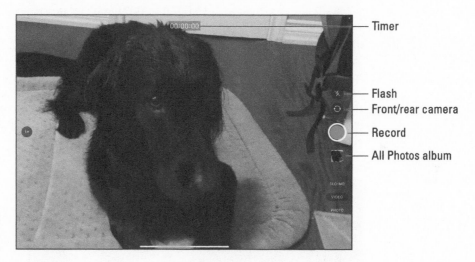

FIGURE 8-6:
Lights, camera,
action.

Timer — 00:00:00

Flash
Front/rear camera
Record
All Photos album

4. **Tap the red record button again to stop recording.**

   Your video is automatically saved to the All Photos album, alongside any other saved videos and digital stills that land in the Photos app.

TIP

   As of this writing, not every iPad model offers a flash. If yours doesn't, you'll need good lighting to capture the best footage.

Going slow

If you have an iPad model that runs iPadOS, you get another shooting benefit: the capability to capture video in slow motion, which I think is truly nifty. Now you can play back in slow motion your kid's amazing catch in the varsity football game.

Depending on your iPad, you'll be able to shoot at 120 frames per second (fps) at 720p or 1080p, or even 240fps at 720p or 1080p. However, the frame rate and resolution you're using to record your slow-motion video won't matter unless you're a professional videographer. And remember that the best camera to use is always the camera you have with you, so set your camera to Slo-Mo and grab the action!

But first things first: To shoot in slow motion, launch the Camera app and select Slo-Mo as your shooting format of choice. Shoot your slow-motion footage the same way you shoot at regular speeds. Note that the white circle surrounding the red shutter icon has teeny-tiny lines around it.

To check out your handiwork, tap the All Photos album (labeled in Figure 8-6), and then tap the slow-motion video you want to watch. The video starts playing at normal speed, and then slows at a point determined by the iPad. To change when slow-motion begins and ends, tap Edit and slide the vertical bars just above the frame viewer, as shown in Figure 8-7. (When the vertical lines are close, the video plays at a normal speed; when the lines are spread apart, the video plays slowly.) Note that when you play back a segment in slow motion, any accompanying audio is slowed too. Tap Revert to go back to the point at which the iPad arranged for the video to start going slow.

FIGURE 8-7: Adjusting your slow-motion playback.

Going fast

The time-lapse camera feature on your iPad has the opposite effect of slo-mo, enabling you to capture a scene and play it back at a warp speed. Even better, every iPad covered in this book sports the Time-Lapse option. To make a time-lapse video, choose the Time-Lapse option the same way you select other shooting modes, and then tap the record icon. The app captures photos at dynamically selected intervals. When you're ready to watch the sped-up sequence, tap play as you do with any other video.

Editing what you shot

I assume you captured some really great footage, but you probably shot some stuff that belongs on the cutting room floor as well. No big whoop — you can perform simple edits right on your iPad. Tap the All Photos album just below the shutter button in the Camera app to find your recordings. Or tap the Camera app, tap the Albums tab at the bottom of the screen, and then tap the Videos section on the left side of the screen. When you record slo-mo or time-lapse videos, iPadOS creates an album for them so you can find them quickly. Select your video, and then:

1. **If the on-screen controls are not visible, tap the video recording.**

2. **Tap the Edit button.**

3. **Drag the start and end points along the frame viewer at the bottom of the screen to select only the video you want to keep.**

    The lines turn yellow.

4. **Tap Done and then tap either Save Video or Save Video as New Clip (as shown in Figure 8-8).**

    If you choose Save Video, Photos will alter the original file — be careful when choosing this option. Save Video as New Clip creates a newly trimmed video clip; the original video remains intact. The new clip is stored in the All Photos, Videos, Slo-Mo, or Time-Lapse album.

5. **To discard your changes, tap Cancel.**

TIP

For more ambitious editing on the iPad, consider iMovie for iPad, a free app closely related to iMovie for Mac computers. Among its tricks: You can produce Hollywood-style movie trailers, just like on a Mac.

WARNING

Any video edited with the iPadOS version of iMovie must have originated on an iOS or iPadOS device. You can't mix in footage shot with a digital camera or obtained elsewhere.

FIGURE 8-8:
Getting a trim.

Sharing video

You can play back in portrait or landscape mode what you've just shot. And if the video is any good, you'll likely want to share it with a wider audience. To do so, open the All Photos album, Videos album, or another album, and tap the thumbnail for the video in question. Tap the share icon, and you can email the video (if the video file isn't too large), send it as a Message (see Chapter 5), or keep a copy in Notes.

And you have many other options: You can save the video to iCloud or share it in numerous other places, including Twitter, Facebook, Flickr, YouTube, Vimeo, and (if a Chinese keyboard has been enabled) the Chinese services Youku and Tudou. You can also view your video as part of a slideshow (see Chapter 9) or, if you have an Apple TV box, dispatch it to a big-screen television via AirPlay.

Seeing Is Believing with FaceTime

I bet you can come up with a lengthy list of people you'd love to be able to eyeball in real time from afar. Maybe the list includes your old college roommate or your grandparents, who've long since retired to a warm climate. That's the beauty of FaceTime, the video chat app. FaceTime exploits the two cameras built into the iPad, each serving a different purpose. The front camera — the FaceTime camera as it's called — lets you talk face to face. The back camera shows what you're seeing to the person you're talking to.

To take advantage of FaceTime, here's what you need:

>> **Access to Wi-Fi or cellular:** The people you're talking to need internet access, too. On an iOS or iPadOS device, you need Wi-Fi or a cellular connection and an internet connection on your iPad. You also need at least a 1Mbps upstream and downstream connection for HD-quality video calls; faster is always going to be better.

WARNING

Using FaceTime over a cellular connection can quickly run through your monthly data allotment and prove hazardous to your budget. However, you can do an audio-only FaceTime call, which can cut down significantly on your data usage.

>> **FaceTime on recipient's device:** You can do FaceTime video only with someone capable of receiving a FaceTime video call. That person must have an iPad 2 or later, an Intel-based Mac computer (OS X 10.6.6 or later), a recent-model iPod touch, or an iPhone 4 or later. You can also send a link to a Windows user and that person can join your call by pasting the link into a web browser.

Getting started with FaceTime

Now, let's get started with FaceTime by tapping the FaceTime icon on the Home screen to launch the app. If you haven't signed in with your Apple ID, head to Settings ⇨ Apple ID and sign in. If you need to create an account, tap Don't Have an Apple ID or Forgot It?

REMEMBER

If this is the first time you've used a particular email address for FaceTime, Apple sends an email to that address to verify the account. Tap (or click) Verify Now and enter your Apple ID and password to complete the FaceTime setup. If the email address resides in Mail on the iPad, you're already good to go.

If you have multiple email addresses, callers can use any of them for FaceTime. To add an email address after the initial setup in iPadOS, tap Settings ⇨ *your-name* ⇨ Name, Phone Numbers, Email. Then sign in to your account, if asked. In the Reachable At section, tap Edit. Tap Add Email or Phone Number to add email addresses or phone numbers. Apple will send confirmation messages to both.

You can turn FaceTime on or off by going to Settings ⇨ FaceTime. Tap the Face-Time toggle so it displays green to turn it on or white to turn it off. If you leave FaceTime activated, however, you don't have to sign in every time you launch the app.

Making a FaceTime call

Now the real fun begins — making a video call. (I say "video call" because you can also make FaceTime audio calls.) Follow these steps:

1. **Tap the FaceTime icon on the Home screen or ask Siri to open the app on your behalf.**

   You can check out what you look like before making a FaceTime call because the front FaceTime camera activates and puts what it sees on the screen. So put on a happy face, because you're about to been seen and heard by a loved one!

   Any recent calls you've made or received are displayed in a list on the left side of the screen.

2. **Choose someone to call:**

   - *Your recent calls list:* If you've already made or received a call, tap anyone in your recent calls list to FaceTime that person again. Below the name of each person in the list is the method you used to call the person before (FaceTime or a cellular call). Tapping an entry in this list will duplicate that method of calling.

     Or tap the *i*-in-a-circle to access the full entry in your contacts. At the top of the contacts list you'll see several ways to contact the person: message, call (as in cellular phone call), FaceTime, mail, and Apple Pay.

   - *Your contacts:* Tap the New FaceTime button and the list of recent calls will become the New FaceTime pane. You have two ways to find someone.

     One, start typing a name in the To field, and iPadOS will display all potential matches from your contacts. The more of the person's name you type, the more accurate those suggestions will be. Tap the name you want, and two green buttons appear on the screen. Tap the Audio button to make an audio-only FaceTime call to that person, or tap the Video button to make a video call.

     Two, you can tap the circle with a plus sign to show all your contacts, where you can choose the specific person you want. Tap a name in your contacts list, and you will get the person's entry in your contacts, including multiple ways to contact the person: message, cellular phone call, FaceTime, mail, and Apple Pay.

   - *Create Link:* Tap this button to send a link to someone who doesn't have FaceTime (such as a Windows user). That person can then paste the link into a web browser to join your call.

3. **Tap FaceTime.**

4. **If necessary, move the picture-in-picture window.**

   When a call is underway, you can see what you look like to the other person through a small picture-in-picture window, which you can drag to any corner of the video call window. The small window lets you know if your mug has dropped out of sight.

5. **(Optional) To toggle between the front and rear cameras, tap the camera icon (labeled in Figure 8-9).**

6. **Tap the Leave button when you're ready to hang up.**

   While you're on a FaceTime call, the following tips will be handy:

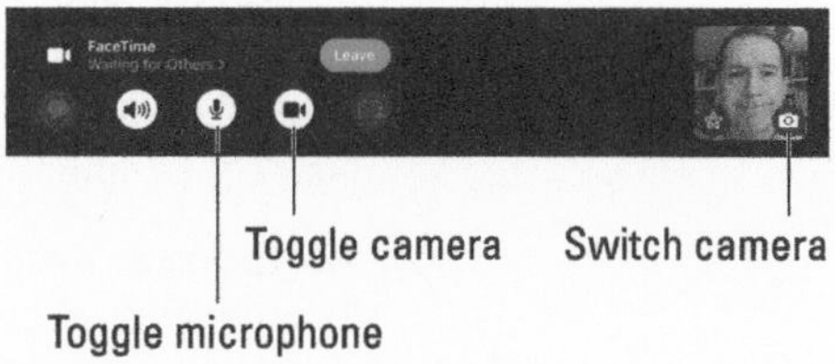

Toggle camera   Switch camera

Toggle microphone

FIGURE 8-9:
Tap the screen to see the FaceTime controls.

- **Rotate the iPad to its side to change the orientation.** In landscape mode, you're more likely to see everybody at once.

- **Silence or mute a call by tapping the microphone icon.** Be aware that you can still be seen even though you're not heard (and you can still see and hear the other person).

TIP

- **Momentarily check out another iPad app by pressing the Home button or swiping up from the bottom of the screen (if your device doesn't have a Home button) and then tapping the icon for the app.** At this juncture, you can still talk over FaceTime, but you can no longer see the person. You also won't be visible to them, which lets them know you're not currently in the FaceTime app. Tap the green bar at the top of the iPad screen to bring the person and the FaceTime app back in front of you.

Through the split view feature in iPadOS, you can conduct and view a FaceTime video call while engaged in other activities on the iPad.

TIP

Caller ID on FaceTime works just like caller ID on a regular phone call. You can choose the email address or phone number you want displayed when you call that person via FaceTime. To set your caller ID info, go to Settings ⇨ FaceTime and, under Caller ID, tap the phone number or email address you want to use.

Receiving a FaceTime call

Of course, you can get FaceTime calls as well as make them. FaceTime doesn't have to be open for you to receive a video call. Here's how incoming calls work:

>> **Hearing the call:** When a call comes in, the caller's name, phone number, or email address is prominently displayed on the iPad's screen, as shown in Figure 8-10, and the iPad rings.

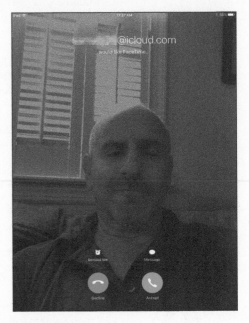

FIGURE 8-10:
Tap the green button to accept the call.

>> **Accepting or declining the call:** Tap the green Accept button to answer the call or Decline if you'd rather not. If your iPad is locked when a FaceTime call comes in, answer by sliding the Slide to Answer button to the right, or decline by doing nothing and waiting for the caller to give up. You can also tap Message to send a canned iMessage *(Sorry, I can't talk right now; I'm on my way; Can I call you later?)* or a custom message. Or you can tap Remind Me to be reminded in one hour that you may want to call the person back.

>> **Silencing the ring:** You can press the top button on the iPad to silence the incoming ring. If you know you don't want to be disturbed by FaceTime calls before you even hear a ring, visit Control Center (see Chapter 14) to put your iPad on mute. You can also turn on the do not disturb feature in Control Center to silence incoming FaceTime calls.

>> **Blocking unwanted callers:** If a person who keeps trying to FaceTime you becomes bothersome, you can block that person. Go to Settings ⇨ FaceTime ⇨ Blocked Contacts ⇨ Add New, and choose the person's name from your contacts. In the FaceTime app, you can block a caller who shows up on your caller list by tapping the *i*-in-a-circle next to the caller's name and then tapping Block This Caller.

>> **Removing people from the call list:** If you don't want to block a caller but don't want the person clogging up your call list, tap Edit, tap the circle next to the person's name so that a check mark appears, and then tap Delete.

TIP

You can also receive calls to your iPhone on your iPad, as long as they're on the same Wi-Fi network. Go to Settings ➪ FaceTime ➪ Calls from iPhone and change the option so the button turns to green.

Although I heavily endorse the use of FaceTime, I'd be remiss if I didn't acknowledge other video-calling services you can easily take advantage of on your iPad. These include Microsoft-owned Skype, Google's Chat, Facebook Messenger, Whatsapp, LINE, and Snapchat.

With that, I hereby silence this chapter. But you can do more with the cameras on your iPad, and I get to that in Chapter 9.

Chapter **9**

Photography on a Larger Scale

E verywhere you go these days, somebody — or, most likely, a whole bunch of somebodies — has a smartphone a foot or so in front of their face. What are they doing? Why, taking photos, of course. So many photos. This citizen photography (some have called it *smartphoneography,* a term that doesn't exactly trip lightly off the tongue) is a hallmark of the age, but it's almost entirely a smartphone phenomenon. Why? Because the size and weight of even the largest smartphone make it easy to snap a photo at will.

Alas, you can't say that about your iPad. Sure, the iPad mini is reasonably wieldy, but your average iPad or iPad Pro makes an awfully awkward camera. An awkward camera, yes, but not a bad camera. After all, the 11-inch iPad Pro and third-generation (and later) 12.9-inch iPad Pro have a 12-megapixel camera with back-side illumination, an impressive $f/1.8$ aperture, and a multi-element lens. The iPad mini 4, iPad mini 5, iPad 9.7 inch, and iPad 10.2 inch have an 8-megapixel camera with an $f/2.4$ aperture; the sixth-generation iPad mini and iPad Air have a 12-megapixel camera, an $f/1.8$ aperture, and a five-element lens. These specs are impressive, so go ahead and use your iPad as a camera. You'll be glad you did.

In this chapter, you delve into the details for taking photos with your iPad. However, you spend most of your time working with your iPad's long list of features that enable you to view, share, and edit your photos. I also give you a quick introduction to the barrel-full-of-monkeys-level of fun you can have with the Photo Booth app.

Shooting Pictures

You can start shooting pictures on the iPad in a few ways. Let's cut to the chase immediately:

1. **Fire up the camera itself. Choose one of the following:**

   - On the Home screen, tap the Camera icon.

   - On the lock screen, swipe from right to left.

   - Drag Control Center down from the top-right corner of the screen and tap the Camera icon.

   - Ask Siri (read Chapter 14) to open the Camera app for you.

   However you get here, your iPad has turned into the tablet equivalent of a point-and-shoot camera, although in a much bigger form factor. You're also effectively peering through one of the largest viewfinders imaginable!

2. **Use the camera's display to frame your image.**

3. **Select a shooting format:**

   - *Photo:* Think snapshot.

   - *Portrait:* Decreases the depth of field to blur the background, which brings more attention to your subject. This feature is only available on the iPad Pro (all 11-inch models and the third-generation and later 12.9-inch models).

   - *Square:* Gives you a picture formatted to make nice with the popular Instagram photo-sharing app.

   - *Pano:* Short for panorama, lets you capture epic vistas.

   - *Video, Slo-Mo,* or *Time Lapse:* I kindly refer you to Chapter 8.

   You move from one format to another by swiping up or down along the right edge of the screen (or the middle of the screen) so that the format you've chosen is highlighted in yellow.

4. **Snap your image by tapping the white round camera button.**

The button is at the middle-right edge of the screen whether you're holding the iPad in portrait mode or landscape mode (see Figure 9-1).

The image you shot lands in the All Photos album, labeled in Figure 9-1. I explain what you can do with the images on the iPad later in this chapter.

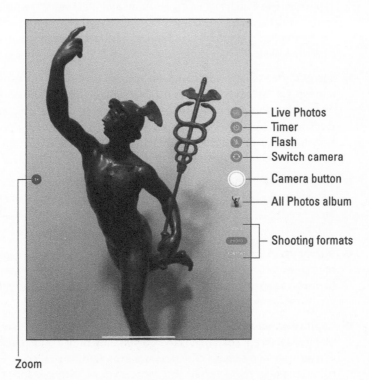

Live Photos
Timer
Flash
Switch camera
Camera button
All Photos album
Shooting formats

Zoom

FIGURE 9-1: Using the iPad as a camera.

Here are some tips for working with the Camera app:

>> **Adjust the focal point.** Tap the portion of the screen in which you see the face or object you want as the image's focal point. A small rectangle surrounds your selection, and the iPad adjusts the exposure and focus for that part of the image. (The rectangle is not visible in Figure 9-1.) Your iPad can detect up to ten faces in a picture. Behind the scenes, the camera is balancing the exposure across each face. If you want to lock the focus and exposure settings while taking a picture, long-press the screen at your desired focal point until the rectangle pulses and AE/AF Lock appears at the top of the screen. After you take your shot, tap the screen again to make AE/AF Lock disappear.

TIP

Next to the focus box is a sun icon. When the sunny exposure icon is visible, drag your finger up or down against the screen to increase or decrease the brightness in a scene.

» **Zoom in or out.** Spread two fingers on the screen to zoom in or pinch two fingers to zoom out. Alternatively, long-press the 1x button on the left side of the screen and then drag the dial counterclockwise to zoom in or clockwise to zoom out. The iPad has a 5X digital zoom and the iPad Pro has a 2x optical zoom, which basically crops and resizes an image. Such zooms are lower quality than optical zooms on many digital cameras. Be aware that zooming works only with the rear camera.

» **See gridlines to help you compose your picture.** Tap Settings ⇨ Camera and tap the Grid switch on (green). The Camera app now shows two vertical and two horizontal gridlines that divide the screen into nine rectangles. Gridlines can help you frame a shot by using the photographic principle known as the rule of thirds (where you place your subject on one of the gridlines instead of in the middle of the screen).

TIP

» **Toggle between the front and rear cameras.** Tap the switch camera icon (labeled in Figure 9-1). The front camera is of lower quality than its rear cousin but is more than adequate for most things, including FaceTime and Photo Booth.

» **Burst out.** In the blink of an eye, burst mode on the iPad can capture a burst of pictures — up to ten continuous images per second. Long-press the camera button to keep on capturing those images. This feature works with the front FaceTime camera and the rear camera.

» **Capture panoramas.** If you're traveling to San Francisco, you'll want a picture of the magnificent span that is the Golden Gate Bridge. At a family reunion, you want that epic image of your entire extended clan. I recommend the panorama feature, which lets you shoot up to 240 degrees and stitch together a high-resolution image of up to 43 megapixels.

To get going, drag the screen so that Pano becomes your shooting mode of choice. The word *Pano* will be in yellow. Position the tablet so it's where you want your pano to begin and tap the camera button when you're ready. Steadily pan in the direction of the arrow. (Tap the arrow if you prefer panning in the opposite direction.) Try to keep the arrow just above the yellow horizontal line. When you've finished shooting your pano, tap the camera button again to stop.

» **Geotag your photos.** The iPad is pretty smart when it comes to geography. Turn on Location Services (in Settings ⇨ Privacy ⇨ Location Services) and then tap Camera to see the specific location settings for the Camera app. Pictures you take with the iPad cameras will now be *geotagged*, or identified by where they were shot.

WARNING

TIP

Think long and hard before permitting images to be geotagged if you plan on sharing them with people from whom you want to keep your address and other locations private — especially if you plan on sharing the photos online.

To remove location data from a photo, open the Photos app, display the photo, tap the *i* (information) icon, tap Adjust, and then tap No Location.

» **Use the self-timer.** Many physical cameras have a self-timer that lets you be part of a picture. The self-timer built into the Camera app adds this functionality to your iPad, whether you're using the front or rear camera.

Tap the timer icon and choose 3 seconds or 10 seconds as the time interval between when you press the camera button and when the picture is captured. You'll see a countdown on the screen leading up to that moment. To turn off the self-timer, tap the Off button.

You can also add pictures to your iPad in several other ways. Alas, one of these methods involves buying an accessory. In the following sections, I zoom in on the details.

Syncing pix

An entire chapter (Chapter 3) is devoted to synchronizing data with the iPad, so I don't dwell on the topic here. But I'd be remiss if I didn't at least mention it in this chapter. (The assumption in this section is that you already know how to get pictures onto your computer.)

When the iPad is connected to your computer, click the Photos tab on the iPad Device page in iTunes on the Mac or PC. Then select a source from the Sync Photos From pop-up menu.

Connecting a digital camera or memory card

Almost all the digital cameras I'm aware of come with a USB cable you can use to transfer images to a computer. Of course, the iPad isn't a regular computer, isn't equipped with a USB port, and doesn't have a memory card slot. So, you'll need an adapter.

For its part, Apple sells an optional Lightning-to-USB-3 camera adapter ($39), a Lightning-to-USB camera adapter ($29), as well as a Lightning-to-SD-card camera reader ($29) for iPad models with the Lightning connector. The SD card reader connector accommodates the SD memory cards common in many digital camera models. You can also buy a USB-C-to-USB adapter for $19 for iPad Pro models with USB-C.

TECHNICAL STUFF

The Lightning connectors support many common photo formats, including JPEG and RAW. The latter is an uncompressed and unprocessed format favored by photo enthusiasts.

Saving images from emails and the web

You can save many of the pictures that arrive in emails or that you come across on the web: Long-press the image and then tap Add to Photos when the menu pops up. Pictures are stored in the All Photos album, which I get to shortly. You can also tap Copy and then paste the image into another app on your device.

Tracking Down Your Pictures

So where exactly do your pictures live on the iPad? I just gave some of the answer away; the images you snap on your iPad first land in a photo album appropriately dubbed All Photos in your Photos app.

In the Photos app, you'll also find pictures you've shared with friends and they've shared with you through the iCloud photo-sharing feature. The photos you imported are readily available and are grouped in the same albums they were in on the computer.

Moreover, every picture you take with your iPad (and other iOS devices) can be stored in an iCloud photo library. You can access any of these pics if you have a Wi-Fi or cellular connection to the internet. No more fretting about images hogging too much storage space on your tablet. What's more, the pictures are stored in the cloud at their full resolution in their original formats. (Apple leaves behind versions ideally sized for your tablet.)

You can still download to the iPad images that you want available when you're not connected to cyberspace.

In this section, I show you not only where to find these pictures but also how to display them and share them with others — and how to dispose of the duds that don't measure up to your lofty photographic standards.

Get ready to literally get your fingers on the pics (without having to worry about smudging them). Open the Photos app either by tapping its icon on the Home screen or by tapping the All Photos album button in the Camera app (labeled in Figure 9-1) and then tapping All Photos. Now display the Photos sidebar by swiping right from the left edge of the screen (portrait orientation) or by rotating your iPad 90 degrees into landscape orientation and tapping the Sidebar icon. The sidebar offers a fistful of icons for navigating Photos: Library, For You, People, Search, and more. I describe these options, and several more, in this information-packed section.

Choosing albums

Tap All Albums to pull up a list of all the albums you've created on your iPad, with a premade album called Recents at the upper left, as shown in Figure 9-2.

FIGURE 9-2:
Recents is a premade album at the top of your list of photos on the Albums tab.

Tap an album listing to open it. You'll see the minimalist interface shown in Figure 9-3, which reveals the by-now-familiar Recents album.

Browse the thumbnails to find the picture or video you want and then tap it. I show you all the cool things you can do from there.

REMEMBER

You'll know when a thumbnail represents a video rather than a still image because the thumbnail includes the length of the video.

Meanwhile, you can tell whether a photo is part of a burst binge in a couple of ways. The first is exposed here in All Photos. The thumbnail that represents this sequence of shots will appear as though it's sitting on a stack of photos. Tap the thumbnail to open the burst. In the second way, the word *Burst* appears in the upper left of an image you've opened, with a numerical count of burst photos in parentheses. Tap Select to choose which of the burst images you want to keep.

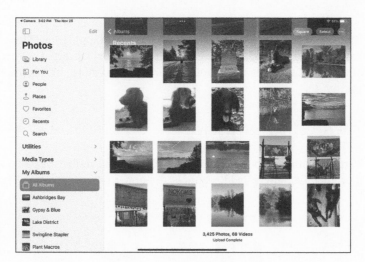

If you can't locate the thumbnail for a photo you have in mind, flick up or down to scroll through the pictures rapidly, or use a slower dragging motion to pore through the images more deliberately.

To return to the list of albums, tap < (back) in the upper-left corner to return to the current album, and then tap Albums. Once you're back in the Albums screen, you can create an album by tapping + (add) in the upper-left corner (refer to Figure 9-2), tapping New Album, typing a name for the album, and then tapping Save. To select pictures (or videos) to add to your newly minted album, tap their thumbnails.

Shortly, you see how to add pictures to an existing album.

REMEMBER

Albums you create on the iPad reside only on the iPad. They can't be synced or copied to your PC or Mac, at least without work-arounds through a third-party app such as Dropbox.

Navigating your pics

Placing pictures into photo albums has been the way of the world forever. But albums aren't the only organizing structure that makes sense. For example, Apple has cooked up a simple but ingenious interface for presenting pictures that's essentially a timeline grouped by years, months, and days.

This timeline breakdown is designed to help you drill down to the photos you want. When you tap on a given year, Photos shifts over to the Months tab. If, say, you're viewing your photos in October 2022 and you tap 2018, the Photos app will take you to October 2018 as a starting point. If you were viewing photos in January, the Photos app would take you straight to January for the year you tapped. Tapping a month shifts you over to the Days tab, where you can scroll through the photos you took in that month.

To scroll through your photos with a focus on visuals, you'll want to use the All Photos tab, where everything is laid out chronologically.

Figure 9-4 shows side-by-side-by-side views of years, months, and days.

FIGURE 9-4:
View your
photos by
years (left),
months
(center), and
days (right).

Through all these views, you'll see location information headings that get more specific as you move from years to days, assuming your iPad knows where the pictures were taken. (Go to Settings ⇨ Privacy ⇨ Location Services ⇨ Camera and tap While Using the App to have the location of your photos saved when you take them.)

In the Photos app sidebar, you can tap Places. Apple will fire up a map and show you how many pictures were taken in that location, as shown in Figure 9-5.

To quickly skim all the pictures in a particular year, press and drag your finger across the year thumbnail.

FIGURE 9-5:
Finding pictures on a map.

You can also tap a thumbnail in days or all photos view to see icons for sharing the picture, making it a favorite, discarding it, and editing it, as shown in Figure 9-6. Tap again and those picture controls disappear and the picture is bordered on the top and bottom by black bars.

FIGURE 9-6: You can share, discard, or edit a photo.

Making memories

Hidden within everyone's photo collection are the crown jewels, those images that trigger the most precious memories. The Photos app in iPadOS has a Memories feature that can help gather such memories automatically. Tap the For You tab to take a photographic trip down memory lane.

How does it work? The Photos app scans your picture library and collects images of vacations and birthday parties, as well as whatever the app deems are the best pictures you took during a given year or shorter time frame.

In Figure 9-7, for example, the Memories feature built memories based on trips to the California coast and Texas. Within such memories, you can play a Memories movie that the app automatically generates, complete with theme music, titles, and transitions. You can edit those movies too, by changing the title, music, duration, and photos in the movies. Apple promises to deliver up to three new memories daily if you're actively adding photos to your library.

Inside a memory, you can view pictures the app thinks are related, as well as by the people in them or by place (with photos plotted on a map).

In grouping photos into albums and such, Apple exploits advanced computer machine learning using facial, object, and scene recognition along with location data to make intelligent choices.

If you cherish any of the memories that Apple has kindly put together on your behalf, tap Add to Favorite Memories at the bottom so you can easily access it whenever you choose. If you change your mind, tap Remove from Favorite Memories. And if you don't like a memory from the start — perhaps it's too bittersweet — tap Delete Memory to get rid of it, though the individual pictures remain in your collection.

FIGURE 9-7:
Thanks for the Photos memories.

TIP

Want to see memories built around holiday events in your home country? Go to Settings ➪ Photos and tap the Show Holiday Events switch on.

Live photos

Did you know photos can come alive? It's true. A live photo looks like a normal photo, but if you tap and hold down on one, it turns into a 3-second video. It's practically magic, just like the books about the kid with the lightning bolt scar on his forehead.

Live photos require an iPad Pro or iPad 9.7-inch or newer model. To put the Camera app in live photo mode, tap the top icon (labeled in Figure 9-1). The live photos feature is active when the icon is yellow. When you take a photo, your iPad will capture 1.5 seconds before you press the button and 1.5 seconds after you press the button and make your photo live! It's a terrific effect, and I'm confident you'll be delighted and amazed by it. When you want to stop taking live photos, just tap that icon again.

A moment for HEIF

iPadOS includes a big under-the-hood feature called High Efficiency Image File Format (HEIF) for still images. HEIF's calling card is smaller photos with the same or higher quality as before. Plus, they support editing Live Photos in new and unique ways.

HEIF is used internally by the Photos app on Macs and by the Camera and Photos apps on iPads running iPadOS. You can't currently export files in the HEIF format, and iPadOS intelligently exports more common file formats. In other words, you don't need to worry about HEIF; it's just something Apple is using to make photos take up less space. I expect this to change over time, because HEIF is an industry standard like its predecessor, JPEG.

Searching for pictures

Your iPad has one more feature to help you find a given photo among the thousands or tens of thousands you've shot. You can search your entire photo library. Open the Photos app sidebar and tap Search.

Apple has kindly grouped some of your pictures into potentially helpful search categories: People, Places, and Categories. What you see may be different, depending on the kinds of photos you have on your iPad. To perform a search for particular photos, tap inside the Search box and type a search term with the on-screen keyboard, perhaps the date or the time a photo was taken or the location where it was shot.

But the big breakthrough comes with the capability to search pictures by what's in them: mountains, beaches, lakes, cats, whatever.

TECHNICAL STUFF

When your iPad is locked and plugged in to power (in other words, when you aren't otherwise using it), it uses some impressive machine learning to identify these elements in your photos. The process happens in the background, essentially invisible to you, and the work is performed locally, on your iPad, rather than on Apple's servers.

TIP

You can also enlist Siri to search for specific photos. For example, tell your obedient voice assistant something like, "Show me all the pictures I took at the baby shower."

Sharing your photos

Apple recognizes that you might want to share your best images with friends and family and have those pictures automatically appear on their devices. iCloud photo sharing enables you to create albums of pictures and videos for sharing and to receive photo streams other people make available to you. Here's how:

1. On the Home screen, tap Settings ⇨ Photos.

2. Tap the iCloud Photos switch to on (if it isn't already).

3. Tap the Shared Albums switch on.

4. Open the Photos app, display the sidebar, and open the Shared Albums list. Then tap All Shared Albums.

5. Tap + near the upper-left corner of the screen to open the iCloud dialog, and then type a name for your stream.

   The name is your call, but I recommend something descriptive, along the lines of *My Trip to Paris* (and you should be so lucky).

6. Tap Next and choose who will receive your stream.

   You can type a phone number, a text address, or an email address, or choose one of your contacts by tapping the +-in-a-circle in the To field of the iCloud pop-up window.

7. Above the To field, tap Create.

8. Add photos as follows:

   a. *Display the sidebar and tap the shared album you just created.*

   b. *Tap the +-in-a-square. When your Photos Library appears, tap each photo you want to include.* You can choose from All Photos or Albums.

   c. *Tap Done.*

9. (Optional) Enter a comment.

10. Tap Post.

   The recipient will receive an email and can choose to subscribe to your shared album by tapping the button shown.

TIP

I recommend checking out the activity view at the top of the Shared tab. It provides a nice summary of photos you and your pals posted.

Admiring Your Pictures

Photographs are meant to be seen, not buried in the digital equivalent of a shoe-box. The iPad affords you some neat ways to manipulate, view, and share your best photos.

Maneuvering and manipulating photos

When you're viewing individual pictures in albums, you can display the picture controls by tapping the screen. But you can do a lot of picture maneuvering without summoning those controls. Here are some options:

» **Navigate photos:** Swipe left to move to the next photo in the album; swipe right to move to the previous photo in the album.

» **View portrait photos in portrait mode and landscape photos in landscape mode:** Most photos — especially those shot with an iPad or iPhone — are oriented as portrait or landscape. When you come across a portrait photo, for best viewing be sure to rotate your iPad into portrait mode; when you come to a landscape photo, rotate the device back to landscape mode and the photo readjusts accordingly.

» **Zoom:** Double-tap to zoom in on an image and make it larger. Double-tap again to zoom out and make it smaller. Alternatively, on the photo, spread two fingers to zoom in and pinch two fingers to zoom out.

» **Pan and scroll:** This cool little feature was once practically guaranteed to make you the life of the party. Now it's commonplace, if no less cool. After you zoom in on a picture, drag it around the screen with your finger, bringing the part of the image you most care about front and center. In this way, you can zoom in on Fido's adorable face as opposed to, say, the unflattering picture of the person holding the dog.

Launching a slideshow

Those of us who store a lot of photographs on computers are familiar with running slideshows of those images. It's a breeze to replicate the experience using the iPad's Photos app:

1. **Open the album that contains the photos you want to include in your slideshow.**

   By default, Photos assumes that you want every photo and video in that album to be part of the slideshow.

2. **To cherry-pick the pictures in the slideshow, tap Select and then tap each image you want to include so that a check mark appears.**

   If you want to save the selected pics in a new album, tap the share icon and then tap Add to Album to make a new album.

3. **Start the slideshow:**

   - *If you're showing the entire album:* Tap the three dots in the upper-right corner and then tap Slideshow.

   - *If you're showing selected photos:* Tap Share (shown in the margin) and then tap Slideshow.

4. **Tap the screen to display the controls and then tap Pause.**

5. **Tap Options.**

6. **Choose a theme and the music (if any) you'd like to accompany the slideshow.**

   You have five theme choices (Origami, Magazine, Dissolve, Push, Ken Burns). Why not try them all, to see what you like? You can go with Apple's theme music or choose from your Music stash.

7. **If you want the slideshow to start over from the beginning rather than end automatically after the last photo, tap the Repeat switch on.**

8. **Drag the slider to set the amount of time each photo appears onscreen.**

   How long each photo appears is determined by how you drag the slider in Options: To keep the photos onscreen longer, drag the slider to the left (towards the tortoise icon); to change photos faster, drag the slider to the right (towards the hare icon).

9. **Choose where you get to see the slideshow.**

   You can view the slideshow on the iPad or have it beamed wirelessly to an Apple TV on your network. Tap the icon in the upper right to make that selection.

10. **Tap the play icon to resume the slideshow.**

Tap Done when you've finished watching. That's it! Enjoy the show.

Storing pictures in the (i)Cloud

Any photo you take with the iPad can be automatically stored in the cloud and pushed to another iPad or to your PC, Mac, iPhone, iPod touch, or Apple TV (third generation or later). Pictures are uploaded when your iCloud devices are connected to Wi-Fi.

Using the iCloud photo library has a catch: You have to pay for storage. You get 5GB of iCloud storage gratis, but shutterbugs will use that up in a flash. So, you'll likely spring for one of the following monthly plans: 50GB of storage for 99¢, 200GB for $2.99, 1TB for $2.99, or 2TB for $9.99 a month.

Photos taken on the iPad aren't whisked to iCloud until you leave the Camera app. That way, you get a chance to delete pictures you'd rather not have turn up everywhere. But after you leave the Camera app, all the photos there are saved in the All Photos album (in the list of Albums in the Photos app), including pictures that arrived as email attachments you saved as well as screen captures taken on the iPad.

You can save pictures in the All Photos album to any other album on the tablet. Start by tapping the Select button at the upper-right corner of the screen. Next, tap each photo you want to move. Tap the share icon (shown in the margin), tap Add to Album in the Share dialog that shows up, and then choose the album destination for your chosen images.

If for some reason the pictures you snap with the iPad are not uploaded, go to Settings ➪ Photos, and make sure the iCloud Photos switch is on.

Editing and Deleting Photos

Although the Photos app is never going to serve as an editing substitute for, say, Adobe Photoshop, you can use it to dramatically (and simply) apply touch-ups and alter the composition of your pictures. You can also remove those embarrassing photos that you don't want to share. The next few sections explain the details.

Editing photos

In iPadOS, Apple has simplified access to the editing controls, displaying them as soon as you tap Edit. As shown in Figure 9-8, you're taken immediately to the Adjust controls. Tap whichever control you want, such as contrast, exposure, or brightness, and then drag the slider for that control until you reach a level you're satisfied with — you see the effect on the image as you drag the slider. Tap Done when you're finished or Cancel to start over.

To start, choose an image and tap Edit. You'll see the Adjust screen, as Figure 9-8 reveals.

FIGURE 9-8:
Use the edit
controls to
make your
photos look
their best.

The screen sports the following icons:

>> **Live Photo:** Edit the keyframe of your Live Photo. Tap Done when you're satisfied with your choice.

>> **Adjust light, color, B&W:** Apple provides numerous editing controls to adjust brilliance, exposure, highlights, shadows, brightness, contrast, and black point (light); saturation, vibrance, warmth, tint, sharpness, definition, noise reduction, and vignette.

>> **Add a filter:** Choose from Vivid, Dramatic, Mono, Silvertone, and Noir filters. Some, such as Vivid and Dramatic, have Warm and Cool variations. Better yet, you can apply these after the fact. If you're not satisfied after applying a filter, tap Original or Cancel to go back to the original.

>> **Rotate, straighten, and crop:** Summon three additional icons that allow you to rotate the image, change the perspective of the image, or skew the image. See Figure 9-9.

>> **Auto-enhance:** Tapping the auto-enhance icon lets the iPad take a stab at making your image look better. Apple lightens or darkens the picture, tweaks color saturation, and more. Tap Done if you like the result.

>> **Exposure:** Adjust your photo's light exposure. All the way up and you'll wash out your photo. All the way down, and your photo becomes much darker. Tap Done when you've adjusted it to your liking or move to another adjustment.

>> **Brilliance:** Adjust the vibrancy of your photo. Tap Done if you like the result or move to another adjustment.

>> **Highlights:** Adjust tonal range of just the highlights in your photo. Tap Done if you like the result or move to another adjustment.

» **Shadows:** Adjust the tonal range of just the shadows in your photo. Tap Done if you like the result or move to another adjustment.

TIP

If you aren't satisfied with any of the edits you've applied to your pictures, you can always tap Cancel followed by Discard Changes to restore the original. If you tap Done instead and apply the changes, you can still change your mind later. Open the image, tap the Edit icon, tap Revert, and then tap Revert to Original, which will remove all edits made to the pic.

Editing live photos

With some simple controls that look a lot like the editing tools discussed in the preceding section, you can trim the length of a live photo, set the keyframe, apply effects, turn off sound, and more.

The biggest difference in editing a Live Photo and a regular photo is setting the *keyframe,* which is the still you see when you're not tapping and holding down on a live photo. To change the keyframe, tap your live photo, and then tap the Edit button in the upper right of the screen. In addition to the familiar editing and filter options at the bottom of the screen, you'll see a live photo icon on the left side of the screen. Tap that icon to get a video timeline that will look familiar if you read Chapter 8, which covers video features of the iPad.

One of the frames in that timeline will have a white square around it. Just tap and drag that square along the timeline until you get a frame you like. When you've finished editing, tap the Make Key Photo button, which appears above the timeline. Then tap Done in the upper-right corner, and your live photo will be represented by its new keyframe.

To mute sound in your live photo, tap the volume button, which is near the top-left corner, as shown in Figure 9-10. To convert your live photo to a boring old regular photo, tap the live icon on the left side of the screen. To trim the length of your live photo, grab the handles at either end of the timeline and move them where you want. Otherwise, the editing tools are the same as described previously.

FIGURE 9-10:
Set the keyframe in a live photo by sliding the box on the timeline.

Deleting photos

Okay, so I told a tiny fib by intimating that photos are meant to be seen. I should have amended that statement by saying that *some* pictures are meant to be seen. Others, you can't get rid of fast enough. Fortunately, the iPad makes it a cinch to bury the evidence:

1. **Display the objectionable photograph.**

2. **Tap to display the picture controls, if they're not already displayed.**

3. **Tap the trash icon.**

    Photos asks you to confirm the deletion.

4. **Tap Delete Photo (or, if you change your mind, tap anywhere else to cancel).**

    In an instant, the photo is mercifully disposed of. It's also deleted from the iCloud photo library across all your devices.

More (Not So) Stupid Picture Tricks

You can take advantage of the photos on the iPad in a few more ways. In each case, you tap the picture and make sure the picture controls are displayed. Then tap the share icon (shown in the margin) to display the choices shown in Figure 9-11. (Not all the options are visible in the figure.)

FIGURE 9-11:
Look at what else I can do!

Here's a rundown of each choice:

>> **AirDrop:** AirDrop is a neat wireless method for sharing photos, videos, or other files with folks who happen to be nearby and also have an iOS 7 or later device or a Mac running macOS High Sierra or later. You turn on the feature in Control Center (see Chapter 2) and choose whether to make your iPad discoverable to everyone or just contacts who are in the vicinity. Tap a photo to select it and then tap the photo or icon representing the person or the device with whom you're trying to share the image, such as Paul's iMac in Figure 9-11. That person will receive an invitation to accept the photograph or reject it on their device. If the photo is accepted, the picture lands on the person's device almost immediately.

>> **Messages:** Tap the Messages option, and the picture is embedded in your outgoing message; you need to enter the phone number, email address, or name of the person to whom you're sending the picture. iPadOS also suggests people you might want to share your image with based on past history and recent iMessage chats. In Figure 9-11, this iPad thinks I might want to send the image to one of the contacts just below the selection preview.

>> **Mail:** Some photos are so precious that you just have to share them with family members and friends. When you tap Mail, the picture is embedded in the body of an outgoing email message. Use the virtual keyboard to enter the email addresses, subject line, and any comments you want to add — you know, something profound, such as "Isn't this a great photo?" After tapping Send, you have the option to change the image size (small, medium, or large) or keep the actual size. Consider the trade-offs: A smaller-sized image may get

through any limits imposed by your or the recipient's internet service provider or company. But if you can get the largest image through, you'll give the recipient the full picture (forgive the pun) in all its glory. (Check out Chapter 5 for more info on using email.)

» **Notes:** You can add your chosen image to the Notes app.

» **Reminders:** This icon sends your image to the Reminders app to create a new reminder with that image embedded in it.

» **Books:** Tap the Books app icon to add your image to the Books library.

» **Twitter:** Lots of people send pictures with their tweets these days. The iPad makes it a breeze. Tap Twitter and your picture is embedded in an outgoing tweet. Just add your words, sticking to Twitter's character limit of 280, and tap Post.

» **Facebook:** Lots (and I mean lots) of people also share photos on the world's largest social network. After your Facebook account is configured, you too can post there from your iPad.

» **Flickr:** The Yahoo!-owned service is another popular photo-sharing destination.

» **Copy Photo:** Copy the image and then paste it into an email or elsewhere.

» **Add to Shared Album:** Post the photo to a shared album.

» **Add to Album:** Move the photo to another album.

» **Duplicate:** You may want to duplicate a photo so that you can edit it while keeping the original.

» **Hide:** Don't want the image to be seen (but don't want to delete it either)? Tap Hide and then tap Hide Photo. The selected pic will be hidden from the days, months, and years views but still visible in albums view.

» **Slideshow:** I discuss slideshows earlier in this chapter. Here is another starting point for a slideshow, which can be accompanied by an optional musical soundtrack.

» **AirPlay:** Own an Apple TV set-top box? You can use AirPlay to stream photos from your iPad to the TV.

» **Use as Wallpaper:** The Apple-supplied background images on the iPad can't measure up to pictures of your spouse, kids, or pet. When you tap Use as Wallpaper, you see what the present image looks like as the iPad's background picture. You're given the opportunity to move the picture around and resize it, through the now-familiar action of dragging or pinching against the screen with your fingers. You can even see how the picture looks against the time and date that appear on the lock screen. Another option is to take advantage of the Perspective Zoom setting, which lets you exploit a parallax animation effect in which the picture moves as you move the iPad. Tap the screen to toggle the setting on or off. When you're satisfied with what the wallpaper looks like, tap the Set button. Options appear that let you use the photo as wallpaper for the lock screen, the Home screen, or both, as shown in Figure 9-12. Per usual, you can also tap Cancel. (You find out more about wallpaper in Chapter 15.)

FIGURE 9-12:
Beautifying the iPad with wallpaper.

>> **Copy iCloud Link:** Copy the web address of the photo to the clipboard for pasting into another app.

>> **Adjust Date & Time:** Modify the date and time assigned to the photo.

>> **Adjust Location:** Change the location assigned to the photo.

>> **Save to Files:** If you didn't shoot the image in question on your iPad but want to add it to the device, tap the Save to Files and then tap either iCloud Drive or On My iPad.

>> **Assign to Contact:** If you assign a picture to someone in your contacts list, the picture you assign pops up whenever you receive a FaceTime call or iMessage from that person. Tap Assign to Contact. Your list of contacts appears on the screen. Scroll through the list to find the person who matches the picture of the moment. As with the Use as Wallpaper option (described next), you can drag and resize the picture to get it just right. Then tap Set Photo.

You can also assign a photo to a contact by starting out in Contacts. To change the picture you assigned to a person, tap the person's name in the contacts list, tap Edit, and then tap the person's thumbnail picture, which also carries the label Edit. From there, you can take another photo with the iPad's digital camera, select another photo from one of your albums, edit the photo you're already using (by resizing and dragging it to a new position), or delete the photo you no longer want.

>> **Print:** If you have an AirPrint-capable printer, tap Print to print the photo. You can choose how many copies of the print you want to duplicate.

Sometimes you want to make decisions about multiple pictures at the same time, whether you're sharing them online, copying or printing them, adding them to a new album, or deleting them in bulk. Here's a convenient way to do so. Launch the Photos app and either tap a specific album in the app or open a days view or all photos view so that you see thumbnails of your pictures. Next, tap Select at the upper right, and then tap each thumbnail on which you're planning to take action, so that a check mark appears. As you do, the count for each picture you select increases. From here, you can delete them, or you can tap the share icon to share pictures on a social network in bulk, email them, send them via a message, or copy or print them, as discussed previously. The options that appear may vary depending on how many pictures you've selected — for example, the number of photos you can email is limited.

Entering the Photo Booth

Remember the old-fashioned photo booths at the local Five and Dime? Remember the Five and Dime? Okay, if you don't remember such variety stores, your parents probably do, and if they don't, their parents no doubt do. The point is that photo booths (which do still exist) are fun places to ham it up solo or with a friend as the machine captures and spits out wallet-size pictures.

With the Photo Booth app, Apple has cooked up a modern alternative to a real photo booth. The app is a close cousin to a similar application on the Mac. Here's how Photo Booth works:

1. **Tap the Photo Booth icon on the Home screen.**

   You get the tic-tac-toe-style grid shown in Figure 9-13.

2. **Point the front-facing camera at your face.**

   You see your mug through a prism of eight rather wacky special effects: Thermal Camera, Mirror, X-Ray, Kaleidoscope, Light Tunnel, Squeeze, Twirl, and Stretch. The center square (what is this, *Hollywood Squares?*) is the only one in which you come off looking normal — or, as I like to kid, like you're supposed to look. Some of the effects make you look scary; some, merely goofy.

   You can also use the rear camera in Photo Booth to subject your friends to this form of, um, visual abuse.

3. **Choose one of the special effects (or stick with Normal) by tapping one of the thumbnails.**

   I chose Mirror for the example shown in Figure 9-14 because, after all, two dogs are better than one. You can pinch or spread the image to further doctor the effect.

   TIP

   If you're not satisfied with the effect you've chosen, tap the icon at the lower-left corner of the app to return to the Photo Booth grid and select another.

4. **When you have your bizarre look just right, tap the camera button on the screen to snap the picture.**

   Your pic lands in both the All Photos album and the Selfies album.

FIGURE 9-13:
Photo booths of yesteryear weren't like this.

From the All Photos album or from right here in Photo Booth, pictures can be shared in all the usual places or deleted, which you might want to seriously consider, given the distortions you've just applied to your face.

Nah, I'm only kidding. Keep the image and take a lot more. Photo Booth may be a blast from the past, but I think it's just a blast.

Before leaving this photography section, I want to steer you to the App Store, which you explore in greater depth in Chapter 10. Hundreds, probably thousands, of photography-related apps are available there, a whole host of them free. That's too many to mention here, but I know you'll find terrific photo apps just by wandering around the place. Head to the Photo & Video category to get started.

And there you have it. You have just passed Photography 101 on the iPad. I trust that the coursework was, forgive another pun, a snap.

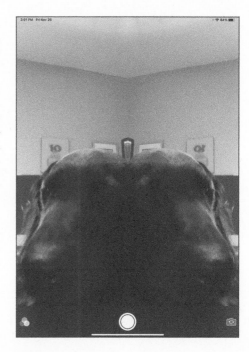

FIGURE 9-14:
When one dog just isn't enough.

4

Putting the iPad to Work

Chapter **10**

Harnessing the Power of Apps

Your iPad comes with an impressive collection of built-in apps, including Safari, Mail, Messages, Calendar, Photos, Music, and Notes. A default installation of iPadOS comes with more than 30 apps. Surely no one needs more than that, amirite?

No, I'm not. For one thing, you might want to use a third-party app instead of one of Apple's default apps. For example, maybe you prefer to use Google Chrome or Mozilla Firefox as your web browser. Maybe you're a diehard Microsoft Outlook fan. Maybe you get your musical kicks from Spotify.

For another, you might have tasks you want to perform on your iPad for which none of the default apps are suitable. Maybe you want to play a game, host a virtual meeting, or just Netflix and chill. That's fine because the App Store is home to nearly 2 million apps, which means that no matter what you want to do with your iPad, there is, as the kids say, an app for that.

In this chapter, you get a bird's-eye view of third-party (that is, non-Apple) apps and your iPad. You don't learn about specific apps. Instead, you find out how to find and download apps on your iPad, and you discover some basics for managing your apps. I also introduce you to your iPad's collection of widgets.

Tapping the Magic of Apps

Apps enable you to use your iPad as a game console, a streaming Netflix player, a recipe finder, a sketchbook, and much, much more. You can run three categories of apps on your iPad:

>> **App made exclusively for the iPad:** This app is the rarest kind, so you find fewer of these than the other two types. This type of app won't run on an iPhone or iPod touch, so you can't even install it on these devices.

>> **App made to work properly on an iPad, iPhone, or iPod touch:** This so-called *universal app* can run on any of the three device types at native resolution.

>> **App made for the iPhone and iPod touch:** This app runs on your iPad but only at iPhone or iPod touch resolution rather than the full resolution of your iPad, as shown in Figure 10-1.

TIP

You can double the size of an iPhone or iPod touch app by tapping the full-screen icon (two arrows facing away from each other) in the lower-right corner of the screen. To return the device to native size, tap the normal icon (two arrows facing toward each other). Figure 10-1 shows you what an iPhone or iPod touch app looks like on an iPad screen.

FIGURE 10-1: iPhone and iPod touch apps run at a smaller size (left) but can be increased to double size (right).

Full screen

Normal

You can obtain and install apps for your iPad in two ways:

>> App Store app on your iPad

>> Automatic download

To switch on automatic downloads on the iPad, tap Settings ⇨ App Store. In the Automatic Downloads section, tap the Apps switch to on. Now all apps you buy on other iPadOS and iOS devices will automagically appear on your iPad.

TIP

After you've obtained an app from the App Store, you can download it to up to ten iOS devices (as long as you log in with the same Apple account or use Family Sharing).

Finding Apps in the App Store

Finding apps with your iPad is easy. The only requirement is that you have an internet connection of some sort — Wi-Fi or wireless data network — so that you can access the App Store and browse, search, download, and install apps.

Browsing the App Store

To get started, tap the App Store icon (shown in the margin) on your iPad's Home screen. After you launch the App Store, you see five icons at the bottom of the screen, representing five ways to interact with the store, as shown in Figure 10-2. The first three icons — Today, Games, and Apps — offer three ways to browse the virtual shelves of the App Store. (I get to the fourth and fifth icons, Arcade and Search, shortly.)

FIGURE 10-2:
The icons across the bottom represent different ways to browse the App Store.

The Today section, shown in Figure 10-2, highlights curated selections from the App Store, including App of the Day and Game of the Day, themed collections such as Top Games of the Week, and staff favorites (not shown in the figure).

The Games section lets you browse games in categories such as AR Games, New Games We Love, and Essential Game Picks, to name a few. Scroll down and you'll find sections for Top Paid Games, Top Free Games, Top Game Categories, and more.

The Apps section is like déjà vu all over again if you've already visited the Games section. It also contains categories such as iPad Essentials and Made for Kids, as shown in Figure 10-3. Scroll down a little farther and you'll find Top Paid Apps, Top Free Apps, Top App Categories, and more.

Most pages in the App Store display more apps than can fit on the screen at once. For example, the iPad Essentials section in Figure 10-3 contains more than the four apps you can see. A few tools help you navigate the Games, Apps, and other sections of the App Store:

>> **Swipe from right to left** to see more apps in most categories.

FIGURE 10-3:
The Apps section displays apps organized by themes, such as New to iPad.

>> **Swipe up the screen** to scroll down and see additional categories.

>> **Tap the See All link** at the top right of most sections to (what else?) see all the apps in that section on one screen at the same time.

Playing in the arcade

Apple introduced Arcade, a subscription game service, with iPadOS. It's the fourth icon at the bottom of the App Store. And it's really cool — let me tell you why!

With Arcade, you get on-demand access to more than 200 games, with Apple adding more every week. These are high-quality, top-tier games. Even better, none of them have in-app purchases, which means you can play the entire game without having to spend a penny outside the Arcade subscription itself. You'll find racing games, fighting games, strategy games, simulations, puzzles, mysteries, and so much more. These games are original, with most produced exclusively for Arcade.

But here's the best part. Arcade is included with an Apple One subscription or is just $4.99 per month on its own, and that includes everything. (You can get Arcade free for three months if you purchase an iDevice.) To subscribe, tap the Try It Free button in the Arcade section to start a 30-day free trial. If you unsubscribe before the trial ends, you won't be charged. Otherwise, you'll begin paying $4.99 per month through your Apple ID. If you love playing great games, that price makes Arcade a no-brainer.

Searching for apps

Finally, the last option at the bottom of the screen is Search, the magnifying glass icon. If you know exactly what you're looking for (or even approximately what you're looking for), just tap Search to bring up the virtual keyboard, and then type a word or phrase. Then tap the Search key to initiate the search.

That's all there is to it.

Finding details about an app

Now that you know how to browse and search for apps in the App Store, the following sections show you how to find out more about a particular app. After tapping an app icon as you browse the store or in a search result, your iPad displays a details screen like the one shown in Figure 10-4.

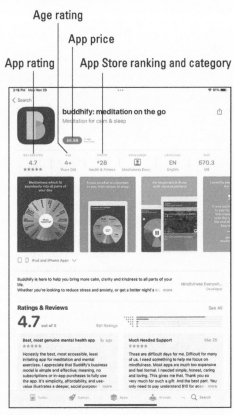

Age rating

App price

App rating

App Store ranking and category

FIGURE 10-4:
The info screen for the buddhify meditation app.

Note the blue More link in the Preview section in Figure 10-4; click More to see a longer description of the app.

Bear in mind that the app description on this screen was written by the app's developer and may be biased. Never fear, gentle reader: In an upcoming section, I show you how to find app reviews written by people who have used the app (and, unfortunately, sometimes people who haven't).

Understanding the age rating

The buddhify app is rated for age 4+, as you can see in Figure 10-4. The rating means that the app may contain content that is unsuitable for children under 4. Other age ratings are 9+, 12+, and 17+, each designed to help parents manage what games and apps their kids are using.

Checking requirements and device support for the app

One more thing: Remember the three categories of apps mentioned at the beginning of the chapter, in the "Tapping the Magic of Apps" section? Scroll down the page to the Information section (not shown in Figure 10-4), tap Compatibility, and you'll find that this app requires iPadOS 10.0 or later.

Reading reviews

The Ratings & Reviews section of the details screen offers reviews written by users of the app. Each review includes a star rating, from zero to five. If an app is rated four stars or higher, you can safely assume that most users are happy with the app.

In Figure 10-4, you can see that this app has a rating of 4.7 stars based on 891 user ratings. That means most of the people who reviewed it think it's a great app. Finally, tap See All to read more user reviews.

REMEMBER

Don't believe everything you read in reviews. People find some amazingly bad reasons to give apps bad — and sometimes good — ratings. Take App Store ratings and reviews with a grain of salt and learn how to look for the reviews that resonate with you. I also like to look for a preponderance of opinions to help weigh the ones to take seriously. Lastly, make sure the review you're reading is for the current version — reviews of older versions may not apply to the new version.

Downloading an app

To download an app to your iPad from the App Store, follow these steps:

1. **To start the download process, tap the blue price button (or the word *Get* or the download from iCloud icon) near the top of the app's details screen.**

   For apps with a price, the price button will morph into a blue Buy button. You might be prompted to sign in to your Apple account, or to use Touch ID or Face ID to authorize the purchase.

2. **Tap the blue Buy button (if the app has a price) or the blue Install button (if the app is free).**

   When the app has finished downloading and is installed on your iPad, the installing icon changes to an Open button.

3. **Tap the Open button to launch the app.**

    If you close the App Store before the app finishes installing, you'll see your new app's icon on the Home screen. (Depending on how many apps you have installed on your iPad, you may need to swipe to another Home screen page to find the new app.) The new app's icon will be dimmed and have the word *Loading* below it, with a pie chart to indicate how much of the app remains to be downloaded (about one third, as shown in the margin).

4. **If the app is rated 17+, click OK on the warning screen that appears after you type your password to confirm that you're 17 or older.**

The app is now on your iPad. If your iPad suddenly loses its memory (unlikely) or you delete the app from your iPad, you can download it again later from the App Store at no charge.

DOWNLOADING OTHER CONTENT ON YOUR IPAD

You may have noticed that the App Store app on your iPad offers nothing but apps.

To obtain music, movies, and TV shows, you use the iTunes Store app; to read stories from newspapers and magazines, you use either the News app or the Safari app (both are included with your iPad).

But to download books and podcasts, you'll need the Books and Podcasts apps, respectively. For what it's worth, these apps work pretty much the same as the App Store. So, now that you understand how to navigate the App Store app, you also know how to use these other Store apps.

Updating apps

Every so often the developer of an iPad app releases an update to add new features or to fix a glitch or security hole. By default, iPadOS keeps all your apps up-to-date by automatically installing app updates soon after they're available. This is a wise choice: You'll always have the latest app features and the latest security patches, so your iPad will be more secure.

To make sure that your iPad is automatically updating your apps, tap Settings ⇨ App Store. In the Automatic Downloads section, make sure the App Updates switch is on.

If, for some reason, you turn off the App Updates switch (because you want to make your life more difficult and less safe, I presume), you can still update your apps by hand. You need to tap your profile button in the upper-right corner of any of the five main sections of the App Store. An account sheet appears with your Apple ID, along with tabs for seeing previously purchased apps, managing subscriptions, redeeming gift cards and gift card codes, sending gift cards by email, and adding funds to your Apple ID.

At the bottom of the screen are recent and pending updates, with app icons, the name of each app, and update notes for the newest update. If an update has already been applied by the App Store, you'll see an Open button, which allows you to launch the app. If the app is waiting to be updated, you'll see an Update button. Tap the Update button to update the app. When the update is complete, the button changes to an Open button.

REMEMBER

If you try to update an app purchased from any Apple ID except your own, you're prompted for that account's ID and password. If you can't provide them, you can't download the update. This doesn't apply, of course, if you've enabled Family Sharing (see Chapter 15).

One last tip: If you download an app and it doesn't work properly (or if you use the app for a while and it then stops working), try deleting it (see the upcoming "Deleting an app" section) and then redownloading it from the App Store. Doing so fixes the problem as often as not.

Working with Apps

Most of what you need to know about apps involves simply installing third-party apps on your iPad. However, you might find it helpful to know how to use App Library, review an app, and delete an app.

Check out App Library

If your iPad Home screen consists of just three or four pages, it's never much of a chore to find the app you need. However, once you have a half dozen pages or more, you might find that you're spending far too much time frantically swiping left and right to find the app you want to use.

One solution is to search for the app you want: Swipe down in the center of the screen to display the Search sheet. Tap a recent app if you see it; otherwise, start typing the app name in the Search box and then tap the app when it shows up in the results.

Another solution is to take advantage of App Library, which you can open either by tapping the App Library icon, which appears on the far-right end of the dock, or by swiping left on the last Home screen page.

REMEMBER

If you don't see the App Library icon on your iPad's dock, tap Settings ⇨ Home Screen & Dock and then tap the Show App Library in Dock switch to On.

As you can see in Figure 10-5, the resulting screen has four main features:

>> A Search box at the top that gives you another way to search for an installed app

>> A Suggestions category that list the apps you use most often

>> A Recently Added category that lists three apps you've installed most recently and a four-app icon that, when tapped, displays all the apps in this category

>> A collection of categories for all your other apps: Games, Utilities, Social, and so on

FIGURE 10-5:
A typical iPad App Library.

TIP

By default, iPadOS doesn't show app icon badges in App Library. If you use App Library frequently, you might want to see those badges so you know if an app has new content you should check out. Tap Settings ⇨ Home Screen & Dock and then, in the Notification Badges section, tap the Show in App Library switch on.

Writing an app review

Sometimes you love or hate an app so much that you want to tell the world about it. In that case, you should write a review. You can do this directly from your iPad.

To write a review from your iPad, follow these steps:

1. **Tap the App Store icon to launch the App Store.**

2. **Navigate to the details screen for the app.**

3. **Tap one to five of the stars at the top of the screen to rate the app.**

   You might have to type your iTunes Store password.

4. **In the Title field, type a title for your review, and in the Review field, type your review.**

5. **Tap the Send button in the upper-right corner of the screen.**

   Whichever way you submit your review, Apple reviews your submission. As long as the review doesn't violate the (unpublished) rules of conduct for app reviews, it appears in a day or two in the App Store in the Reviews section for the particular app.

TIP

You can configure the behavior of many apps in the Settings app. Scroll all the way down the list of settings and you'll find an alphabetical list of apps that have settings; tap an app in the list to see its settings.

Taking an app off the Home screen

If you have an app you use only occasionally, you can tidy up your Home screen a bit by taking that app's icon off the Home screen. The app remains installed on your iPad, but now you must bring up App Library to launch the app.

Here's how to move an app to App Library:

1. **Long-press the app icon.**

2. **Tap Remove App.**

3. **Tap Remove from Home Screen.**

   iPadOS plucks the app's icon from the Home screen. However, the app remains in App Library, so you can still open the app from there.

Deleting an app

If you have an app you no longer use, you can delete it to reduce Home screen clutter. Here's how to delete an app on your iPad:

1. **Long-press the app icon.**

2. **Tap Remove App.**

3. **Tap Delete App.**

   A dialog appears, informing you that deleting this app also deletes all its data.

4. **Tap the Delete button.**

   iPadOS removes the app and its data from your iPad.

Working with Widgets

As long as you're running iPadOS 15 or later on your iPad, your Home screen is populated not only by apps but also by a collection of widgets. A *widget* is a scaled-down version of an app that shows you current info from that app. Here are some examples:

» The Calendar widget shows you today's appointments and what's coming up in the next day or two.

» The Weather widget shows the current conditions in your neck of the woods.

» The News widget shows the current top stories.

» The Photos widget shows a random photo from one of your albums.

Viewing your widgets

You have two ways to view and interact with your widgets:

» Display the first Home screen page, where a subset of your widgets appears at the top.

» From the first Home screen page or from the lock screen, swipe right from the left edge of the screen to open today view, where all your widgets appear in a vertical column on the left side of the screen, as shown in Figure 10-6. Swipe down and up on this column to see more widgets.

Most widgets are there for information purposes only. If you want to open the widget's underlying app, just tap the widget. If the app is part of a *stack* (two or more widgets), swipe up or down within the stack to navigate the widgets.

Adding a widget

Tons of widgets are available, so if one of your installed apps has a widget that's not available either on the first Home screen page or in today view, you can follow these steps to add the widget:

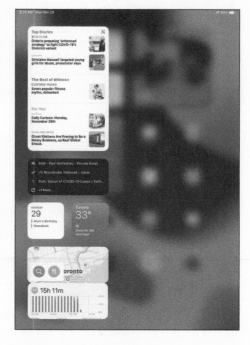

FIGURE 10-6:
You see all your widgets in today view.

1. **Open the widgets for editing:**

   - *If today view is onscreen:* Scroll down to the bottom of the today view column and tap Edit.

   - *If the first Home screen page is onscreen:* Long-press any widget and then tap Edit Home Screen. The widgets and app icons start wiggling.

2. **Tap + in the upper-left corner of the screen.**

   iPadOS displays a widgets sheet with your installed apps listed on the left.

3. **Tap the app with the widget you want to add.**

   Note that you see the first form of the widget at this point. For many widgets, you can swipe left to browse other forms of the widget before adding it.

4. **Tap Add Widget.**

   iPadOS adds the widget.

5. **Tap and drag the new widget to the position you prefer.**

6. **To create a stack, tap and drag the widget and drop it on top of another widget that you want to be in the same stack.**

7. **Tap Done.**

Removing a widget

If you have a widget you no longer use, you can remove it to clean up your first Home screen page and your today view. Here's how to remove a widget:

1. **Long-press the widget icon.**

   You can long-press the widget either on the first Home screen page or in today view.

2. **Tap Remove Widget.**

   A dialog appears, reassuring you that removing the widget doesn't delete the app or any of its data.

3. **Tap Remove.**

   iPadOS removes the widget.

Chapter **11**

Staying in Touch with People and Appointments

hate to break the news to you, but your iPad isn't only for fun and games; it also has a serious side. The iPad can remind you of appointments and help you keep all your contacts straight.

Please add a sentence or two about what the reader will learn in this chapter.

Working with the Calendar

The Calendar program lets you keep on top of your appointments and events (birthdays, anniversaries, and the like). You open it by tapping the Calendar icon on the Home screen. The icon is smart in its own right because it changes daily, displaying the day of the week and the date right in the app icon on your Home screen.

You can display five calendar views: year, month, day, week, and a searchable list view, which shows current and future appointments.

Tap one of the four tabs at the top of the screen — Day, Week, Month, or Year — to choose a view. Tap Today, near the top-right corner of the screen (just below the Search box), to return to the current date in any view.

To get to list view, tap the list view icon in the upper-left corner of the screen (and shown in the margin).

You take a closer look at these views in the following sections.

Year view

There's not much to the year view, but it does let you see the current calendar year with today's date circled in red (and the current month and year shown in red type). You can scroll up or down to see prior or future years, but that's about it; unfortunately, in year view, you can't tell on which days you have appointments. Boo. Hiss.

Month view

Tap any of the months visible in year view to jump to that specific month, as shown in Figure 11-1. When your iPad is in month view, you can see which days have appointments or scheduled events. Tap a day to see the list of activities on the agenda for that day, which leads nicely into the next section.

Day view

As just mentioned, you have to tap a date with an entry to see what you have going on in a 24-hour period — though to see an entire day's worth of entries, you might have to scroll

Calendars
Inbox
List View
Add

FIGURE 11-1:
Month view gives you a bird's-eye view of your appointments.

up or down depending on how many entries you have. You can swipe to the left to advance to the next day of the week and beyond; swipe to the right to retreat one or more days; or tap a day near the top of the screen to jump to it.

In the day view, all-day events, birthdays, and events pulled from your Facebook account (if you provide your Facebook credentials) appear in a narrow strip above the timeline for the day.

Your daily appointments span the entire time in which they've been scheduled on your calendar. For example, if an appointment runs from 12:00 p.m. to 1:00 p.m., that hour will be blocked off on the calendar like the *Meeting with Editor* entry shown in Figure 11-2.

You find out how to create calendar entries in a moment, but for now know that you can hold down on an event and drag it to a new time slot should your plans change. If you have overlapping appointments, you'll see more than a single entry claim a given time slot.

Finally, calendar entries are color-coded according to the calendar in which you scheduled the appointment. These color codes will help you distinguish an appointment you made on your travel calendar versus, say, a work, family, or Facebook calendar.

Week view

In week view, shown in Figure 11-3, you can see an entire week at a glance. The current date is circled in red.

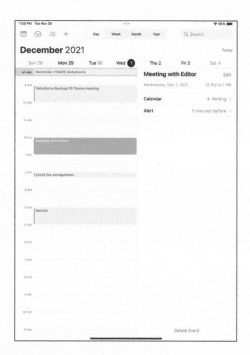

FIGURE 11-2:
Day view.

FIGURE 11-3:
Week view.

TIP

You can arrange to start your weekly view on any day of the week. Tap Settings ⇨ Calendars ⇨ Start   Week On, and then tap the day on which you want to start your week. (Sunday is the default in the United States.)

List view

List view isn't complicated. You can get to this view by tapping the list view icon in the upper-left corner of the screen (and shown in the margin). As you would expect, all your calendar appointments are listed chronologi-cally, as shown in Figure 11-4. If you have a lengthy list, drag up or down with your finger or flick to rapidly scroll through your appointments.

Tap any of the listings to get meeting or appointment details for that entry. If you tap a person's birthday, you see

FIGURE 11-4:
List view.

that person's contact information. Sorry, but you just ran out of excuses for not sending a card.

Adding Calendar Entries

In Chapter 3, you discover pretty much everything there is to know about syncing your iPad, including syncing calendar entries from your Windows machine (using the likes of Microsoft Outlook) or Mac (using Calendar or Outlook) or Google Calendar. If you're syncing your calendar entries with iCloud, you can also manage your calendars at www.icloud.com from any computer or device with a web browser.

In plenty of situations, you can enter appointments on the fly. To add appointments directly to the iPad, follow these steps:

1. **On the Home screen, tap the Calendar icon, and then (optionally) tap the Year, Month, Week, or Day tab.**

2. **Tap + (add) in the upper-left corner of the screen (and labeled in Figure 11-1).**

   The New Event overlay appears, as shown in Figure 11-5.

3. **Tap the Title and Location fields in turn and type as much or as little information as you feel is necessary.**

   Tapping displays the virtual keyboard (if it's not already shown).

   Don't forget you can use dictation or Siri to add a calendar entry. See Chapter 14 for more on dictation and Siri.

TIP

4. **To add start and end times:**

   a. *Tap the Starts field.* A carousel wheel, like the one shown for the Ends time in Figure 11-6, appears below the field you tapped.

   b. *Choose the time the event starts.* Use your finger to roll separate carousel controls for the date, hour, and minute (in 1-minute intervals) and to specify AM or PM. The process is a little like

FIGURE 11-5:
The screen looks like this just before you add an event to your iPad.

FIGURE 11-6:
Controlling the Starts and Ends fields is like manipulating a bike lock.

manipulating a combination bicycle lock or an old-fashioned date stamp used with an inkpad.

c. *Tap the Ends field and choose the time the event ends.*

To enter an all-day milestone (such as a birthday), tap the All-Day switch to turn it on (green). Because the time is no longer relevant for an all-day entry, you won't see Starts, Ends, or Time Zone options.

5. **When you're finished, tap Add.**

I can't think of an easier way to add an entry than to instruct Siri along the lines of "Set a lunch appointment for tomorrow at noon with the Smiths." Siri will be pleased to comply.

That's the minimum you have to do to set up an event. But I bet you want to do more. The Calendar app is at your service:

>> **Change the time zone.** If the correct location isn't already present, tap the Time Zone field and type the name of the city where the appointment is taking place.

>> **Set up a recurring entry.** Tap the Repeat field. Tap to indicate how often the event in question recurs. This setting is good for everything from a weekly appointment, such as an allergy shot, to a yearly event, such as an anniversary.

The options are Every Day, Every Week, Every 2 Weeks, Every Month, and Every Year. Tap the Custom field if you want to further refine those options. Tap Never if you are planning to never repeat this entry again.

>> **Add travel time to and from events.** Tap the Travel Time field and enable the Travel Time switch. A list of durations appears, ranging from five minutes to two hours. Tap a duration to specify your travel time.

>> **Assign the entry to a particular calendar.** Tap Calendar, and then tap the calendar you have in mind (Home or Work, for example).

>> **Invite people to join you.** Tap Invitees to specify who among your contacts will be attending the event.

>> **Set a reminder or alert for the entry.** Tap Alert and tap a time.

Alerts can be set so that you arrive at the time of an event, or 1 week before, 2 days before, 1 day before, 2 hours before, 1 hour before, 30 minutes before, 15 minutes before, or 5 minutes before the event. If it's an all-day entry, you can request alerts 1 day before (at 9:00 a.m.), 2 days before (at 9:00 a.m.), or 1 week before.

When the appointment time rolls around, you hear a sound and see a message like the one shown in Figure 11-7.

TIP

If you're the kind of person who needs an extra nudge, set another reminder by tapping the Second Alert field (which you'll see only if a first alert is already set).

FIGURE 11-7:
Alerts make it hard to forget.

>> **Indicate whether you're busy or free by tapping Show As.** If you're invited to an event, you can tap Availability and then tap Free (if it's shown on your iPad).

>> **Enter a web address.** Tap the URL field (at the bottom of the New Event screen) and type or copy and paste the web address.

>> **Enter notes about the appointment or event.** Tap the Notes field (at the bottom of the screen) and type your note.

Tap Done after you finish entering everything.

Managing your calendars

When you have the hang of creating calendar entries, you can get even more control of the task with these tips:

REMEMBER

>> **Choose a default calendar.** Tap Settings ⇨ Calendar ⇨ Default Calendar and select the calendar you want to use as the default for new events.

>> **Make events appear according to whichever time zone you selected for your calendars.** Tap Settings ⇨ Calendar ⇨ Time Zone Override and then tap the Time Zone Override switch to on. Tap Time Zone and then type the time zone's location, using the keyboard that appears. If you travel long distances for your job, this setting comes in handy.

When Time Zone Override is turned off, events are displayed according to the time zone of your current location.

>> **Customize calendar alert sounds.** Tap Settings ⇨ Sounds ⇨ Calendar Alerts and then choose the sound effect you want to hear when a calendar alert appears.

>> **Set default alert times for birthdays, all-day events, or certain other events.** Tap Settings ⇨ Calendar ⇨ Default Alert Times. For birthdays or other all-day events, you can choose to be alerted at 9:00 a.m. on the day of the event, at 9:00 a.m. one day before, at 9:00 a.m. two days before, or a week before. For other alerts, you can choose a default alert time at the time of

event, 5, 10 15, or 30 minutes before, 1 hour before, 2 hours before, 1 day before, 2 days before, or 1 week before the event.

» **Modify an existing calendar entry.** Tap the entry, tap Edit, and then make whichever changes need to be made.

» **Wipe out a calendar entry.** Tap the event and then tap Delete Event. For a one-time-only event, when Calendar asks you to confirm, tap Delete Event (or tap outside the dialog to cancel the deletion). For a repeating event, you can choose to Delete This Event Only or Delete All Future Events.

Letting your calendar push you around

If you work for a company that uses Microsoft Exchange ActiveSync, calendar entries and meeting invitations from coworkers can be *pushed* to your device so they show up on the screen moments after they're entered, even if they're entered on computers at work. Setting up an account to facilitate this pushing of calendar entries to your iPad is a breeze, although you should check with your company's tech or IT department to make sure your employer allows it. Then follow these steps:

1. **Tap Settings ⇨ Mail ⇨ Accounts ⇨ Add Account.**

2. **From the Add Account list, tap Microsoft Exchange.**

3. **Fill in the email address and account description, and then tap Next.**

4. **Fill in your password and tap Next.**

5. **If required, enter your server address on the next screen that appears.**

   The iPad supports the Microsoft Autodiscovery service, which uses your name and password to automatically determine the address of the Exchange server. The rest of the fields should be filled in with the email address, username, password, and description you just entered.

6. **Tap Next.**

7. **Tap the switch to turn on each information type you want to synchronize using Microsoft Exchange.**

   The options are Mail, Contacts, Calendars, Reminders, and Notes. You should be good to go now, although some employers may require you to add passcodes to safeguard company secrets.

REMEMBER

If you have a business-issued iPad and it's lost or stolen — or you're a double agent working for a rival company — your employer's IT administrators can remotely wipe your device clean after you set up Microsoft Exchange.

One more thing: If you sync via iCloud, Google, or Microsoft Exchange, your calendar entries are automatically pushed to your iPad by the server when received.

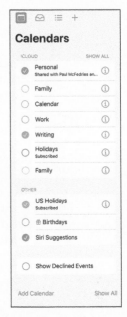

FIGURE 11-8:
Choosing the calendars to display.

Choosing which calendars to display

By tapping the calendars icon in the top-left corner (shown in the margin), you can choose the calendar or calendars to display on your iPad. Tap each calendar you want to include so that a check mark appears next to it, as shown in Figure 11-8. To remove the check mark, tap again.

When you want your entire schedule to be an open book, tap Show All, in the upper right.

From the Calendars list, tap the *i*-in-a-circle for even more tricks. You can change the color assigned to your calendar, share the calendar with a given individual (tap Add Person to do so), make a calendar public (by flipping a switch), or delete the calendar.

Responding to meeting invitations

The iPad has one more important button in the Calendar app. It's the inbox icon in the top-left corner (shown in the margin). If you partake in iCloud, have a Microsoft Exchange account, or have a calendar that adheres to the CalDAV internet standard, you can send and receive a meeting invitation.

If you have any pending invitations, you'll see them when you tap the inbox, which is separated into new invitations and invitations to which you've already replied. You can tap any of the items in the list to see more details about the event to which you've been invited. (Note that the Calendar's inbox is not the same as your email inbox.)

Suppose a meeting invitation arrives from your boss. You can see who else is attending, check scheduling conflicts, and more. Tap Accept to let the meeting organizer know you're attending, tap Decline if you have something better to do (and aren't worried about upsetting the person who signs your paycheck), or tap Maybe if you're waiting for a better offer.

And as I point out previously, you can also invite other folks to attend an event you yourself are putting together.

Meantime, if you run into a conflict, why not ask Siri to change your schedule? For that matter, you can also call upon Siri to remind you when you have your next appointment. Visit Chapter 14 for more on this clever feature.

You can choose to receive an alert every time someone sends you an invitation. Tap Settings ⇨ Notifications ⇨ Calendar ⇨ Customize Notification and make sure the Invitations switch is on.

As mentioned, if you take advantage of iCloud, Google, or Microsoft Exchange, you can keep calendar entries synchronized between your iPhone, iPad, iPod touch and your Mac or PC. When you make a scheduling change on your iPad, it's automatically updated on your computer and other devices, and vice versa.

Subscribing to calendars

You can subscribe to calendars that adhere to the CalDAV and iCalendar (.ics) standards, which are supported by the popular Google and Yahoo! calendars and by the Mac's Calendar app. Although you can read entries on the iPad from the calendars you subscribe to, you can't create entries from the iPad or edit the entries that are already present.

To subscribe to one of these calendars, tap Settings ⇨ Mail ⇨ Accounts ⇨ Add Account. Tap Other and then choose Add CalDAV Account or Add Subscribed Calendar. Next, enter the server where the iPad can find the calendar you have in mind, and if need be, a username, a password, and an optional description.

Finally, some apps, websites, and email messages will offer to add calendar events and subscriptions.

Sifting through Contacts

If you read the chapter on syncing (see Chapter 3), you know how to get the snail-mail addresses, email addresses, and phone numbers that reside on your Mac or PC into your iPad. Assuming you went through that drill already, all those addresses and phone numbers are hanging out in one place. Their not-so-secret hiding place is revealed when you tap the Contacts icon on the Home screen. The following sections guide you from the main screen to whatever you want to do with your contacts' information.

Adding and viewing contacts

To add contacts to your Contacts app, tap the + icon at the top of the screen and type as much or as little profile information as you have for the person. Tap Add Photo to add a picture from your photo albums or collections (or to take a snapshot with your iPad camera). You can edit the information later by tapping the Edit button when a contact's name is highlighted.

A list of your contacts appears in the left panel, with the one you're currently viewing shown in gray; see Figure 11-9. At the top on the right, you can see a mug shot of your contact — if you added one — and the person's address. Below that you'll see the contact's phone number, email address, another address, and birthday (all blurred in Figure 11-9 to protect Jacob's privacy). You also find an area to scribble notes about a contact.

FIGURE 11-9:
A view of all contacts.

TIP

You have three ways to land on a specific contact:

>> **Flick your finger so that the list of contacts on the left side scrolls rapidly up or down,** loosely reminiscent of the spinning Lucky 7s and other pictures on a Las Vegas slot machine. Think of the payout you'd get with that kind of power on a one-armed bandit.

>> **Slide your thumb or another finger along the alphabet on the right edge of the contacts list** or tap one of the teeny-tiny letters to jump to names that begin with that letter.

>> **Start to type the name of a contact in the Search field near the top of the contacts list.** Or type the name of the place where your contact works. When you're at or near the appropriate contact name, stop the scrolling by tapping the screen.

When you tap to stop the scrolling, that tap doesn't select an item in the list. This may seem counterintuitive the first few times you try it, but I got used to it and now I really like it this way. Just think of that first tap as applying the brakes to the scrolling list.

You can change the way your contacts are displayed. Tap Settings ⇨ Contacts. Tap Sort Order or Display Order, and for each one, choose the First, Last option or Last, First option to indicate whether you want to sort or display entries by a contact's first or last name. You can also choose First Name & Last Initial or First Initial & Last Name.

Searching contacts

You can search contacts by entering a first or last name in the Search field or by entering a company name.

You can locate people on your iPad without opening the Contacts app. Swipe down from the middle of the Home screen to pull down your iPad's Search field. Type a name in the Search field, and then tap the name in the search results. You can also ask Siri to find people for you, and even have it compose and send them an email or iMessage, or call them via FaceTime video or audio chat.

Contacting and sharing your contacts

You can initiate an email from Contacts by tapping an email address under a contact's listings. Doing so fires up the Mail program on the iPad, with the person's name already in the To field. For more on the Mail app, I direct you to Chapter 5.

You can also share a contact's profile with another person. Tap the Share Contact button (you may have to scroll down to see it) and use the Mail or Messages app to send the contact's vCard, which is embedded in the body of a new Mail or Messages message. Just add an address and send it on its merry way. A *vCard*, in case you were wondering, is kind of like an electronic business card. You can identify it by its .vcf file format.

You can also share a contact's vCard with iPadOS's drag-and-drop feature. Just press and hold down on a contact in the list, and then drag it to another app (such as Messages or Mail).

Finally, you can tap a contact's snail-mail address to launch the Maps app and see it pinned to a map.

Linking contacts

The people you know most likely have contact entries in more than one account, meaning you might end up with redundant entries for the same person. The iPad solution is to *link* contacts. Find the contact in question, tap Edit, scroll to the bottom of the Edit screen, and tap Link Contacts. Choose the related contact entry and then tap Link. It's worth noting that the linked contacts in each account remain separate and aren't merged.

Removing a contact

Hey, it happens. A person falls out of favor. Maybe the person is a jilted lover. Or maybe you just moved cross-country and will no longer call on the services of your old gardener.

Removing a contact is easy, if unfortunate. Tap a contact and then tap Edit. Scroll to the bottom of the Edit screen and tap Delete Contact. When Contacts asks you to confirm, tap Delete Contact (or tap outside the confirmation to cancel the whole thing).

And that, gentle reader, should be pretty much all you need to work with Contacts. Onward!

Chapter **12**

Indispensable Apps and Utilities

M ost new iPad users shuttle between a few popular apps that come with iPadOS: Safari, Mail, Photos, Music, Calendar, and Contacts. These apps are great and useful, for sure, but your iPad comes with a fistful of other built-in apps. Are they all awesome? Nope, not even close. However, a few are good enough and useful enough to merit the adjective *indispensable*.

That might seem like hyperbole, but in this chapter, I'll try to change your mind. Here you explore five often-overlooked apps that I think you'll find truly useful: Notes, Reminders, Clock, Home, and Measure. You also examine the lock screen, notifications, Personal Hotspot, and AirDrop — four utilities that can make your day-to-day life easier and more productive.

Jotting Things Down with Notes

Notes enables you to create short documents called — wait for it — *notes* that you can save or send through email. These documents could be shopping lists, to-do lists, quick notes, brainstorming ideas, or just about anything you want to get out of your brain and onto (digital) paper. Over the years, Notes has gained many useful features, including "sketch with your finger" mode, checklists, and enclosures. In addition, many apps now allow you to save data directly to the Notes app (after tapping the share icon). Finally, all your notes can be synced across all your enabled Apple devices via iCloud.

To create a note, follow these steps:

1. **On the Home screen, tap the Notes icon.**

2. **Tap the New Note icon in the upper-right corner (and shown in the margin) to start a fresh note.**

   The virtual keyboard appears.

3. **Type your note, such as the one shown in Figure 12-1.**

Figure 12-1 shows off a few features in Notes: a list formatted as a checklist, followed by a table with two columns and two rows, and then some handwriting.

TIP If you're in a hurry or you want to quickly jot something down without having to switch out of your current app, you can also create a Quick Note. Swipe up from the bottom-right corner of the screen to display the Quick Note window on top of your current app. Tap out your note and then tap Done. Now that's quick!

Other things you can do with the Notes app include the following:

» Tap the back icon (<) in the upper-left corner of the screen to see either a list of all your notes or — if you sync Notes with more than one account, such as iCloud, Google, or Yahoo! — folders for each service you sync with.

» When a list of notes is onscreen, tap a folder to see its contents, or tap a note to open and view, edit, or modify it.

» Tap the checklist icon (labeled in Figure 12-1) to create a checklist; select text before you tap it to change existing text into a checklist.

Checklist   Markup   New note

Media   More

Table

Format

FIGURE 12-1:
The Notes app
revealed.

» Tap the media icon (labeled in Figure 12-1) to take a picture with the camera, select a picture from your Photos library, or scan a document to add to the note you're writing. The document scanner automatically senses and scans a document into the Notes app, crops it, and removes any skewing or glare. If you have a recent generation iPad and Apple Pencil, you can then use Apple Pencil to fill in the blanks or sign the document.

» Tap the markup icon (labeled in Figure 12-1) to display the markup tools you can use to create a new finger sketch.

>> Tap the more icon (labeled in Figure 12-1) to scan a document into the note; pin the note to the top of its folder; lock the note with a password so that the note can't be changed; delete the note; send a copy of the note or otherwise share the note via the Share sheet; move the note to another folder; display horizontal or vertical lines (or both) for easier handwriting; or print the note (see Chapter 2 for more about printing).

When the keyboard is displayed, you can

>> Tap the table icon (labeled in Figure 12-1) to create a table with two columns and two rows. To add a new row below the current row, tap inside a current row, tap the three vertical dots that appear just to the left of the row, and then tap Add Row. To add a new column to the right of the current column, tap inside a current column, tap the three horizontal dots that appear just above the column, and then tap Add Column.

>> Tap the format icon (labeled in Figure 12-1) to format text as Title, Heading, Body, Bulleted List, Dashed List, or Numbered List. Select the text before you tap it to change its format. Depending on the cursor's location in the note, you may see other options.

TIP

You can also use Siri to set up and dictate your note by speaking. (You hear more about Siri in Chapter 14.)

As with most iPad apps, your notes are saved automatically while you type them so you can quit Notes at any time without losing a single character.

I'd be remiss if I didn't remind you one last time that you can sync Notes with your Mac and other devices via iCloud. You enable Notes syncing in Settings ⇨ *your name* ⇨ iCloud on your iPad and System Preferences ⇨ Apple ID ⇨ iCloud on your Mac.

TIP

Enable the Notes widget to access your Notes in today view, as described in Chapter 11.

Finally, one of my favorite iPadOS features for those with an Apple Pencil and a compatible iPad: You can tap the lock screen with your Apple Pencil to launch Notes to a blank page so you can begin taking notes instantly. If this doesn't work for you, tap Settings ⇨ Notes and then enable the Access Notes from Lock Screen setting.

You now know what you need to know about creating and managing notes with Notes.

Remembering with Reminders

You can find lots of good to-do list apps in the App Store; if you don't believe me, search for *to-do list.* You'll find more than 200 offerings for the iPad. Many are free, but others sell (and sell briskly, I might add) at prices up to $30 or $40.

What you get for free is Reminders, a simple to-do list app for making and organizing lists, with optional reminders available for items in your lists.

Tap the Reminders icon on your Home screen, and you'll see something that looks like Figure 12-2. Reminders on the right side of the screen belong to a default list called All, as indicated by the list name highlighted on the left side of the screen.

Working with lists

To create a new list, tap Add List at the bottom of the screen, type a name for the list on the virtual keyboard, tap a color circle to set the list color, tap an icon, and then tap Done. You can also modify your list after you've created it by tapping the list, tapping the three-dots-in-circle icon in the upper-right corner of the Reminders screen, and then tapping Show List Info.

FIGURE 12-2:
The Reminders app.

To manage the lists you create, tap the Edit button at the top of the edit list, shown in Figure 12-2. When you do, the left side of the screen goes into edit mode, as shown in Figure 12-3.

From this screen, you can

TIP

>> **Delete a list:** Tap the red minus sign for the list. The list's name slides to the left, revealing a red Delete button.

You can also delete a list without first tapping the Edit button by swiping the list's name from right to left. The red Delete button appears on the right; tap it to delete the list or tap anywhere else to cancel.

» **Reorder (move up or down) lists:** Tap and drag your finger on the three horizontal lines (shown in the margin) to the right of a list's name in edit mode, and then drag the name up or down. When the list's name is where you want it, lift your finger.

Setting up a reminder

Reminders is a straightforward app, and the steps for managing reminders are equally straightforward. Here's how to remind yourself of something:

1. **On the Home screen, tap the Reminders app.**

2. **On the left side of the screen, tap the list to which you want to assign the reminder.**

   If you haven't created your own lists, you'll see the two default lists: All and Scheduled. Otherwise, you'll see a list of all the reminder lists you've created.

   The virtual keyboard appears.

3. **To start a new reminder , tap + New Reminder at the bottom of the list.**

4. **Type your new reminder.**

   Or just ask Siri to remind you. (See Chapter 14 for more about Siri.)

   The item appears in the current reminders list. At this point, your reminder is bare bones; its date, repeat, and priority options have not been activated. To use those features, continue.

5. **Tap the reminder and then tap the little *i*-in-a-circle to set the following options in the details overlay, as shown in Figure 12-4 (not all options are visible):**

   • *Notes:* If you have anything else to add, tap the Notes field (the second text box; the one with "Mmmm, chocolate" in Figure 12-4) and type away.

   • *URL:* If your reminder is associated with a web page, type the page address here.

   • *Date:* Tap to specify a day for this reminder.

   • *Time:* Tap to specify a time for this reminder.

FIGURE 12-3:
Tap the Edit button to create, delete, or reorder your lists.

- *Repeat:* After you specify a day and time for a reminder, a Repeat button appears. Tap it if you want to set a second reminder for a different day or time.

- *Tags:* Tap to add one or more tags to the reminder. Tags make it easy to search for related reminders. When you tap inside the Search box, you see a Tags section that lists all your tags. Tap a tag to see every reminder that uses that tag.

- *Location:* Tap to set a location-based reminder. Select a location and tap the *i*-in-a-circle button to choose either Arriving (the reminder fires when you arrive at the location) or Leaving (the reminder fires when you leave the location).

- *When Messaging:* Tap this switch to on to display the reminder when you start a Messages conversation with a selected contact.

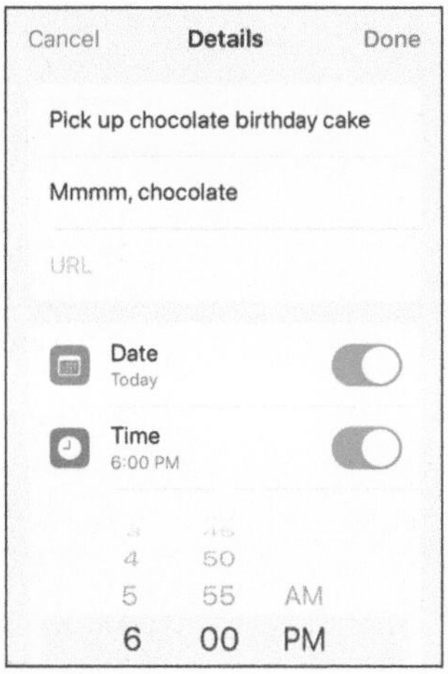

- *Flag:* Tap this switch to on to add a flag icon beside the reminder. Use a flag for important reminders. You can see all your flagged reminders by tapping Flagged near the top-left corner of the Reminders app.

- *Priority:* Tap to specify a priority for this reminder. You can select None, Low, Medium, or High.

- *List:* Tap if you want this reminder to appear in a different list. Then tap the list to which you want to move this reminder.

- *Subtasks:* Tap this setting to add one or more subtasks to the main reminder.

- *Add Image:* Tap this setting to add an image to the reminder from your camera or your library.

FIGURE 12-4: Details for my shiny, new reminder.

6. **After you've set your options, tap the Done button in the upper-right corner of the details overlay.**

Choose the list you want your new reminder to appear in *before* you create the reminder. But if you forget, you can always tap the *i*-in-a-circle icon and choose a different list.

TIP

Viewing and checking off reminders

After you create reminders, the app helps you see what you have and haven't done and enables you to do the following tasks:

» **Check off reminders.** You probably noticed that every reminder you create includes a hollow circle to its left. Tap the circle to indicate that a task has been completed. When you do, Today, Scheduled, and All Numbers will adjust.

» **Search reminders.** To search for a word or phrase in all your reminders, completed or not, tap the Search field at the upper left, type your word or phrase, and then tap the search icon (magnifying glass). Or swipe down from the middle of any Home screen to search for it with Search.

» **Keep reminders on your Mac or PC.** You can create reminders on your Mac or PC with Reminders (macOS Mountain Lion or later), or Tasks in Outlook. And if you're using iCloud, your reminders will always be up to date on all your devices.

That's about it. The Reminders app isn't a bad effort. If it lacks a feature or two that you desire, check out the myriad third-party to-do list apps in the App Store.

Loving the Lock Screen

The lock screen is what you see when you first turn on or wake up your iPad. You can quickly access the features and information you need most from the lock screen, even while the iPad is locked.

From the lock screen, you can do the following without unlocking your iPad first:

» Swipe left to open the camera.

» Swipe right to see today view.

» Drag down from the upper-right corner of the screen to open Control Center.

» Swipe up from the center of the screen to see older notifications.

TIP

To fine-tune what you see on the lock screen, tap Settings ⇨ Touch ID & Passcode (or Settings ⇨ Face ID & Passcode, if your iPad supports Face ID). In the Allow Access When Locked section, use the switches to toggle which features are available in the lock screen.

Navigating Notifications

When your iPad is locked, notifications appear on the lock screen; when it's unlocked, they appear at the top of the screen.

To summon older notifications to the forefront of your iPad screen when it's unlocked, all you need is the magical incantation — that is, a swipe from the top of the screen downward. Go ahead and give it a try. I'll wait.

Here's the rest of what you need to know about navigating notifications:

>> **Open a notification on the lock screen.** Swipe right to open a notification with the appropriate app after authenticating with Touch ID, Face ID, or your passcode.

>> **Open a notification on an unlocked iPad.** Tap the notification to open it in the appropriate program.

>> **Edit or rearrange the widgets in the today view.** Tap the Edit button at the bottom of the screen.

>> **Clear a single notification.** Swipe from right to left and then tap the Clear button.

>> **Clear all notifications.** Swipe right to left to get to the Notification screen and then tap the little x-in-a-circle to the right of the section heading. The x turns into a Clear button; tap the Clear button and all notifications are cleared. If you have notifications from previous days, repeat this procedure for each one.

That's how to summon and use notifications. There's still a bit more to know — including how to change the notification settings for individual apps — but you have to wait until the chapter on settings (which happens to be Chapter 15).

Taming Time with the Clock App

When you see the Clock icon on your iPad's Home screen, you might think that the app just tells you the time. Yep, sure, it does that, but the Clock app also does so much more. For example, it can tell you the current time in just about any city in the world. The app also enables you to set alarms, time events with a stopwatch, start a countdown timer, and more.

To get started, tap the Clock icon on your Home screen. Alternatively, swipe down from the top-right corner of the screen to open Control Center and then tap the timer icon (shown in the margin) to open the Clock app with its timer feature displayed.

The Clock app has four icons across the bottom of the screen: World Clock, Alarm, Stopwatch, and Timer. I talk about each of these features in the next four sections.

Seeing the time anywhere in the world

Want to know the time in Beijing or Bogota? Tap the Clock app's World Clock icon to display the time in numerous cities around the globe, as shown in Figure 12-5. When the clock face is dark, it's nighttime in the city you chose; if the face is white, it's daytime outside.

To add a city to the world clock, tap + in the upper-right corner and then use the virtual keyboard to start typing a city name.

As you type, the iPad displays a list of places where the city or country name includes what you've typed. For example, typing *ve* brings up Andorra la Vella, Andorra; Caracas, Venezuela; and Las Vegas, U.S.A., among others. Keep typing until you see the city you want, and then tap it to add a clock for that location. You can create clocks for as many cities as you like, though

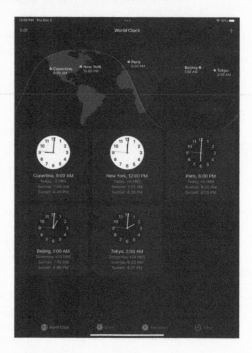

FIGURE 12-5:
What time is it in Paris?

only six cities fit onscreen at a time (in landscape orientation). Note, too, that you can drag the clocks around the screen to set your preferred arrangement.

To remove a city from the list, tap Edit and then tap the red circle with the white horizontal line that appears to the left of the city.

Setting an alarm

Ever try to set the alarm in a hotel room? It's remarkable how complicated setting an alarm can be, on even the most inexpensive clock radio. Like almost everything else, the procedure is way more straightforward on the iPad:

1. **At the bottom of the Clock app, tap the Alarm icon.**

2. **Tap + in the upper-right corner of the screen.**

   The Add Alarm dialog appears.

3. **Choose the time of the alarm by rotating the hour, minute, and AM/PM wheels.**

4. **Tap Save.**

That's what you can do with a regular alarm clock. What's the big deal, you say? Well, you can do even more with your iPad alarm. In the Add Alarm dialog, you can also do the following:

>> **Set the alarm to go off on other days.** Tap Repeat and then tell the iPad the days you want the alarm to be repeated, as in Every Monday, Every Tuesday, Every Wednesday, and so on.

>> **Name your alarm.** If you want to call the alarm something other than, um, Alarm, tap the Label field and use the virtual keyboard to type another descriptor.

>> **Choose your own sound.** Tap Sound to choose the tone that will wake you up. You can even use songs from your Music library and any custom tones stored on your iPad.

>> **Set the snooze to sleep in.** Tap Snooze on (showing green) to display a Snooze button along with the alarm. When your alarm goes off, you can tap the Snooze button to shut down the alarm for nine minutes.

TIP

You can also ask Siri to set the alarm for you. See Chapter 14 to learn how to use Siri.

You know that an alarm has been set and activated because of the tiny status icon (surprise, surprise — it looks like an alarm clock) that appears on the status bar in the upper-right corner of the screen.

An alarm takes precedence over any tracks you're listening to on your iPad. Songs or videos with sound pause when an alarm goes off and resume when you turn off the alarm (or tap the Snooze button).

When your ring/silent switch is set to Silent, your iPad still plays alarms from the Clock app. It stays silent for FaceTime calls, alert sounds, or audio from apps, but it *will* play alarms from the Clock app.

Although it seems obvious, if you want to actually *hear* an alarm, you have to make sure that the iPad volume is turned up loud enough for you to hear.

Timing events with Stopwatch

Are you're helping a friend or family member train for an upcoming track meet? Do you want to know how long it takes to peel a half-dozen carrots (hey, whatever floats your boat)? Whenever you need to time something, the Stopwatch function can provide an assist. Open it by tapping Stopwatch at the bottom of the Clock app.

When you're ready, tap Start to begin the timing. When your trainee arrives at the finish line or you're finished with those carrots, tap Stop to shut off the timing. Note, too, that along the way you can also tap the Lap button as often as needed to monitor the times of individual laps (or carrots).

Starting a countdown timer

Cooking a hard-boiled egg or Thanksgiving turkey? Again, the Clock app comes to the rescue. Tap Timer at the bottom of the Clock app, and then rotate the hours, minutes, and seconds wheels to set the length of time you want to count down. Tap When Timer Ends to choose the ringtone that will signify time's up.

Tap Start when you're ready to begin. You can watch the minutes and seconds wind down on the screen. Or tap Pause to pause the countdown temporarily. If you need to end the timer prematurely, tap Done.

If you're doing anything else on the iPad — admiring photos, say — you hear the ringtone and see a *Timer Done* message on the screen at the appropriate moment. Tap OK to silence the ringtone.

Controlling Smart Appliances with the Home App

The Home app is all about managing HomeKit accessories, which fit into a broader tech trend of connecting devices known as the *Internet of Things (IoT)*. HomeKit is Apple's framework for IoT accessories in and around the house — door locks, lightbulbs, thermostats, and various other products you might like to control with your iPad.

Just launch the Home app on your Home screen, and tap the Add Accessory button in the middle of your screen to get started. If you already have an accessory added to your Home app, tap + at the top of the screen and then tap Add Accessory to add more.

If the device has a HomeKit setup code, you can scan it from the Add Device screen. You can also enter the device's HomeKit code by hand. Be sure to set which room the device is in so you can control your devices by room. Figure 12-6 shows a typical Home setup, with several devices and scenes, which I talk more about shortly.

TIP

If you have an Apple TV or Home-Pod, you can use it as a hub for your HomeKit accessories and access and control most devices from anywhere with internet access. Without Apple TV or HomePod, you can control your accessories only when your iPad is connected to the same Wi-Fi network.

FIGURE 12-6:
The Home app lets you control HomeKit smart devices.

Home scenes allow you to control multiple devices, set timers, or even add geolocation data to your controls. For example, Figure 2-6 has an I'm Going to Bed scene to turn on the bedroom lights and turn off all other lights in the house. The I'm Leaving scene turns on the porch lights and turns off all other lights in the home. You can use Siri to activate any scene or device by name, such as "Hey Siri, I'm going to bed."

To create a scene, tap + at the top right of the screen, and then tap Add Scene. Then choose which devices and other parameters you want for your scene.

At the bottom of the Home app are the following three tabs:

>> **Home:** Displays all scenes and devices (refer to Figure 12-6).

>> **Rooms:** Shows scenes and devices by room. Tap the menu icon in the upper-left to change the displayed room.

>> **Automation:** Offers a more exciting way to control your smart devices. With Home app automation, you can set devices or scenes to occur based on time; people arriving or leaving; or info from a sensor (if a HomeKit-enabled sensor is installed). To create an automation, tap + in the upper right, and then set the devices and parameters you want to control.

Taking the Measure of Things with the Measure App

I think the Measure app is nothing short of magical. You can use it and your iPad's camera to make very accurate measurements of real-world objects. Seriously!

Tap the Measure app icon on the Home screen. The screen is taken over by a view from your iPad's camera with instructions to Move iPad to Start. As you do so, your iPad gets a fix on its surroundings. The Measure app draws dotted lines around certain shapes. You can tap within those dotted lines to get measurements, as shown in Figure 12-7. In the middle of those measurements, the app even provides the area of the shape, .31 square feet in this case.

You can also plot your own points by tapping the + button on the right side of the screen. Add additional points, and the Measure app will give you those measurements. Think about all those times when you wished you had a ruler or measuring tape with you. With the Measure app, now you do!

FIGURE 12-7:
Measure things with just your iPad and the Measure app.

Sharing Your Internet Connection with Personal Hotspot

Personal Hotspot is a feature that lets your iPad with Wi-Fi + Cellular share its cellular high-speed data connection with other devices, including computers, iPod touches, and other iPads.

REMEMBER

If your iPad is Wi-Fi only, feel free to skip this section — the Personal Hotspot option is available only on cellular iPads.

To enable your Personal Hotspot and share your cellular data connection with others, do the following:

1. **On the Home screen, tap Settings ⇨ Cellular Data ⇨ Set Up Personal Hotspot.**

2. **Tap the Allow Others to Join switch to on.**

3. **Tap Wi-Fi Password and create or change the password for the Wi-Fi network you create.**

Now Wi-Fi, Bluetooth, or USB-enabled devices can join your Personal Hotspot network and share your iPad's cellular data connection.

REMEMBER

Your Personal Hotspot network adopts your iPad's name (see Figure 12-8).

FIGURE 12-8:
Devices can join this Personal Hotspot via Wi-Fi, Bluetooth, or USB.

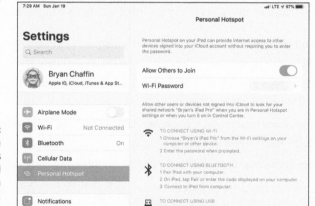

Most carriers offer support for Personal Hotspots in some or all of their data plans in the United States. Some don't, so check with your carrier if you don't see a Personal Hotspot option in the Settings app (and, of course, if your iPad has cellular capabilities).

WARNING

Some carriers don't charge extra for this feature, but the data used by connected devices counts against your monthly data plan allotment.

To see how much cellular data you're using, tap Settings ➪ Cellular Data and scroll down until you see Cellular Data Usage, which displays your cellular usage for the current period as well as data used while roaming.

Dropping In on AirDrop

At various points when you're using your iPad, you encounter AirDrop, a fast, safe, and secure (through encryption) wireless method of sharing photos, videos, contacts, documents, and more with people you are close to physically.

 You just tap the share icon (shown in the margin) in any app that offers one. AirDrop exploits both Wi-Fi and Bluetooth. No advanced setup is required.

REMEMBER

To be part of an AirDrop exchange, you and the recipient must be using an iPhone or iPad running iOS 7 or later, including iPadOS, or a Mac running macOS Yosemite or later.

Taking advantage of this clever feature involves three simple steps:

1. **Turn on the AirDrop feature (if it's not on already) in Settings ➪ General ➪ AirDrop.**

    You have the option to make your device visible to Everyone (within the vicinity) or just to your contacts.

2. **Tap the share icon when it presents itself in an app, and then choose the file or files you want to share.**

3. **Choose someone who has the AirDrop icon added to their avatar.**

    To see all nearby unlocked Apple devices with AirDrop activated, tap the AirDrop icon below the row of possible recipients.

Yes, you can choose more than one person. People in range who are eligible to receive the file are represented on your iPad by a circle.

The AirDrop process hath begun. The people on the receiving end will get a prompt asking them to accept the picture, video, or whatever it is you're offering them.

Assuming they take kindly to your offer and grant permission (by tapping Accept rather than Decline), the file lands on their devices in short order, where it is routed to its proper location. That is, a picture or video ends up in the Photos app, a contact in the Contacts app, and the Passbook pass in the Wallet app.

IN THIS CHAPTER

» Taking a guided tour of the Maps app

» Searching for coffee shops, bakeries, and other nearby essentials

» Putting yourself on the map

» Answering the age-old question: "Can I get there from here?"

Chapter **13**

Navigating the World

The science fiction writer Arthur C. Clarke once said that "any sufficiently advanced technology is indistinguishable from magic." Your iPad is bursting at the seams with advanced technology, but the one trick your iPad does that really does seem like magic is mapping. Not only does your iPad somehow know your exact location, but it also knows the exact location of pretty much everything else in the world *and* it can show you how to get from here to there. Magic? Not really, but it *is* impressive. I'm sure you'll find endless uses for the Maps app.

In this chapter, you explore Maps and discover all that it can do, from mapping addresses, to showing your current location, to getting directions on how to get from A to B (and back).

Mapping Locations

The Maps app is the Grand Central Station of mapping on your iPad. To get this trip started, tap the Maps icon on your iPad's Home screen. You'll come face-to-face with a screen that looks something like the one shown in Figure 13-1, which is essentially just a big map. You use Maps in two main ways:

>> To view locations on the map

>> To get specific directions for getting from one location to another

The next few sections show you numerous ways to map a location. I get to the directions part of the tour a bit later in this chapter.

REMEMBER

Maps isn't the only app that can use your location. Lots of apps, including App Store, Calendar, Camera, Reminders, and Weather, can ask for your permission to use your location. Fortunately, you have complete control over which apps use your location. To learn how to exercise that control, see Chapter 18.

FIGURE 13-1:
Most of your iPad's mapping magic happens in the Maps app.

Mapping a location by searching for it

Maps knows — or seems to know — the location of just about anything. If it's situated somewhere on planet Earth and has an address or a name, chances are you can map it by running a search in the Maps app. Here's how:

1. **Tap inside the Search Maps box near the upper-left corner of the Maps screen.**

2. **Start typing some text that specifies the location.**

   You can type any of the following:

   ● The name of the location

   ● The address of the location

   ● A word or phrase that describes the location

252 PART 4 **Putting the iPad to Work**

As you type, Maps displays a list of locations that match what you've entered so far.

3. **In the search results, tap the location you want to map.**

Maps inserts a pin for the destination on the map and displays an information card with data about the location, as shown in Figure 13-2.

The location's info card often displays a ton of data about the location (the more public the location, the more data you see). The data shown on the card can include the location's phone number, street address, hours of operation, website address, and perhaps a photo or two. The card might also display reviews of the location from Yelp (a service that offers user-generated ratings and reviews of millions of locations around the world).

FIGURE 13-2:
Tap your location in the search results and Maps shows you where it is and displays some info about it.

Dropping a pin

In the preceding section, I went through the steps involved in searching for a specific location. That technique works like a treat provided you have a specific location in mind (and know the address or name of that location). However, sometimes you just want to investigate a block or a neighborhood, not a specific location.

No problem. Maps enables you to create a *dropped pin,* which is a pushpin icon that Maps inserts on any spot that you long-press. Handily, Maps also displays the Dropped Pin information card, which tells you the address of the dropped pin, its latitude and longitude, and the name of any nearby businesses (such as a shop or restaurant).

You also get the location's Look Around icon (if that feature is available for the location) in the lower-right corner so you can peek at what's located where you dropped the pin. (The Look Around feature is discussed next.)

Looking around your destination

The Maps app gives you a kind of bird's-eye view of a location and its surrounding area. That overview is usually enough to allow you to get your bearings, but it's often helpful to come down from the clouds and get right onto the street to see exactly what's there. You could literally get right onto the street by actually traveling to the destination, but what if you want to look around before you go?

You can definitely do that by taking advantage of a Maps feature called Look Around, which shows you still images (taken from a car) of whatever location you're interested in. (Look Around is Apple's equivalent or the Street View feature in Google Maps.) As I write this, Look Around is available in most major cities in the US and Canada, as well as in select locations around the world, including London, Edinburgh, Dublin, and Tokyo.

 To use Look Around, map your location and then tap the Look Around icon in the lower-right corner of the screen (and shown in the margin). With Look Around enabled, use the following techniques to, well, look around:

>> **Pan the scene.** Drag a finger left or right, up or down.

>> **Move forward in the scene.** Tap the screen.

>> **Zoom in or out on the scene.** Pinch or spread two fingers on the screen.

>> **Switch to full-screen mode.** Tap the enter full screen mode icon (two arrows facing away from each other).

>> **Exit full-screen mode:** Tap the exit full screen mode icon (two arrows facing toward each other).

>> **Exit Look Around:** Tap Done.

You are here: Mapping your current location

Go to your local mall and chances are that somewhere near the entrance you'll see a kiosk that contains a map that you can use to locate the store you want. To help you orient yourself, these maps almost always have a "You Are Here" marker that specifies the location on the map and, therefore, the location of *you*.

 When you're in an unfamiliar part of town or in a city you've never visited before, wouldn't it be great to come across a kiosk that has a "You Are Here" marker? Well, if you happen to have your iPad with you, the Maps app can do that! Tap the tracking icon (shown in the margin). Maps navigates to your overall area and then displays a blue beacon that marks your exact location. Tap the tracking icon a second time and Maps orients the map to face in the same direction as your iPad and also rotates the map along with your iPad.

How does your iPad know your current location? It's hideously complex, but it boils down to your iPad having three (or sometimes four) internal hardware doo-dads that can pick up location information from devices. The internal doohickeys are the Bluetooth and Wi-Fi antennas for all iPads, plus the GPS (Global Positioning System) and cellular antennas, if your iPad comes with cellular network hardware. The Bluetooth, Wi-Fi, and cellular antennas pick up location data from nearby Bluetooth beacons, Wi-Fi hotspots, and cellular network towers, respectively. The GPS receiver gets its location data from in-orbit GPS satellites.

Putting a contact on the map

When you add a contact to your iPad's Contacts app (see Chapter 11), you can include a street address for that person or business. That's cool, but it's even cooler to know that you can map that address by following three measly steps:

1. **From your iPad's Home screen, tap the Contacts icon.**

2. **Tap the contact you want to work with.**

   The Contacts app displays the contact data for the person or business.

3. **Tap the street address that you want to map.**

   Your iPad switches to Maps and drops a pin on the contact's address.

Mapping an address from an email message

If you receive an email message that includes a street address (say, as part of the sender's signature), you might want to know where that address is located. You could copy the address from the message and then paste it into the Search Maps text box in the Maps app, but there's no need to go to that much trouble. Instead, you can follow these much easier steps:

1. **In the Mail app, display the message that includes the address.**

   If your tablet is in portrait mode, tap Inbox to see the messages.

2. **Long-press the address in the message to display a list of actions.**

3. **If the address is displayed as a link (underlined and in blue), tap it. Otherwise, tap Open in Maps.**

   Maps opens and drops a pin on the address.

Saving a location as a favorite

If you know the address of the location you want to map, you can add a pushpin for that location by opening Maps and running a search on the address. That is, tap the Search Maps box, type the address, and then tap the location in the search results.

That's no big deal for one-time-only searches, but what about a location you map frequently? Typing that address over and over would get old in a hurry, I assure you. You can save time and tapping by telling Maps to save the location in its favorites list, which means you can access it, usually, with just a few taps.

Use either of the following techniques to add a location to the favorites list:

» Map the location you want to save and then tap Add to Favorites in the location's information card.

» In the Favorites section that appears under the Search Maps text box, tap Add, search for the location you want to add, and tap it in the search results. Use the Details pane to name the favorite, and then tap Done.

To map a favorite location, follow these steps:

1. **If you have a location's information card displayed, tap X (close) in the upper-right corner to close the card.**

2. **If you don't see the favorite you want in the Favorites section (just below the Search Maps text box), tap More.**

   Maps displays the Favorites pane.

3. **Tap the location you want to map.**

   Maps displays the appropriate map and adds a pin for the location.

Sharing a map

To send someone a map via email, text message, AirDrop, or some other sharing method, follow these steps:

1. **Map the location you want to send.**

2. **In the location's information card, tap Share.**

   Maps displays a list of ways to share the map.

3. **Tap the method you want to use to share the map.**

   If the method you choose is not text-based (if you choose AirDrop, for example), you're done.

4. **If the method is text-based (such as an email or text), fill in the rest of your message and send it.**

Mapping locations with Siri voice commands

The Siri voice–activated assistant (see Chapter 14) can be used to control Maps with straightforward voice commands. You can display a location, get directions, and even display traffic information. Press and hold down on the top button (if your iPad supports Face ID) or the Home button (for all other iPad models) until Siri appears.

Here are some commands you can use for mapping locations:

» **To display a location in Maps:** Say "Show *location*" (or "Map *location*" or "Find *location*" or "Where is *location*"), where *location* is an address, a name, or a Maps favorite.

» **To get directions:** Say "Directions to *location*," where *location* is an address, a name, or a Maps favorite.

» **To see the current traffic conditions:** Say "Traffic *location*," where *location* can be a specific place or somewhere local, such as "around here" or "nearby."

» **To get your current location:** Say "Where am I?" or "Show my current location."

Getting There from Here: Navigating with Maps

You'll often map locations just to see where they are. However, most of the time, you'll bring up a location on the map because you want to go there, by car, transit, walking, or whatever.

When you map a destination — using an address search, a name search, a dropped pin, or a tap on a contact or email address — and you know your way around town, just knowing where the destination is located might be enough to enable you to navigate there on your own.

But if the destination is far away or in an unfamiliar town, you'll likely need some help with navigation duties. Maps can ride shotgun with you not only by showing you a route to the destination but also by providing the distance and time it should take and by giving you street-by-street, turn-by-turn instructions, whether you're driving or walking. It's one of the sweetest Maps features, and the next few sections provide the details.

Getting directions to a location

Here are the basic steps to follow to get directions to a location:

1. **Use Maps to add a pushpin for your destination.**

   Use whatever method works best for you: search for an address or a name, drop a pin, tap a contact or email address, or tap a favorite.

2. **On the location's information card, tap Directions.**

   Maps displays several possible routes, as shown in Figure 13-3.

3. **To use a different starting point:**

   a. *Tap the From location (which defaults to My Location, meaning your current location).* Maps opens the Change Route pane.

   b. *In the From box, select or enter a new location.*

   c. *Tap Route.* Maps returns to the routes and updates them to account for your new starting point.

Drive   Transit

Walk   Bicycle   Choose map

FIGURE 13-3:
Maps offers a few driving routes originating from your current location.

↑↓

If you need directions from the destination rather than to it, tap your From location to open the Change Route pane, tap the swap icon (shown in the margin) to swap the To and From locations, and then tap Route.

4. **Tap the icon for the type of directions you want: drive, walk, transit, or bicycle.**

   These icons are labeled in Figure 13-3.

5. **Tap the Go button for the route you want to take.**

   Maps displays the first leg of the journey.

Maps features turn-by-turn directions. This means that as you approach each turn, Siri tells you what to do next, such as "In 400 feet, turn right onto Main Street." Maps also follows along the route, so you can see where you're going and which turn is coming up. By tapping the screen, you can see your estimated time of arrival, remaining travel time, and distance remaining.

Getting live traffic information

Okay, it's pretty darn amazing that your iPad can tell you precisely where you are and how to get somewhere else. However, in most cities, it's the getting some-where else part that's the problem. Why? One word: traffic. Maps may tell you the trip should take 10 minutes, but that could easily turn into a half-hour or more if you run into a traffic jam.

That's life in the big city, right? Maybe not. If you're in a major North American city, Maps can most likely supply you with — wait for it — real-time traffic con-ditions. This amazing tool can help you avoid traffic messes and find alternative routes to your destination. The Maps app can also display traffic construction spots, and it gathers real-time information from Maps users to generate even more accurate traffic data. If you're in the middle of turn-by-turn directions, Maps will even recognize an upcoming traffic delay and offer an alternative route around it!

To see the traffic data, tap the icon that appears above the tracking icon in the upper-right corner of the screen (refer to Figure 13-3); the icon changes depend-ing on the currently selected map (drive, walk, transit, or bicycle). In the Choose Map dialog that appears, tap Driving (if it's not selected already) and then tap X (close).

Maps now displays the following:

>> An orange line to indicate traffic slowdowns.

>> A red line to indicate very heavy traffic.

>> Roadwork icons to indicate construction sites. Tap a roadwork icon to see more information about the work, as shown in Figure 13-4.

Getting directions with Siri voice commands

You can also use Siri to get directions and display traffic information. Tap and hold the top button (if your iPad supports Face ID) or the Home button (for all other iPad models) until Siri appears.

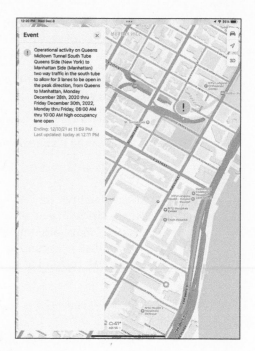

FIGURE 13-4:
Tap a roadwork icon to see info about the construction.

Here are the commands you can use:

>> **To get directions:** Say "Directions to *location*," where *location* is an address, a name, or a Maps favorite.

>> **To see the current traffic conditions:** Say "Traffic *location*," where *location* can be a specific place or somewhere local, such as "around here" or "nearby."

Chapter **14**

Taking Control

When you want your iPad to do your bidding, you usually put the magic of multitouch to work: You tap this, double-tap that, swipe something else, and so on. These and other touchscreen gestures such as pinching and spreading aren't difficult, but doesn't it sometimes feel like you have to perform a seemingly endless litany of gestures to accomplish some tasks? We're all going to end up with calluses on our fingers if we keep this up!

Or you can try a smarter approach and take advantage of some iPad features that drastically reduce or even eliminate the number of gestures you perform to make some tasks happen.

The first of these features is Control Center, which you can open with a quick swipe. Control Center offers one- or two-tap access to many common iPad settings, including Wi-Fi, Bluetooth, Focus, brightness, and volume.

The second feature is Siri, the intelligent, voice-activated virtual personal assistant living like a kind of digital genie inside your iPad. Siri responds to your voice commands for tasks such as opening an app, setting an alarm, scheduling an appointment, and retrieving information. It sounds like the stuff of science fiction and, well, I suppose it is.

Finally, you can also dictate text instead of typing it using the virtual keyboard.

In this chapter, you investigate all these ways of controlling your iPad.

Controlling Control Center

As its name suggests, Control Center is a repository for controls, tools, and settings you'll need frequently. To access Control Center, swipe down from the upper-right corner of your screen — any screen, even the lock screen. (If Control Center doesn't work for you on any screen, open the Settings app, tap Control Center, and then tap the Access within Apps switch to on.)

REMEMBER

However — and I bet you were waiting for some kind of *however* — some apps disallow access to Control Center. When that happens, you'll have to press the Home button (if your iPad has one) or swipe up from the bottom of the screen to go back to the Home screen. Now swipe down from the upper-right corner to display Control Center.

When you open Control Center, you see a blurry background version of whatever was just on the screen with Control Center itself taking up most of the upper-right quadrant.

Two groups of icons appear, along with more individual icons. The first group is for the iPad's radios: airplane mode, cellular data (if your iPad is a Wi-Fi + Cellular model), Wi-Fi, and Bluetooth. If you have a Wi-Fi–only iPad, the cellular data icon is replaced with an AirDrop icon, as shown in Figure 14-1. If you long-press that group, you'll get expanded controls that add AirDrop and Personal Hotspot, as shown in Figure 14-2, which was taken on an iPad with Wi-Fi + Cellular.

The ability to long-press icons or icon groupings is a hallmark feature in Control Center. It allows iPadOS to give you expanded access when you need it, while keeping Control Center neat and tidy the rest of the time. Take a minute to long-press all the icons to see what's there!

TIP

Tapping the Wi-Fi or Bluetooth icon in iPadOS's Control Center does not turn off those radios on your iPad. Instead, it disconnects your iPad from any connected Wi-Fi network or Bluetooth devices, respectively, while leaving the radios themselves on. To truly turn off those radios — say, to save battery life — you need to go to Settings.

The second Control Center group appears to the right of the radio controls and contains the music controls: previous, play, and next. Long-press the music control group, and you get a volume slider, a slider for controlling where you are in the song, a list of AirPlay speakers or Apple TVs on your network, and an additional AirPlay icon for a different way of choosing AirPlay output.

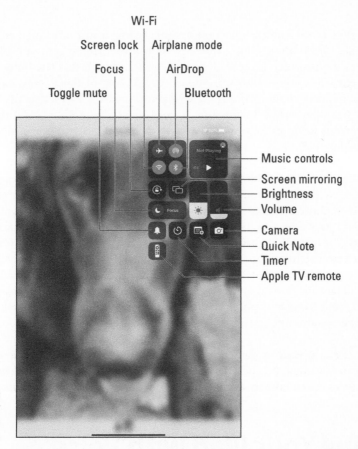

Toggle mute

Focus

Screen lock

Wi-Fi

Airplane mode

AirDrop

Bluetooth

Music controls

Screen mirroring

Brightness

Volume

Camera

Quick Note

Timer

Apple TV remote

FIGURE 14-1:
Control Center
is merely a
swipe away.

Immediately below the music controls are brightness and volume sliders that look more like a thermometer metaphor than a slider metaphor. Drag up or down on either control to change screen brightness and volume, respectively. If you long-press the volume slider, you just get a bigger volume slider. Long-pressing the brightness slider (which is discussed in more depth in Chapter 15) adds icons for dark mode, night shift, and true tone.

To the left of the brightness and volume sliders are the screen lock icon and an icon for activating screen mirroring, where you can choose an Apple TV or other compatible device to mirror your iPad's screen. Below these two controls is the Focus icon. You can tap the Focus icon to see icons for each focus you've set up, such as do not disturb, driving, personal, and work.

FIGURE 14-2:
Expand Control Center groups and icons by tapping and holding down.

Below these icons a collection of other icons, a sort of a catch-all for everything else: toggle mute, timer, Quick Note, camera, Home app, Apple TV remote, and flashlight, which is on iPads with a rear camera flash. (The Home app and flashlight icons aren't shown in Figure 14-1.) Most of these icons expand when you long-press them. The expanded camera control is particularly useful because it has options for Take Selfie, Record Video, Take Photo, and then either Take Portrait Selfie or Record Slo-Mo (which of the last two you see depends on your iPad model).

And this is where things get customizable. Choose Settings ⇨ Control Center. You can use the Show Home Controls switch to toggle the Home app's controls on and off in Control Center. You also get a list of controls specific to your iPad that you can remove or add, including accessibility shortcuts, alarm, dark mode, guided access, magnifier, hearing, screen recording, stopwatch, and text size. Tap the red circle with a minus sign to remove a control. Tap the green circle with a plus sign to add a control. You can add all of them if you want, but your Control Center will be a mess. Also, in the Included Controls section, you can rearrange the order of these icons by tapping the three little lines next to any control and dragging it where you want.

TIP

You can permit or deny access to Control Center on the lock screen in Settings. Go to Settings ⇨ Touch ID & Passcode (or Face ID & Passcode). Then, in the Allow Access When Locked section, toggle the Control Center switch on or off.

Controlling Your iPad with Voice Commands? Siri-ously!

Siri is Apple's voice-controlled virtual personal assistant that stands ready, willing, and able to carry out your voice commands, no questions asked (usually).

Summoning Siri

TIP

You can't turn Siri off, but you can control how you access it in Settings ⇨ Siri & Search. You'll see on/off switches for Listen for "Hey Siri," Press Home for Siri (if your iPad has a Home button), Press Top Button for Siri (of your iPad doesn't have a Home button), and Allow Siri When Locked. You look at each of these methods in this section.

REMEMBER

Siri requires internet access.

A lot of factors go into Siri's accuracy in understanding you, including surrounding sounds and unfamiliar accents. You also need to be comfortable with the fact that Apple is recording what you say, though the company anonymizes Siri data through something called differential privacy, which allows Apple to collect anonymized data and mix it with signal noise in such a way that it can't be tracked back to individual users.

You can call Siri into action in a few ways. The traditional way is to press and hold down on the Home button (or the top button if you own an iPad Pro with Face ID) until you hear a tone. Siri then listens for your query. How do you know Siri is listening? You see the orb shown in Figure 14-3 in the bottom-right corner of your screen. You have about five seconds to start talking, after which Siri goes back to sleep.

FIGURE 14-3: When you see this orb, you know that Siri is listening.

If you tap the Listen for "Hey Siri" switch to on, you can summon Siri also by merely saying, "Hey Siri." You can even keep going with your question or command by saying something like, "Hey Siri, FaceTime Mom."

Siri also responds when you press and hold down on the call button on most Bluetooth headsets. If you have Apple AirPods, two sharp taps on the outside of either AirPod will activate Siri. If you have AirPods Pro, you can use "Hey Siri."

What happens next is up to you. You can ask a wide range of questions or issue voice commands. Note that after you ask your first question, the Siri orb stays onscreen in the lower-right corner, although Siri stops listening after it answers your query. Tap the orb to put Siri back in listening mode.

Siri relies on voice recognition and artificial intelligence (its, not yours). The voice genie responds in a conversational manner, and Siri sounds amazing in iPadOS. But using Siri isn't always a hands-free experience. Spoken words are sometimes supplemented by information on the iPad screen (as you see in the next section).

Siri seeks answers using sources such as Google, Wikipedia, Yelp, Yahoo!, Open Table, Twitter, and WolframAlpha, making Siri your personal search agent for your iPad's content or outside information. For instance, ask Siri to find all the videos you shot at your kid's graduation party and it'll oblige (at least if you tagged them correctly).

Siri on the iPad can also launch apps — Apple's own as well as third-party apps. From your contacts, Siri might be able to determine who your spouse, coworkers, and friends are, as well as knowing where you live. You might say, "Show me how to get home," and Siri will fire up Maps to help you on your way. Or you can say, "Find a good Italian restaurant near Barbara's house," and Siri will serve up a list, sorted by Yelp rating. Using Open Table, Siri can even make a restaurant reservation.

Apple has also opened up Siri to third-party app developers. For example, you can have Siri arrange a ride through Uber or Lyft, or pay a debt on your behalf through Apple or apps such as Venmo or Square Cash.

If you ask about a favorite sports team, Siri will retrieve the score of the team's last game or the game in progress. And if you're rummaging through a longish email that you can't quite get through at the moment, you can have Siri set a reminder for you to follow up later in the evening.

Figuring out what to ask

The beauty of Siri is that there's no designated protocol you must follow when talking to it. Asking, "Will I need an umbrella tomorrow?" produces the same result as, "What is the weather forecast around here?" Siri makes its share of mistakes, of course, but Apple's long-view approach is making Siri better at understanding the meaning of your words.

Another cool feature is that Siri can identify the name and artist of the musical track that's playing. Just ask Siri what song is playing and it'll name that tune. When the song is properly identified, you even get a chance to buy it.

If you're not sure what to ask, invoke Siri and then say "Help." Siri displays the Siri's Here to Help dialog, which you can tap to display a web page that has some sample questions or commands, as shown in Figure 14-4. You can tap any of the links on the page to see even more samples.

FIGURE 14-4:
Siri can help out in many ways.

Here are some ways Siri can lend a hand . . . um, I mean a voice:

>> **FaceTime:** "FaceTime *phone number* my wife."

>> **Music:** "Play Frank Sinatra" or "Play Apple Music." "What song is this?" "Rate this song three stars."

>> **Messages:** "Send a message to Nancy to reschedule lunch."

>> **Apple Pay:** "Apple Pay $10 to Johnny Appleseed."

>> **Translation:** "Translate 'I miss you so' in French."

>> **Sports:** "Did the Warriors win?"

>> **Calendar:** "Set up a meeting for 9 a.m. to discuss funding."

>> **Reminders:** "Remind me to take my medicine at 8 a.m. tomorrow."

>> **Maps:** "Find an ATM near here."

>> **Mail:** "Mail the tenant about the recent rent check."

>> **Photos:** "Show me the photos I took at Samuel's birthday party."

>> **Stocks:** "What's Apple's stock price?"

>> **Web search:** "Who was the 19th president of the United States?"

>> **Knowledge:** "How many calories are in a blueberry muffin?"

>> **Clock:** "Wake me up at 8:30 in the morning."

>> **Trivia:** "Who won the Academy Award for Best Actor in 2003?"

>> **Twitter:** "Send tweet, 'Going on vacation,' smiley-face emoticon" or "What is trending on Twitter?"

Correcting mistakes

As I point out earlier, as good as Siri is, it sometimes needs to be corrected. Fortunately, you can correct its mistakes fairly easily. The simplest way is to tap the microphone icon and try your query again.

You can also tap your question on your iPad's screen to edit or fix what Siri thinks you said. If a word or phrase is underlined, you can use the keyboard to make a correction. Apple will also offer suggestions when you tap the underlined material: "Maybe you meant . . . ." After you have make the edit, tap Done on the virtual keyboard, and Siri will give you a new response based on that edit.

Siri also seeks your permission before sending a dictated message. That's a safeguard you might come to appreciate. If you need to modify the message, you can do so by saying such things as, "Change Tuesday to Wednesday" or "Add: I'm excited to see you, exclamation mark" — obligingly, *I'm excited to see you!* will be added.

Making Siri smarter

From Settings ⇨ Siri & Search ⇨ Language, you can tell Siri which language you want to converse in. Siri is available in English (with many country variations), as well as versions of Chinese, Danish, Dutch, Finnish, French, German, Hebrew, Italian, Japanese, Korean, Malay, Norwegian, Portuguese, Russian, Spanish, Swedish, Thai, and Turkish.

You can also request voice feedback from Siri all the time, or just when you're using a hands-free headset. If you want, you can silence the feedback when the mute switch is on. You'll still get voice feedback if using the Hey Siri command.

In the My Info field in Settings, you can tell Siri who you are. When you tap My Info, your contacts list appears. Tap your own name in Contacts.

You can also choose whether Siri has a male or female voice. If you're using English, you can even choose Siri's accent: American, Australian, British, Indian, Irish, or South African.

WARNING

You can call upon Siri from the lock screen too. (That's the default setting, anyway.) Consider this feature a mixed blessing. Not having to type a passcode to get Siri to do its thing is convenient. On the other hand, if your iPad ends up with the wrong person, that person would be able to use Siri to send an email or a message in your name, post to Facebook, or tweet, bypassing whatever passcode security you thought was in place. If you find this potential scenario scary, tap Settings ⇨ Siri & Search and turn off the option for Allow Siri When Locked so that it's white instead of green. For more on Settings, read Chapter 15.

Using Dictation

All iPads that run iPadOS offer a dictation function, so you can speak to your iPad and have the words you say translated into text. It's easy and works pretty well. Even if you're comfortable with the virtual keyboard or use an accessory keyboard, dictation is often the fastest way to get your words into your iPad.

When you want to use your voice to enter text, tap the microphone key on the virtual keyboard that appears in the app you're using. Begin speaking right away. A sound wave appears in place of the virtual keyboard as you talk.

The first time you tap the microphone key, a dialog appears asking if you want to enable dictation. Why might you choose not to enable it? Your voice input, contacts, and location are shared with Apple, which makes some people uncomfortable.

You can always enable or disable dictation later. Go to Settings ➪ General ➪ Keyboard and tap to turn the Enable Dictation switch on or off. If you set the switch to off, you won't see the microphone key on the keyboard.

REMEMBER

For some iPad models, dictation works only if you're connected to the internet. If you're not connected, the microphone key will appear dimmed. How do you know if you iPad can do dictation offline? Open Settings, tap General, and then tap Keyboard. Under the Enable Dictation switch, look for the following text: "Dictation processes many voice inputs on iPad." If you see this text, it means your iPad can process dictation locally (although it might still send some search queries to Apple's servers, if they're available).

Some apps don't display the microphone key on the keyboard. If you don't see a microphone key, the app doesn't accept dictated input.

When you've finished dictating your text, tap Done to end the dictation and return to your regular keyboard.

TIP

Here are a couple of ways you can improve your dictation experience:

>> You can speak punctuation by saying it. So, remember to say, "period," "question mark," or whatever at the end of your sentences. You can also insert commas, semicolons, dashes, and other punctuation by saying their names.

>> The better your iPad hears you, the better your results will be:

- A wired headset with a microphone is great when you have a lot of ambient noise nearby.

- A Bluetooth headset or Apple's AirPods or AirPods Pro may be better than the built-in microphone.

- If you use the iPad's built-in mic, make sure the iPad case or your fingers aren't covering it.

WARNING

When dictation is enabled, information is shared with Apple's servers if your iPad can't process speech locally. This hasn't stopped me from taking advantage of dictation, but if you have particular privacy concerns, it's helpful to keep this in mind.

5

The Secret Life of an iPad

Explore every single iPad setting that's not discussed in depth elsewhere in the book.

Gaze longingly at some of the iPad accessories I use and recommend.

Peruse my comprehensive guide to troubleshooting the iPad.

Chapter **15**

Tweaking Settings

W hen you liberate a new iPad from its box and turn it on for the first time, you run through a short series of screens to configure a few settings, and then you're ready to go. One of the perks of getting an iPad is that you can be up-and-surfing (or whatever) in just a few minutes.

However, the cost of that short on ramp is an iPad configured by Apple to suit the most common users. Yes, that mercifully brief setup procedure enabled you to customize your iPad a bit, but those options are just a few of the hundreds of settings offered by iPadOS via the Settings app. Yep: *hundreds*.

Sure, tons of those settings redefine the word *esoteric* and should come with a "For geeks only" label. However, just as many settings redefine the word *useful* and should have an "Everyone is welcome" label. You can take advantage of these more useful settings to make your iPad more efficient, less bothersome, and more suited to your personal style.

In this chapter, you break open the Settings app and explore what it has to offer to make your iPad life better. Because I cover some settings elsewhere in this book, I don't dwell on every setting here. Nor do I describe every setting in the order in which Apple lists them. But you still have plenty to digest to help you make the iPad your own.

Checking Out the Settings Screen

To get the party started, tap the Settings icon on your iPad's Home screen. When you first open Settings, you see a display something like Figure 15-1, with a scrollable list of categories and apps on the left and a pane on the right that corresponds to whichever category or app is selected (which, in Figure 15-1, is the General category). I say "something like" because Settings on your iPad may differ slightly from what's shown here.

You must scroll down to see the entire list of categories and apps. Also, if you see a greater-than symbol (>) to the right of a listing, the listing has a bunch of options. Throughout this chapter, you tap the > symbol to check out those options.

As you scroll to the bottom of the list on the left, you come to all the settings pertaining to some of the specific third-party apps you've added to the iPad. (See Chapter 10.) These settings aren't visible in Figure 15-1.

FIGURE 15-1:
The Settings app offers a list of categories and apps on the left and the selected app's or category's settings on the right.

tings aren't visible in Figure 15-1. We all have different collections of apps on our iPads, so settings related to those programs will also be different.

Apple ID Settings

The first thing to note in the Settings app is the section at the top with your Apple ID info. You'll see your name, the profile photo you selected when you set up your device, and a partial description of the settings available in your Apple ID settings.

Tap your Apple ID settings, and you'll find a variety of settings for both your Apple ID and Apple services, as shown in Figure 15-2:

» **Profile photo:** Tap your profile photo (which, if you don't have a photo yet, will just be your initials) and then tap Take Photo, Choose Photo, or Browse to create or select an image to use.

» **Name, Phone Numbers, Email:** Edit the name, phone numbers, and email addresses associated with your Apple ID.

» **Password & Security:** Reset your password, manage a trusted phone number for your Apple ID account, and turn on or off two-factor authentication. (I recommend that you turn it on.)

» **Payment & Shipping:** Manage which credit cards you have attached to your iCloud account. Included is a place to enter your shipping address for Apple Store purchases.

» **Subscriptions:** Manage your app subscriptions.

» **iCloud:** The amount of total and available storage. Tap Manage Storage to, well, manage your iCloud storage, taking note of all your iOS and iPadOS backups. If need be, you can buy more storage; tap Change Storage Plan to get started.

» **Media & Purchases:** Tap this setting and then tap View Account to see settings associated with media and purchases via the App Store, iTunes Store, and Apple Books.

» **Find My:** Manage the Find My feature specific to the device you're using at the moment. You can also set which of your Apple devices is used to determine where you are when it comes to sharing your location. You can also see everyone you might have shared your location with.

» **Family Sharing:** Manage or set up your iCloud Family Sharing plan.

» **Device list:** View a handy list of every device associated with your Apple ID. Tap through to any of them and you'll see the device's Find My settings, model name, operating system version, and serial number. You can also remove any device from your account except the iPad you're using.

» **Sign Out:** Sign out of your Apple ID and erase data on the iPad associated with that Apple ID. You may have to scroll down to see this option.

Your personal settings

Settings for your Apple services

Settings for your devices associated with this Apple ID

FIGURE 15-2:
Apple ID
Settings.

Controlling Your iPad's Antennas

Your iPad's innards are stuffed with sensors and other electronic gewgaws, including some antennas that your iPad uses to exchange data. There's an antenna for Wi-Fi signals, another for Bluetooth connections, and a cellular antenna on iPad models that support cellular networks. The next few sections take you through a few settings for controlling your iPad's antennas.

Flying with airplane mode

Your iPad offers settings to keep you on the good side of air-traffic communications systems. No matter which iPad you have — Wi-Fi only or a model with cellular — you have airplane mode.

Using a cellular radio or Wi-Fi on an airplane is restricted to when the pilot says it's okay. But nothing is wrong with using an iPad on a plane to read, listen to music, watch videos, peruse pictures, or play games. None of these activities require Wi-Fi, Bluetooth, or cellular data, so go ahead and enable airplane mode by tapping the Airplane Mode switch on.

Enabling airplane mode initially disables each of the iPad's radios: Wi-Fi, Bluetooth, and cellular (depending on the model). While your iPad is in airplane mode, you can't surf the web, get a map location, send or receive emails, sync through iCloud, use the iTunes or App Store, or do anything else that requires an internet connection. If a silver lining exists here, it's that the iPad's long-lasting battery will last even longer — good news if the flight you're on is a long one.

One quirk of airplane mode is that if you turn it on and then enable Wi-Fi, Bluetooth, or both, iPadOS leaves those features enabled the next time you turn on airplane mode.

How do you know when airplane mode is on? The appearance of a tiny airplane icon on the status bar at the upper-right corner of the screen is your reminder that airplane mode is turned on. Just remember to turn it off when you're back on the ground.

If in-flight Wi-Fi is available on your flight, which is increasingly the case, you can turn on Wi-Fi independently, as I describe in the next section, leaving the rest of your iPad's wireless radio safely disabled. Bluetooth, which I get to shortly, can also be enabled independently.

Working with Wi-Fi connections

Wi-Fi is typically the fastest wireless network you can use to surf the web, send email, and perform other internet tricks on the iPad. You use the Wi-Fi setting to determine which Wi-Fi networks are available to you and which one to join. To see your iPad's Wi-Fi settings, tap the Wi-Fi category in the Settings app.

At the top of the Wi-Fi settings page, you can tap the Wi-Fi switch to toggle the Wi-Fi antenna on and off. When the Wi-Fi switch is on, all Wi-Fi networks in range are displayed, as shown in Figure 15-3.

FIGURE 15-3:
When the Wi-Fi switch is on, you see a list of the nearby Wi-Fi networks.

Tap the Wi-Fi switch off whenever you don't have access to a network and don't want to drain the battery (because when Wi-Fi is on, your iPad constantly searches for nearby Wi-Fi networks). You can easily toggle Wi-Fi on and off in Control Center. When you're in a hotel, at an airport, or at another location, you might still have to enter a password after joining even if the lock icon is not present.

A signal-strength indicator can help you choose the network to connect to if more than one is listed; tap the appropriate Wi-Fi network when you reach a decision. If a network is password-protected, you see a lock icon and need the passcode to access it.

Be careful when joining open networks (such as those in coffee shops or other public places) as well as networks you don't know. Malicious actors might try to snoop on any unencrypted data on a network you don't control.

You can also turn on and off the Ask to Join Networks setting. However, networks your iPad is already familiar with are joined automatically, whether the Ask to Join Networks feature is toggled on or off. If the Ask feature is off and no known networks are available, you have to select a new network manually. If the Ask feature is on, your iPad will ask if you want to join new networks as they become available. Either way, you see a list with the same Wi-Fi networks in range.

If you used a particular network automatically in the past but no longer want your iPad to join it, tap the *i*-in-a-circle next to the network in question (in Wi-Fi settings) and then tap Forget This Network. The iPad develops a quick case of selective amnesia.

In some instances, you have to supply other technical information about a network you hope to glom onto. You encounter a bunch of nasty-sounding terms: DHCP, BootP, Static, IP Address, Subnet Mask, Router, DNS, Search Domains, Client ID, and HTTP Proxy. Chances are none of this info is on the tip of your tongue — but that's okay. For one thing, it's a good bet that you'll never need to know this stuff. What's more, even if you *do* have to fill in or adjust these settings, a network administrator or techie friend can probably help you.

Sometimes you may want to connect to a network that's closed and not shown on the Wi-Fi list. If that's the case, tap Other and use the keyboard to enter the network name. Then tap to choose the type of security setting the network is using (if any). Your choices are WEP, WPA, WPA2, WPA Enterprise, and WPA2 Enterprise. Again, the terminology isn't the friendliest, but I figure that someone nearby can lend a hand.

Connecting to unfamiliar open networks carries risks. Malicious hackers may be able to get to your personal or business data. Be careful when joining unknown networks, especially open ones.

If no Wi-Fi network is available, you have to rely on a cellular connection if you have a cellular iPad model. If you don't — or you're out of reach of a cellular network — you can't rocket into cyberspace until you regain access to a network.

Making Bluetooth connections

Of all the peculiar terms you may encounter in techdom, *Bluetooth* is one of my favorites. The name is derived from Harald Blåtand, a tenth-century Danish monarch, who, the story goes, helped unite warring factions. And, I'm told, *Blåtand* translates to *Bluetooth* in English. (Bluetooth is all about collaboration between different types of devices — get it?)

Blåtand was ahead of his time. Although I can't imagine he ever used a tablet computer, he now has an entire short-range wireless technology named in his honor. On the iPad, you can use Bluetooth to communicate wirelessly with a compatible Bluetooth headset, such as Apple's AirPods and AirPods Pro, or to use an optional wireless keyboard, such as Apple's Smart Keyboard. Such accessories are made by Apple and others.

To ensure that your iPad works with a Bluetooth device, it typically has to be wirelessly *paired,* or coupled, with the chosen device. If you're using a third-party accessory, follow the instructions that came with that device so it becomes *discoverable,* or ready to be paired with your iPad. Then, in the Settings app, tap the Bluetooth category and make sure the Bluetooth switch is on so that the iPad can find such nearby devices and the devices can find the iPad. The nearby Bluetooth devices that your iPad finds are displayed in the Other Devices section of the Bluetooth settings screen, as shown in Figure 15-4. Once you pair with a device, it appears in the My Devices section.

FIGURE 15-4:
Paired and nearby Bluetooth devices appear in the Bluetooth setting screen.

Tap a Bluetooth device to initiate the pairing. (Unless the device already appears in the My Devices section, which means your iPad and the device are already paired so you're good to go.) In some cases, the Bluetooth device requires you to enter a passkey. (This is usually the case with Bluetooth keyboards, for example.) You won't need a passkey to pair every kind of device, though. You won't need a passkey when pairing the iPad with a wireless speaker, for example. Most Bluetooth devices work up to a range of about 30 feet and don't require line of sight.

Unless you turn Bluetooth off, it's on by default. To see if it's on, pull down from the top-right corner of the screen to access Control Center. The Bluetooth icon (shown in the margin) shows blue in Control Center when Bluetooth is on. To disconnect any Bluetooth devices currently connected to your iPad, tap the Bluetooth icon in Control Center so that it turns white. Note, however, that this does not turn off Bluetooth on your iPad — it only disconnects from connected devices. To turn off Bluetooth, which saves battery life, go to Settings ➪ Bluetooth and tap the Bluetooth switch to off.

While you're in Settings ➪ Bluetooth, check out the list of Bluetooth devices you've previously paired to your iPad. To unpair a device, tap the device's *i*-in-a-circle icon, and then tap Forget This Device.

The iPad can use Bluetooth in other ways. One is through *peer-to-peer* connectivity, so you can engage in multiplayer games with other nearby iPad, iPhone, or iPod touch users. You can also exchange business cards, share pictures, and send short notes. In addition, you don't even have to pair the devices as you do with a headset or wireless keyboard.

TECHNICAL
STUFF

You can't use Bluetooth to exchange files or sync between an iPad and a computer. Nor can you use it to print stuff from the iPad on a Bluetooth printer (although the AirPrint feature handles that chore in some instances). That's because the iPad doesn't support any of the Bluetooth *profiles* (or specifications) required to allow such wireless stunts to take place — at least not as of this writing.

You may also see devices that communicate with the iPad through a flavor of Bluetooth called Bluetooth Low Energy (BLE), Bluetooth Smart, or Bluetooth Smart Ready. Apple's iBeacon technology is based on BLE and is a way to tap into your location, another topic for later in this chapter.

You can wirelessly share files also through AirDrop, as noted in Chapter 12 and elsewhere in this book.

Roaming among cellular data options

If you have a cellular model iPad, you'll see another group of settings. The options appear on the right pane of the Settings screen when you tap the Cellular Data category:

>> **Cellular Data:** If you know you don't need the cellular network when you're out and about or are in an area where you don't have access to the network, turn it off. Your battery will thank you later. But even if you have access to a

speedy cellular network, be prudent; in a 4G environment where you can easily consume gobs of data, your data allowance may run out all too quickly. And if you haven't set up your cellular data plan yet, you can get started by tapping the carrier of your choice directly in Settings ⇨ Cellular Data. Data rates apply.

>> **Data Roaming:** You may unwittingly rack up lofty roaming fees when exchanging email, surfing with Safari, or engaging in other data-heavy activities while traveling abroad. Turn off Data Roaming to avoid such potential charges.

TIP

>> **Manage Account:** Tap Manage *your carrier* Account to see or edit your account information or to add more data.

>> **Add a SIM PIN:** The tiny *SIM,* or *Subscriber Identity Module,* card inside your iPad with cellular holds important data about your cellular account. To add a PIN or a passcode to lock your SIM card, tap SIM PIN. That way, if someone gets hold of your SIM, the person can't use it in another iPad without the passcode.

REMEMBER

If you assign a PIN to your SIM, you have to enter it to turn the iPad on or off, which some might consider a minor hassle. And be aware that the SIM PIN is different from and may be in addition to any passcode you set for the iPad, as described later in this chapter.

>> **Cellular Data:** You can use your cellular connection for iCloud documents, iTunes, a Safari reading list, and most third-party apps. You can see just how much data you're using on your apps and, if need be, shut down an app that's sucking up way too much. You can also decide whether or not to use cellular connections for FaceTime. Use the setting at the bottom of the Cellular Data panel to turn on Wi-Fi Assist, which lets your iPad automatically employ cellular data when your Wi-Fi connection is poor.

>> **Personal Hotspot:** Share your iPad's data connection with any other devices you carry. Just know that extra charges may apply — and even if they don't, you'll rack up that much extra data. You or the owner of the device piggyback-ing on your internet connection must enter the designated password generated by the iPad for the Hotspot connection to make nice. You can use the hotspot feature via Wi-Fi or Bluetooth, or by connecting a USB-C-to-USB or Lightning-to-USB cable. See Chapter 12 to find out how to use Personal Hotspot.

Managing Alerts and Notifications

Developers can send you alerts related to the apps you've installed on your iPad. Such alerts are typically in text form but may include sounds as well. The idea is that you'll receive notifications even when the app they apply to isn't running. A notification may also appear as a numbered badge on the app's Home screen icon. The downside to keeping notifications turned on is that they can be distracting.

Customizing app notifications

You manage notifications on an app-by-app basis. To do so, open the Settings app, tap the Notifications category, and then tap the app you want to manage. All installed apps that can take advantage of notifications (see Chapter 12) appear on the right, as shown in Figure 15-5. Tap an app and choose whether or not to allow notifications by enabling or disabling the Allow Notifications option. If you choose not to permit notifications for select apps, you'll see the Off in the list next to those app names.

Tap any app to adjust its settings. In Figure 15-6, you see notification settings for the Calendar app, as indicated by the word Calendar at the top of the screen. Some apps may offer more options than you see here, while other apps may offer fewer options.

FIGURE 15-5:
Notify the iPad of your notification intentions.

To help you get started, here's a rundown of the options shown in Figure 15-6, starting at the top:

>> **Allow Notifications:** Tap this switch on or off to enable or disable notifications for the selected app.

>> **Always Deliver Immediately:** When this switch is on, iPadOS delivers time-based notifications right away and leaves them onscreen for an hour so you'll be much less likely to miss them.

» **Alerts:** This section enables you to customize the notification alert options:

- Lock Screen: Deselect this check box if you don't want this app's notifications to appear on the Lock screen.

- Notification Center: Deselect this check box if you don't want this app's notifications to appear in Notification Center.

- Banners: Deselect this check box if you don't want this app's notifications to appear onscreen as a banner.

- Banner Style: Choose between temporary banners, which stay at the top of your screen for a few seconds before automatically disappearing, and persistent banners, which stay at the top of your screen until you perform an action, such as flicking them away or tapping them to go to the app. Note that you see the Banner Style setting only if you leave the Banners check box selected.

FIGURE 15-6:
The notification settings for Calendar.

- Sounds: Choose from a variety of sounds for many Apple notifications. Apps such as Instagram, however, give you control over only whether or not you hear the sound they chose.

- Badges: Display the number of pending alerts on the app's icon on your Home screen.

» **Show Previews:** See a preview of whatever you're being notified about. In the case of Instagram, the preview would be a thumbnail image of the post you're being alerted about.

» **Notification Grouping:** Allow your iPad to group notifications as it sees fit or to group them by app, or simply turn Notification Grouping off for the selected app.

» **Customize Notifications:** Choose which features of the app can generate notifications.

Apps that don't take advantage of the settings in Settings ⇨ Notifications can still offer notifications, but you'll have to scroll down to the apps section on the left side of Settings and tap the app you want to alter.

If you find you went overboard with notifications to the point where they become annoying or distracting, don't fret. You can always go back and redo any notifications you've set up.

Many notifications are interactive, so you can respond to them on the spot. For example, you can reply to an incoming email or iMessage without having to drop by the underlying app.

Setting sound settings

Consider the Sounds category as the iPad's soundstage. There, you can turn audio alerts on or off for a variety of functions: ringtones, text tones, new email, sent mail, calendar and reminder alerts, Facebook posts, tweets, and AirDrop. You can also decide whether you want to hear lock sounds and keyboard clicks.

You can alter the ringtone you hear for FaceTime calls and the text tone you hear for iMessages. If you want more, visit the iTunes Store to buy more, typically for $0.99 and $1.29 a pop. You can also create your own ringtones in GarageBand on an iPad.

To set a custom tone for individuals in the Contacts app, tap Contacts ⇨ *your contact* ⇨ Edit, tap either the Ringtone or the Text Tone option, and then tap the sound effect you want to use. Tap Done when you're finished.

To raise the decibel level of alerts, drag the Ringer and Alerts volume slider to the right. Drag in the opposite direction to bring down the noise. An alternative way to adjust sound levels is to use the physical volume buttons on the side of the iPad, as long as you're not already using the Music or TV app to listen to music or watch video, respectively.

You can enable and disable the use of physical buttons to alter the volume by using the Change with Buttons switch, below the volume slider.

Coming into focus

Apple understands that sometimes you don't want to be bothered by notifications or other distractions, no matter how unobtrusive they might be. The result is a feature aptly named Focus, which you can find by tapping Settings ⇨ Focus. The idea behind Focus is to silence your iPad's alerts and notifications, leaving you free to, yep, *focus* on your work.

You configure Focus in one or all of the following ways:

>> **Do Not Disturb:** Tap Do Not Disturb and then tap the Do Not Disturb switch to on and a moon icon appears in the status bar. With Do Not Disturb on, you can rest assured that your alerts are silenced until you turn the setting off. Other options in the Do Not Disturb settings screen enable you to schedule when Do Not Disturb kicks in and when it turns off. You can also allow notifications from selected people and apps.

>> **Driving:** If you take your iPad with you while driving, the next time you get in the car, tap Driving and then tap the Driving switch to on to silence alerts and notifications while you're behind the wheel.

>> **Personal:** To configure Focus for your personal time, tap Personal. The first time you do this, Settings takes you through a brief setup procedure. After that, you can turn on the personal focus by tapping the Personal switch to on.

>> **Work:** To configure Focus for your work time, tap Work. The first time you do this, Settings takes you through a setup procedure. After that, you can turn on the work focus by tapping the Work switch to On.

>> **Custom:** Tap + in the upper-right corner and then choose an area of focus such as Mindfulness or Reading. You can also choose Custom to create your own focus. Follow the screens to set up your new focus.

REMEMBER

All of your focus features are available via Control Center. Simply swipe down from the top-right corner of the iPad screen, and then tap Focus.

Location, Location, Location Services

By using the onboard Maps, Camera, or Find Friends app (or any number of third-party apps), the iPad makes good use of knowing where you are. With Location Services turned on, your iPad has the capability to deliver traffic information and suggest popular destinations in your vicinity. And at your discretion, you can share your location with others.

The Wi-Fi–only iPad can find your general whereabouts by triangulating signals from Wi-Fi base stations and Bluetooth beacons. iPads with cellular capabilities use Wi-Fi, Bluetooth, plus built-in GPS to help determine your location.

If such statements creep you out a little, don't fret. To protect your right to privacy, when you launch an app that would like to use location data, you see a dialog similar to the one displayed in Figure 15-7. Here, the Calendar app is requesting permission to use the iPad's location tools to determine your location. Most of the time you see the following four options:

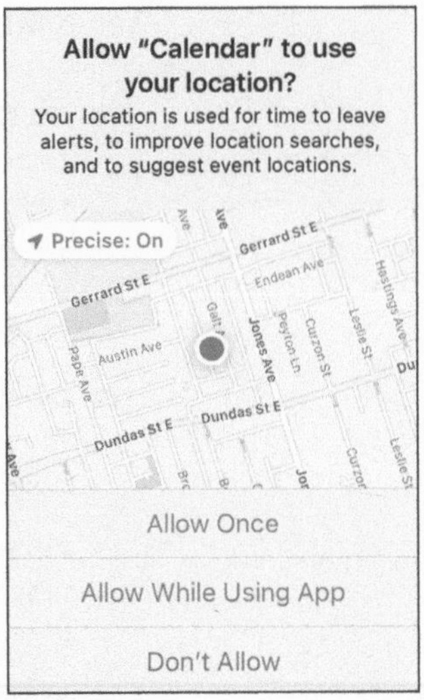

>> **Precise:** Determines whether the app can use your exact location (to within about 10 meters, or about 30 feet) or just an approximate location (to within about 2 kilometers — about a mile and a quarter — in urban locations and to within about 10 kilometers — about 6 miles — in rural locations). Tap Precise to toggle this setting between on and off.

>> **Allow Once:** Allows the app to use your location just this time. The app will ask again the next time you run it.

>> **Allow While Using App:** Allows the app to use your location, but only when you're using the app. When you switch to a different app, the previous app no longer has access to your location.

>> **Don't Allow:** Prevents the app from using your location.

You can also turn off Location Services in Settings ➪ Privacy ➪ Location Services.

Be aware as well that some apps will ask for access when you're in the midst of using them. Consider the request carefully before allowing such access.

While visiting the Privacy settings, you may want to consult the privacy listings for individual apps and functions on your iPad: If any third-party apps request access to these services, they show up here.

Meantime, tap Settings ➪ Privacy ➪ Location Services to enable or disable various other location preferences, ranging from compass calibration to location-based Apple ads.

You can also choose to share your location with family members and friends in the Messages and Find My Friends apps, and as part of Family Sharing.

From time to time on the iPad, you can land in the same destination multiple ways. For example, you can access the same privacy settings via the restrictions settings that I address later in this chapter.

Allow "Calendar" to use your location?

Your location is used for time to leave alerts, to improve location searches, and to suggest event locations.

Allow Once

Allow While Using App

Don't Allow

FIGURE 15-7:
Calendar wants to know where you are.

Settings for Your Senses

A number of settings control what the iPad looks and sounds like.

Display & Brightness

The brightness slider shown in Figure 15-8 appears when the Display & Brightness category is highlighted. Who doesn't want a bright, vibrant screen? Alas, the brightest screens exact a trade-off: Before you drag the control to the max, remember that brighter screens sap the life from your battery more quickly.

TIP

That's why I recommend activating True Tone in Settings ⇨ Display & Brightness. This setting automatically adjusts the screen according to the lighting environment in which you're using the iPad, saving considerable battery power.

The Night Shift setting is also found here (as well as in Control Center). As a reminder, it shifts the colors of the display after dark to help you get a good night's sleep, or so the theory goes.

FIGURE 15-8:
Sliding this control adjusts screen brightness.

If the app you're spending time in supports dynamic type, you can adjust the type size by tapping Text Size and then dragging the slider that appears. Under Display & Brightness, you'll also find a switch for making text bold.

Tap Auto-Lock under Display & Brightness, and you can set how much time elapses before the iPad automatically locks or turns off the display. Your choices are 15 minutes, 10 minutes, 5 minutes, or 2 minutes. Or you can set it so the iPad never locks automatically.

TIP

If you work for a company that insists on a passcode (see the next section), the Never Auto-Lock option isn't in the list that your iPad displays.

Home Screen & Dock

The Home Screen & Dock section has five settings that can significantly change your overall iPad experience:

>> **Use Large App Icons:** Leave this switch off to have smaller but more icons on each of your Home screen pages. Tap this switch to on to have larger icons on each Home screen page.

>> **Newly Downloaded Apps:** The default location for new apps is the Home screen, so in this section the Add to Home Screen option is selected; if you prefer that your new apps just go the App Library, tap App Library Only.

>> **Show App Library in Dock:** Tap this switch to off to remove the App Library from the dock. You can still display the App Library by swiping left on the last Home screen page.

>> **Show Suggested and Recent Apps in Dock:** Display on the right side of the dock apps that Siri thinks you might want, as well as recently opened apps. Learn more about this feature in Chapter 1.

>> **Show in App Library:** Tap this switch to on to configure App Library to show notification badges on app icons that have this notification type enabled.

Accessibility

The Accessibility tools on your iPad are targeted at helping people with certain needs. There's a lot to dig into, so I encourage you to explore the various choices on your own, especially if you or a loved one have a particular area of need.

VoiceOver

The VoiceOver screen reader describes aloud what's on the screen. It can read email messages, web pages, and more. With VoiceOver active, you tap an item on the screen to select it. VoiceOver places a black rectangle around the item and either speaks the name or describes an item. For example, if you tap Display & Brightness, the VoiceOver voice speaks the words "Display and brightness button." VoiceOver even lets you know when you position the iPad in landscape or portrait mode and when your screen is locked or unlocked.

Within the VoiceOver setting, you have several options. For instance, you can drag a Speaking Rate slider to speed up or slow down the speech. You can also determine the kind of typing feedback you get: characters, words, characters and words, or no feedback. Additional switches let you turn on sound effects, change the pitch, and choose the default speech accent. For example, you can choose an English accent common to Australia, the United Kingdom, Ireland, or South Africa, along with, of course, the United States. You have additional speech choices from within these countries.

You have to know a new set of finger gestures when VoiceOver is on, which may seem difficult, especially when you first start using VoiceOver. This requirement makes a lot of sense because you want to be able to hear descriptions on the screen before you activate buttons. Different VoiceOver gestures use different numbers of fingers, and Apple recommends that you experiment with different techniques to see what works best for you. After enabling VoiceOver, you can tap and then double-tap the VoiceOver Practice button to display the VoiceOver Practice screen and practice the gestures.

I list just a few of the many available gestures here:

- **Tap:** Select the item.

- **Double-tap:** Activate a selected icon or button to launch an app, turn a switch from on to off, and more.

- **Two-finger tap:** Stop speaking.

- **Rotate two fingers:** This gesture has multiple outcomes that depend on how you set the rotor control gesture. To select your options, head to Settings ⇨ Accessibility ⇨ VoiceOver ⇨ Rotor. The rotor control gesture is similar to turning a dial: You rotate two fingertips on the screen. The purpose is to switch to a different set of commands or features. Suppose you're reading text in an email. By alternately spinning the rotor, you can switch between hearing the body of a message read aloud word by word or character by character. After you set the parameters, flick up or down to hear stuff read back. When you type an email, the flicking up and down gestures serve a different purpose: The gestures move the cursor left or right within the text.

- **Two-finger swipe up:** Read everything from the top of the screen.

- **Two-finger swipe down:** Read everything from your current position on the screen.

- **Three-finger swipe up or down:** Scroll a page.

Zoom

The Zoom feature offers a screen magnifier for those who are visually challenged. To zoom, double-tap the screen with *three* fingers. Drag three fingers to move around the screen. To increase magnification, use three fingers to tap and drag up. Tap with three fingers and drag down to decrease magnification. You can tap a

Zoom Controller switch for quick access to zoom controls. You can also choose to zoom full screen or zoom only a window. And you can drag a slider to choose your maximum zoom level, up to 15x.

Display & Text Size

This section offers a variety of controls for changing your text size, making it bolder, adding shapes to text-based buttons, reducing transparency, and a lot more.

Motion

Tap the Motion section to reveal controls that enable you to control how much motion appears on the iPad screen. The settings you see depend on your iPad model, but usually include Reduce Motion, Auto-Play Message Effects, Auto-Play Video Previews, and Limit Frame Rate.

Spoken Content

Tap the Spoken Content section to reveal controls for Speak Selection, Speak Screen, Typing Feedback, Voices, Speaking Rate, and Pronunciations. When the Speak Selection setting is on, the iPad speaks any text you select. With Speak Screen enabled, you can swipe down with two fingers from the top of the screen to have all the contents of the current screen read out loud. Typing Feedback allows you to hear what you type as you type it, and there are several controls for fine-tuning this feature. A slider control allows you to adjust the speaking rate for all of the spoken content. And the Pronunciations section allows you to fine-tune how specific phrases and words are pronounced.

Audio Descriptions

Toggling the Audio Descriptions switch on enables the iPad to automatically play audio descriptions when available.

Touch

Tap the Touch section to find controls for enabling the following features:

>> **AssistiveTouch:** Use an adaptive accessory, such as a joystick, because of difficulties touching the screen. A movable dot appears; tap the dot to access certain features, such as notifications or Home. You can also create custom gestures through AssistiveTouch.

>> **Haptic Touch:** Customize the length of time before your iPad recognizes a long-press.

- **Touch Accommodations:** Customize the touch sensitivity of your iPad. For example, you can change the amount of time you must touch the screen before your touch is recognized. You can also change how long your iPad treats multiple touches as a single touch. And you can enable a Tap Assistance option to allow any single finger gesture to perform a tap before a timeout period, which you can customize, expires.

- **Tap to Wake (available only on iPad models without a Home button):** Tap your screen to wake it up, a must on iPad Pro models with Face ID and no Home button.

- **Shake to Undo:** Undo your last action with a shake of your iPad.

- **Call Audio Routing:** This feature is set to Automatic by default, and I recommend you leave it there. Tap it, however, to manually set where audio phone calls you answer on your iPad get routed, regardless of the speakers or headset you are using when the call comes in. When set to Automatic, your iPad will intelligently send audio phone calls to whatever speakers you are using.

Face ID & Attention (iPad models with Face ID only)

Tap the Face ID & Attention section to reveal a switch named Attention Aware Features. I recommend you leave this on, as it is by default. When activated, this feature will check to see if you're looking at your iPad before dimming the screen or lowering the alert volume.

Switch Control

Several controls are represented under the Switch Control setting. The general idea is that you can use a single switch or multiple switches to select text, tap, drag, type, and perform other functions. However, turning on Switch Control changes the gestures and techniques you use to control your tablet and are presumably already familiar with. For example, the iPad can scan by or highlight items on the screen until you select one. Or you can take advantage of scanning crosshairs to select a location on the screen. You can also manually move from item to item by using multiple switches, with each switch set to handle a specific action. I recommend poking around this setting to examine these and other options.

Voice Control

When activated, Voice Control allows you to control your iPad with your voice. This way of interacting with and controlling your iPad is different than the usual method, and you'll see multiple controls for customizing this feature.

Top Button (iPad models with Face ID) or Home Button

Tap this section for controls that change the how your top or Home button works:

» **Click Speed:** Choose between Default, Slow, and Slowest to change how fast your iPad should interpret when you press the top or Home button. This setting is relevant when you press the top or Home button more than one time to activate a feature.

» **Press and Hold to Speak:** On by default, press and holding down your top or Home button will enable Siri. Tap this setting to Off to disable Siri when pressing and holding down the top or Home button.

Apple TV Remote

Tap the Apple TV Remote option to use directional buttons instead of swipe gestures when using the Apple TV Remote app on your iPad. Toggle it on (green) to use directional buttons or leave it white to use swiping gestures by default.

Keyboards

Tap the Keyboards section for access to controls that change the way hardware keyboards perform. There's also a control for having virtual keyboards display lowercase letters when the Shift key isn't pressed.

AirPods

The AirPods section of Accessibility settings allows you to control press speed, press and hold down duration, and noise cancellation with one AirPod if you have AirPod Pros.

Hearing Devices

The Hearing Devices section allows you to connect to Apple-certified hearing aids through Bluetooth. The Hearing Aid Compatibility setting improves audio quality with some connected hearing aids.

Sound Recognition

Tap this switch to on and then select one or more sounds that you want your iPad to recognize for you, such as a fire or smoke alarm, a cat or dog, or a door bell.

Audio & Visual

The Audio & Visual section of Accessibility has five controls:

» **Headphone Accommodations:** Customize audio settings for your headphones.

» **Background Sounds:** Specify a background sound to play — such as the sound or rain or the ocean — to help you focus or relax.

» **Mono Audio:** Combine the right and left audio channels so that both channels can be heard in either earbud of any headset you plug in. This setting is helpful if you suffer hearing loss in one ear.

» **Balance:** Use the slider control to adjust the audio balance between the left and right output channels.

» **Visual:** Toggle the LED Flash for Alerts to have the LED on the back of your iPad flash for any alerts. (iPads with rear LED flashes only.)

Subtitles and Captioning

The Subtitles and Captioning setting lets you turn on the Closed Captions + SDH switch to summon closed-captioning or subtitles. You can also choose and preview the subtitle style and create your own subtitle style.

Guided Access

The Guided Access setting can limit iPad usage to a single app and also restrict touch input on certain areas of the screen. You can set a passcode to use when Guided Access is enabled and use Touch ID of Face ID (on compatible models) to end it.

Siri

The Siri section of Accessibility has the following controls:

» **Type to Siri:** Siri allows you to type your requests when you press and hold down the top button. When enabled, the ability to type your Siri requests is in addition to Siri listening as normal.

» **Voice Feedback:** Choose between Always On and Hands-Free Only for Siri responding to you with voice feedback when your iPad is muted.

» **Always Listen for "Hey Siri":** When this switch is on, your iPad listens for you to say "Hey Siri" even when it's face down or covered.

>> **Show Apps Behind Siri:** When this switch is on, your iPad keep the current app visible while you interact with Siri.

Accessibility Shortcut

Double-pressing the Home button launches multitasking. But you can set up the iPad so that triple-pressing the Home button — or triple-pressing the top button for iPad models that don't have a Home button — turns on an accessibility feature that you specify. Tap each accessibility feature you want to turn on when you triple-press. If you turn on two or more features, triple-clicking opens the Accessibility Shortcuts dialog so that you can choose which feature to use.

Wallpaper

Choosing wallpaper is a neat way to dress up the iPad according to your aesthetic preferences. You'll find colorful dynamic animated wallpapers with floating bubbles that add a subtle dizzying effect. But stunning as they are, these images may not hold a candle to the masterpieces in your own photo albums (more about those in Chapter 9). And animations consume more power.

You can sample the pretty patterns and dynamic designs that the iPad has already chosen for you, as follows:

1. **Tap Settings ⇨ Wallpaper and then tap Choose a New Wallpaper.**

   A list of your photo albums appears, along with Apple's own wallpaper.

2. **Tap Dynamic or Stills or tap one of your own photo albums in the list.**

   I chose Stills to bring up the thumbnails shown in Figure 15-9.

3. **Tap a thumbnail image.**

   That image fills the screen.

4. **Turn Perspective Zoom on or off, as needed.**

FIGURE 15-9:
Choosing a majestic background.

Note that Perspective Zoom is not an option if you're setting a dynamic wallpaper image.

5. **Tap Set and choose Set Lock Screen, Set Home Screen, or Set Both. Or to return to the thumbnail page without changing your Home or lock screen, tap Cancel.**

Siri & Search

If you love Siri, the chatty personal digital assistant who can remind you whether to take an umbrella or clue you in on how the Giants are faring in the NFL, see Chapter 14, where I devote a good chunk of the chapter to learning more about Siri. Here in Settings, you can change its voice from female to male, choose a default language, let Siri know your name, and decide whether to summon it through the "Hey Siri" command.

You can also tell the iPad which apps you want to search for by flipping the switch for each one. There are switches here to turn on Siri Suggestions for Search, Lookup, and your lock screen.

I address Search in Chapter 2 and Siri in Chapter 14. As a reminder, you can initiate a search on the iPad by dragging down from near the top of the screen.

Monitoring Screen Time

Screen Time consists of two sets of tools. One shows you how much time you and other users are spending on your iPad, and the other allows you to set restrictions on how much time you, your children, your employees, or your students spend on their iPad and what each person can do during that time:

>> **Screen Time:** See a report of your daily average use of your iPad for the current week. Tap See All Activity to get a more detailed report, including how much time you've spent in individual apps. You can also see the average number of times you've picked up your iPad, as well as the average number of notifications you received. All of these tools are designed to help you take control of your own screen time, or the screen time of your children, employees, or students.

>> **Restrictions:** Screen Time allows you to set restrictions on how and when your iPad is used:

   • *Downtime:* Set limits on when your iPad can be used. You can block your iPad from use at different times and days of the week — or every day of the week.

- *App Limits:* Choose apps you want to limit on your iPad. You can limit individual apps, a category of apps, or all apps. When you've selected the apps you want to limit, tap Next to set the number of minutes or hours (or both) that those apps can be used during a given day.

- *Communication Limits:* Set limits on who you can communicate with via the phone, Messages, and FaceTime apps.

- *Always Allowed:* Choose apps that can always be accessed on your iPad, regardless of other restrictions you've set.

- *Content & Privacy Restrictions:* Dive deep into a number of settings designed to protect your privacy or the privacy of your children, employees, or students. A vast number of settings are here, and I encourage you to explore them fully.

You can also set a passcode for accessing Screen Time. If you're setting up Screen Time for your children, employees, or students, the Screen Time passcode should be different than the passcode that unlocks your iPad to prevent them from undoing the restrictions you so carefully set.

Further down in the Screen Time settings is Share Across Devices. Leave this switch on if you want to copy your Screen Time settings across every device signed into your iCloud account. Tap Set Up Screen Time for Family if you want to configure Screen Time only for iCloud accounts set up for Family Sharing.

If you want to turn off Screen Time, tap Settings ⇨ Screen Time ⇨ Turn Off Screen Time at the bottom of the Screen Time settings.

Exploring Settings in General

Certain miscellaneous settings are difficult to pigeonhole. Apple wisely lumped these under the General settings moniker. Here's a closer look at your options.

About

This section, as shown in Figure 15-10, is all about the About setting. And About is full of trivial (and not-so-trivial) information *about* the device. What you find here is straightforward:

>> **Name:** The name of your device, which you can edit. This name will appear on your network and in the share interface when using AirDrop to transfer files.

» **Software version:** The version of iPadOS running on your iPad.

» **Model Name:** Apple's official name for your iPad model.

» **Model Number:** The official model number for your iPad.

» **Serial Number:** The serial number of your iPad.

» **Network (Wi-Fi + Cellular versions only):** The cellular network you are subscribed to, if any.

» **Songs:** The number of songs stored on your iPad.

» **Videos:** The number of videos stored on your iPad.

» **Photos:** The number of photos stored on your iPad.

» **Applications:** The number of apps installed on your iPad.

» **Capacity:** Because of the way the device is formatted, you always have a little less storage than the advertised amount of flash memory.

» **Available:** The amount of storage you haven't yet used on your iPad.

» **Carrier (Wi-Fi + Cellular versions only):** This may seem redundant with the Network entry described previously in this list, but it's the difference between which company you are paying and which network your iPad is connected to.

» **Cellular Data Number:** For billing purposes only.

» **Wi-Fi Address:** The address assigned to your internal Wi-Fi radio, which you might need for joining a network that uses a whitelist. To copy the address, long-press the Wi-Fi Address setting and then tap the Copy button that appears.

» **Bluetooth:** The address assigned to your internal Bluetooth radio. If you need to use this address, long-press the Bluetooth Address setting and then tap the Copy button that appears.

FIGURE 15-10:
You find info about your iPad under About.

- » **SEID:** An identifier for the Secure Element used in the Apple Pay mobile payments system.

- » **EID (Wi-Fi + Cellular versions only):** An identifier tied to your SIM card.

- » **Certificate Trust Settings:** Esoteric information relating to security and encrypted data.

Software Update

The Software Update section is for updates to iPadOS. When Apple releases an update, you can find it here. If you don't want your iPad to install updates automatically, tap Automatic Updates and then tap the Install iPadOS Updates switch to off.

AirDrop

In the AirDrop setting, tap Receiving Off to turn off AirDrop on your iPad. Tap Contacts Only so that only people you know can send you an AirDrop file. Tap Everyone to allow any Tom, Dick, or Harriet to send you files — I don't recommend this option.

AirPlay & Handoff

The Handoff feature lets you start a task (such as typing an email) on your iPad, on another device running iOS 8 or later (including iPadOS), or on a Mac computer running macOS Yosemite or later, and resume the task on another compatible iOS device, iPadOS device, or Mac. All the devices have to be running the same iCloud account. On the tablet, you'll be able to resume with the app from your lock screen or app switcher. On a Mac, you'll see the appropriate app on the dock.

iPad Storage

The About setting (covered earlier) gives you a lot of information about your device. But after you back out of About and return to the main General settings, you can find out how your iPad is using its storage. You can see what type of files take up how much space, and even see which apps are hogging the most storage and delete those you're no longer using.

Background App Refresh

Some apps continue to run in the background even when you're not actively engaged with them. If you have a Wi-Fi iPad, flip the Background App Refresh switch on to allow such apps to update content when an active Wi-Fi connection is available. If you have a Wi-Fi + Cellular iPad, tap the Background App Refresh button, and then tap Wi-Fi to update content only over Wi-Fi, or tap Wi-Fi & Cellular Data to update content over either Wi-Fi or the cellular network.

WARNING

If you have a cellular iPad and you choose the Wi-Fi & Cellular Data option, be aware that updating app content over the cellular network can eat into your cellular data plan in a hurry.

As it turns out, your iPad is pretty smart about when to refresh apps. iPadOS detects patterns based on how you use your iPad. It learns when your tablet is typically inactive — at night perhaps when you're in slumberland. And in some cases, apps are refreshed when you enter a particular location.

You can also turn on or off Background App Refresh for any individual app listed under this setting. Flip the switch to make the determination for each given app.

Date & Time

Tap Date & Time to reveal several settings for your iPad's clock:

» **24-Hour Time:** Display a 24-hour clock. Toggle to white if you prefer a 12-hour clock.

» **Show AM/PM in Status Bar:** Include the AM/PM designation. This setting is visible only if you are using a 12-hour clock.

» **Show Date in Status Bar:** Display today's date in the status bar.

» **Set Automatically:** Set the clock to the time on Apple's servers. I strongly recommend that you use this feature.

» **Time Zone:** Manually set your time zone. If you're using the Set Automatically feature, this option will show your current time zone, and you can't change it.

Keyboard

Tap Settings ⇨ General ⇨ Keyboard to see the following options covering typing on your virtual keyboard:

- **Keyboards:** Use an international keyboard (see Chapter 2). You can also choose the layout of your English keyboards in this setting, substitute the default keyboard on your iPad to, for example, Swype, SwiftKey, or Fleksy. For more on adding a third-party keyboard, consult Chapter 2.

- **Hardware Keyboard:** Tap this setting to configure an external keyboard connected to your iPad.

- **Text Replacement:** Create shortcuts that will expand into longer text. The default entry is "omw." If you leave this entry as it is, whenever you type "omw," it will automatically expand to "On my way!" Tap the + icon at the top right of the screen to add your own text replacements. Tap the Edit button at the bottom of the screen to delete text replacement entries.

- **Auto-Capitalization:** Automatically capitalize the first letter of the first word you type after ending the preceding sentence with a period, a question mark, or an exclamation point. Auto-capitalization is on by default.

- **Auto-Correction:** The iPad takes a stab at what it thinks you meant to type.

- **Check Spelling:** iPadOS checks spelling while you type.

- **Enable Caps Lock:** All letters are uppercased LIKE THIS if you double-tap the shift key. (The shift key is the one with the arrow pointing up.) Tap shift again to exit caps lock.

- **Shortcuts:** The iPad's virtual keyboard will display a shortcut bar with controls to copy and paste the text you've selected text, or to make that text bold, italic, or underline. Don't confuse this Shortcuts setting with the "." Shortcut setting described later.

- **Predictive:** The iPad keyboard suggests certain words that you might want to type next. Tap a suggested word to accept it. You can also flip the Predictive switch on or off from the keyboard itself.

- **Smart Punctuation:** Your iPad will automatically format smart quotes and smart apostrophes as you type.

- **Enable Key Flicks:** Use a downward flick to type alternate characters on your keyboard.

- **Slide on Floating Keyboard to Type:** Slide your finger across your iPad's floating keyboard to type.

- » **Delete Slide-to-Type by Word:** Delete entire words from Slide-to-Type when you use the delete key, as opposed to deleting one letter at a time.

- » **"." Shortcut:** A period is inserted followed by a space when you double-tap the space bar. This setting is turned on by default; if you've never tried it, give it a shot.

- » **Enable Dictation:** Use your iPad's microphone — or the microphone in a connected headset — to dictate your textual input.

- » **Dictation Shortcut:** If you have an external keyboard connected to your iPad, use this setting to specify the keyboard shortcut to press to enable dictation.

- » **Memoji Stickers:** Enable memoji stickers in your keyboard. See Chapter 6 for more on memoji stickers.

Fonts

Your iPad comes with multiple fonts installed, but you can also find fonts in the App Store (both free and not). Tap the Fonts setting to see any third-party fonts you've installed and to see a link to the App Store where you can search for more fonts.

Language & Region

In the Language & Region section, you can set the language in which the iPad displays text, plus the date and time format for the region in question. You can choose a Gregorian, Japanese, or Buddhist calendar, too.

Dictionary

Tap the Dictionary setting to see both the dictionaries enabled on your iPad by default and the long list of optional dictionaries you can enable. Choosing an international keyboard will often enable additional dictionaries.

VPN & Device Management

Tap Settings ⇨ General ⇨ VPN to set up or manage a VPN.

TECHNICAL STUFF

A *VPN*, or *virtual private network*, is a way for you to securely access your company's network behind the firewall — using an encrypted internet connection that acts as a secure tunnel for data. Some people use VPNs to encrypt their traffic or evade regional restrictions on content.

Before you attempt to configure a VPN on your own, consider these two other possibilities:

>> If you're setting up a school or corporate VPN, an administrator may provide you with a profile file (via am email attachment or a website download) that you open to install a correctly configured connection for that VPN.

>> If you use a commercial VPN service, the VPN host may provide an app that handles the complexities for you.

Failing either of those scenarios, you can configure a VPN on the iPad by following these steps:

1. **Tap Settings ⇨ General ⇨ VPN & Device Management ⇨ VPN ⇨ Add VPN Configuration.**

2. **Tap one of the protocol options.**

   The iPad software supports the protocols *IKEv2* (Internet Key Exchange), *L2TP* (Layer 2 Tunneling Protocol), and *IPSec,* which apparently provides the kind of security that satisfies network administrators.

3. **Using configuration settings provided by your company or VPN provider, fill in the appropriate server information, account, password, and other information.**

4. **Choose whether to turn on RSA SecurID authentication, if the option presents itself.**

   Better yet, lend your iPad to the techies where you work and let them fill in the blanks on your behalf.

After you configure your iPad for VPN usage, you can turn that capability on or off by tapping (yep) the VPN switch in Settings.

Legal & Regulatory

If you find yourself unable to sleep, be sure and tap the Legal & Regulatory section to read all the fine print that legions of lawyers have managed to cram into your iPad. Yeah, it's that exciting.

Transfer or Reset iPad

As a little kid playing sports, I ended an argument by agreeing to a do-over. Well, the Reset settings, found by tapping Settings ⇨ General ⇨ Reset on the iPad, are one big do-over. Now that you're (presumably) grown up, think long and hard about the consequences before implementing do-over settings. Regardless, you may encounter good reasons for starting over; some of these are addressed in Chapter 17.

Here are your reset options:

>> **Prepare for New iPad:** Tap Get Started to prepare to transfer this iPad's data and settings to a new iPad.

>> **Reset:** Displays a menu with the following options:

- **Reset All Settings:** Restore all settings to their factory defaults. Data and media is not deleted.

- **Reset Network Settings:** Delete the current network settings and restore them to their factory defaults.

- **Subscriber Services:** Reprovision (or refresh) your account and reset your authentication code. This option does not appear on all models.

- **Reset Keyboard Dictionary:** Remove added words from the dictionary. Remember that the iPad keyboard is intelligent, and one reason why it's so smart is that it learns from you. When you reject words that the iPad keyboard suggests, it figures that the words you banged out should be added to the keyboard dictionary.

- **Reset Home Screen Layout:** Revert all Home screen icons to the way they were at the factory.

- **Reset Location & Privacy:** Restore your iPad's location and privacy settings to their factory defaults.

>> **Erase All Content and Settings:** Reset all settings *and* wipe out all your data.

Shut Down

In addition to being able to use your top and Home buttons, or top and volume up buttons, to shut down your iPad, you can also use the Shut Down setting in your General settings to shut down your device. To shut down your iPad, tap Shut Down, then slide the slide to power off slider from left to right. Your iPad will promptly shut down. Tap the Cancel (X) button at the bottom of your screen to back out of the shutdown process.

Customizing Control Center

In Chapter 14, I sing the praises of Control Center, the convenient utility that is no further away than a down swipe from the upper-right corner of the screen. In Settings ⇨ Control Center, you get to decide whether to make Control Center accessible from the lock screen and whether you can access it within apps. The switches for making these determinations are pretty straightforward.

Setting Up Touch ID (or Face ID) & Passcode

If you want to prevent others from using your iPad, you can set a passcode by tapping Settings ⇨ Touch ID & Passcode and then tapping Turn Passcode On. iPad models with Face ID will instead have a Face ID & Passcode setting. By default, you use the virtual keypad to enter and confirm your passcode. After you do so, you'll see options for when and how you use Touch ID or Face ID, as well as options for changing your passcode and resetting Touch ID or Face ID.

If you've already set up Touch ID or Face ID, you'll see options for using that feature for iPad Unlock, iTunes & App Store, Wallet & Apple Pay, and Password Autofill. By default, these options are toggled on (green). You can toggle each option off if you want, but I recommend that you leave them on.

Below those toggles are settings that control your fingerprint scan. By default, you have just the one fingerprint you initially set up for Touch ID, probably called Finger 1. Tap Settings ⇨ Touch ID & Passcode ⇨ Finger 1 to rename that fingerprint scan or delete it.

You can add up to five fingerprints (yours and people you trust with whom you share the iPad). Tap Add a Fingerprint and go through the training session that you likely encountered back when you set up your iPad (consult Chapter 2 for details). If the iPad doesn't recognize your finger, you see Try Again at the top of the screen. You get three wrong tries before you're forced to use a traditional passcode instead, at least for this session.

If you have Face ID, you can reset Face ID or set up an alternate appearance. This might be useful if Face ID has a hard time recognizing you in makeup, for instance.

You can also determine whether a passcode is required immediately, after 1 minute, after 5 minutes, 15 minutes, 1 hour, or 4 hours. Shorter times are more secure, of course. On the topic of security, the iPad can be set to automatically erase your data if someone makes ten failed passcode attempts.

You can also change the passcode or turn it off later (unless your employer dictates otherwise), but you need to know the present passcode to apply any changes. If you forget the passcode, you have to restore the iPad software, as I describe in Chapter 17.

From the Touch ID (or Face ID) & Passcode setting, you can determine whether to allow access to the Today View, the Notifications Center, Control Center, or Siri, Home control, returning missed calls, and USB accessories when the iPad is locked.

As an added security measure, a regular passcode is required the first time you try to get past a lock screen after restarting the tablet.

Promoting Harmony through Family Sharing

Earlier under Screen Time, I show you how to impose an iron fist when it comes to permitting iPad usage at home. Now I'm going to try to make everybody in the clan happy again.

Setting up Family Sharing

Visit iCloud settings and consider setting up Family Sharing with up to six members of your family. Adults and kids can partake, but one grown-up must take charge as the family organizer. I figure it might as well be you, the person reading this book. You'll be the person presenting your iCloud Apple ID username and password, and the one on the hook for paying for iTunes, Books, and App Store purchases. As the family organizer, you can turn on Ask to Buy so that you can approve (or deny) purchases or download requests from other members of your clan.

When Family Sharing has been implemented, you can all share a calendar, photos, reminders, and your respective locations. Family Sharing may also help find a missing device through the important Find My iPad feature, which I describe at the end of this chapter.

WARNING

Should you leave Family Sharing, your account is removed from the group and you can no longer share content with everybody else. You won't be able to use DRM-protected music, movies, TV shows, books, or apps that another member purchased. And you won't be able to access the family calendar, reminders, or photos.

Family Sharing works on devices with iOS 8 and later, including iPadOS, and macOS Yosemite and later on a Mac.

Sorting and displaying contacts

Do you think of the folks in your contacts list by first name or last name? The answer to that question will probably determine whether you choose to sort or display your contacts list alphabetically by last name or first name.

In Settings, tap Contacts, tap Sort Order, then tap Last, First or First, Last. You can determine whether you want to display a first name or last name first by tapping Display Order and then choosing First, Last or Last, First. You can also go with a short name to fit more names on the screen. You can choose a first name and last initial, first initial and last name, first name only, or last name only. If you prefer nicknames, you can choose those instead, when available.

Configuring Transactional Settings

You use your iPad to shop and pay for stuff, areas where the following settings apply.

App Store

In the App Store section, you decide whether your iPad should automatically download apps and app updates. And if you give the okay, you can choose whether to tap into your cellular network (if applicable) when downloading these items.

Wallet & Apple Pay

If you have an iPad with Touch ID or Face ID and want to take advantage of Apple Pay (Apple's mobile payments system), add a new credit or debit card in the Wallet & Apple Pay section. Apple Pay lets you make secure online purchases right from your tablet.

You can also manage your Apple Cash settings, including tying in a bank for sending and receiving money through Messages using Apple Pay. For an in-depth discussion of Apple Pay and Apple Pay Cash, see Chapter 6.

Locating a Lost iPad with Find My iPad

I hope you never have to use the Find My iPad feature — though I have to say that it's darn cool. If you inadvertently leave your iPad in a taxi or restaurant, Find My iPad may just help you retrieve it. You need a free iCloud account and your iPad must be connected to a network of some kind.

Well, that's *almost* all you need. Tap Settings ⇨ Apple ID ⇨ Find My ⇨ Find My iPad and make sure the Find My iPad switch is on. To increase your chances of finding a lost iPad, leave the Find My Network switch on and tap the Send Last Location switch to on.

Now, suppose you lost your tablet — and I can only assume that you're beside yourself. Follow these steps to see whether Find My iPad can help you:

1. **Log on to your iCloud account at www.icloud.com from any browser on your computer.**

2. **Click the Find iPhone icon.**

    Yes, even though the feature is Find My iPad on the iPad, it shows up as Find iPhone on the iCloud site. Don't worry; it will still locate your iPad — and, for that matter, a lost iPhone, a Mac, and sometimes even lost AirPods or AirPods Pro.

    Assuming your tablet is turned on and in the coverage area, its general whereabouts turn up on a map in standard or satellite view, or a hybrid of the two. In my tests, Find My iPad found my iPads quickly.

    Even seeing your iPad on a map may not help you much, especially if the device is lost somewhere in midtown Manhattan. Take heart.

3. **Click your lost iPad.**

    iCloud displays options for your iPad.

4. **Click the Lost Mode button.**

    If your iPad doesn't have a passcode, iCloud prompts you to enter a passcode to lock the iPad.

5. **Enter the passcode twice.**

   iCloud asks you to enter a phone number where you can be reached.

6. **Type a phone number and tap Next.**

   iCloud prompts you to enter a message that will appear on the iPad screen.

7. **Type a plea to the Good Samaritan who (you hope) picked up your iPad.**

   Apple has already prepared a simple message indicating that the iPad is lost, but you can change or remove the message and substitute your own plea for the return of your tablet.

8. **Click Done.**

   iCloud locks your iPad and displays the message on the lost iPad's screen.

TIP

To get someone's attention, you can also sound an alarm that plays for two minutes, even if the volume is off. Tap Play Sound to make it happen. Hey, that alarm may come in handy if the iPad turns up under a couch in your house. Stranger things have happened.

TIP

The Find My feature (which finds any iOS or iPadOS device, as well as any friends or family who have shared their location with you) is also available as an app on your iPad as well as on any iOS and macOS device.

After all this labor, if the iPad is seemingly gone for good, click Erase iPad at the iCloud site to delete your personal data from afar and return the iPad to its factory settings.

Meanwhile, the person who found (or possibly stole) your iPad can't reactivate the device to use as their own, or to peddle, unless that person successfully types in *your* Apple ID.

Even if you choose to erase the device remotely, it can still display a custom message with the information needed for someone to return it to you. If, indeed, you ever get your iPad back, you can always restore the information from an iTunes backup on your Mac or PC or iCloud.

Chapter **16**

Accessorizing Your Tablet

A nyone who has purchased a new car in recent years is aware that it's not always a picnic trying to escape the showroom without the salesperson trying to get you to part with a few extra bucks. You can only imagine what the markup is on roof racks and navigation systems.

I don't suppose you'll get a hard sell when you snap up a new iPad at an Apple Store (or elsewhere). But Apple and several other companies are all too happy to outfit whichever iPad model you choose with extra doodads, from wireless keyboards and stands to battery chargers and carrying cases. So just as your car might benefit from dealer (or third-party) options, so too might your iPad benefit from a variety of spare parts.

Accessories from Apple

My roster of worthwhile accessories begins with the options that carry the Apple logo:

» **Apple Smart Cover:** No iPad has ever shipped with a case in the box, which has helped build a thriving industry of third-party cases in addition to Apple's optional cases and covers. Let's start with Apple's *Smart Cover*, an ultra-thin cover for just the screen that attaches to your iPad magnetically. Flip the cover open (even just a little), and your iPad wakes instantly; flip it shut, and your iPad goes right to sleep. The Smart Cover is available in numerous bright colors in polyurethane ($39–$49) or leather ($69).

» **Apple Magic Keyboard for iPad Pro:** The various virtual keyboards that pop up just as you need them on the iPad Pro are fine for shorter typing tasks, whether it's composing emails or tapping a few notes. For longer assignments, however, I am more comfortable pounding away on a real-deal physical keyboard.

The Apple Magic Keyboard is a way to use a decent-enough physical keyboard without physically tethering it to the iPad. It operates from up to 30 feet away from the iPad via Bluetooth, the wireless technology I discuss in Chapter 15. The keyboard has a built-in lithium-ion battery, which you can charge by plugging it into the supplied USB-C port on a computer or (via an adapter) to your iPad. Apple claims battery life of a month or more. The Apple Magic Keyboard comes in two flavors: the $299 Magic Keyboard for iPad Pro 11-inch (3rd generation) and iPad Air (4th generation) and the $349 Magic Keyboard for iPad Pro 12.9-inch (5th generation).

That said, many compatible Bluetooth keyboards and keyboard covers and cases can be used with any iPad, plus smarter cases for Pro models and iPad 10.2-inch, such as . . .

» **Apple Smart Keyboard:** Apple's special keyboard-and-cover combinations for iPad are the aptly named Smart Keyboard folio for iPad Pro and Smart Keyboard for iPad Air (2019) and iPad (10.2-inch). Pricing for Apple's current iPad models are $159 (iPad Air and iPad), $179 (iPad Pro 11-inch), and $199 (iPad Pro 12.9-inch).

The keyboard connects to the iPad via the smart connector on the edge of the Smart Keyboard and on the side of the iPad models just listed. And beyond typing, you get the added benefit of using the Smart Keyboard as your Smart Cover.

» **Camera connector:** iPads don't include a USB port or an SD memory card slot, which happen to be the most popular methods for getting pictures (and videos) from a digital camera onto a computer. Apple offers the

Lightning-to-USB camera adapter ($29), the Lightning-to-USB-3 camera adapter ($39), the Lightning-to-SD-card camera reader ($29), and the USB-C-to-SD-card reader ($39).

>> **Travel adapter:** If you're traveling abroad, consider the Apple World Travel Adapter Kit. The $29 kit includes the proper prongs and adapters for numerous countries around the globe, and it lets you juice up not only your iPad but also iPhones, iPod touches, and Macs.

Listening and Talking

You've surely noticed that your iPad didn't include earphones or a headset. Fortunately, you can find a seemingly unlimited number of third-party options, as well as Apple's popular AirPods and AirPods Pro. I talk about some of my favorite options in the next section.

Wired headphones, earphones, and headsets

Search Amazon for *headphones, earphones,* or *headsets,* and you'll find thousands of each available at prices ranging from $10 to more than $1,000. Or if you prefer to shop in a bricks-and-mortar store, Target, Best Buy, and the Apple Store all have decent selections, with prices starting at less than $20.

TIP

Much as I love the shopping experience at Apple Stores, you won't find any bargains there because Apple-branded products are rarely discounted, including the company's own Beats brand of headphones.

Lots of wired earphones and headphones are on the markets. Past editions of this book have focused on wired earphones and headphones. But — and I know you felt a *but* coming — wireless earphones and headphones are all the rage these days, and I tell you more about them in the next section.

Bluetooth stereo headphones, earphones, and headsets

Bluetooth headphones have steadily improved over the years. You get higher audio quality if you're using expensive wired headphones, but unless you're an audiophile, you'll probably find that Bluetooth headsets sound good. Apple's Beats by Dre have wireless earphones starting at $99.95, and Apple's own AirPods are $159. AirPods Pro ($249) add an in-ear seal, active noise cancellation, and higher sound quality than the original AirPods.

Hundreds of models from other companies are available for a lot less, too. Do a search on Amazon, and you'll find many options under $100, with some starting at just $11.88. You can also find Bluetooth over-the-ear or on-ear headphones, with many models as low as $40.

Listening with Speakers

You can connect just about any speakers to your iPad, but if you want decent sound, I suggest you look only at *powered* speakers, not *passive* (unpowered) ones. Powered speakers contain their own amplification circuitry and can deliver much better sound than unpowered speakers. Prices range from under $100 to hundreds (or even thousands) of dollars. Most speaker systems designed for use with your computer, iPod touch, or iPhone work well as long as they have an auxiliary input or a dock connector that can accommodate your iPad.

Desktop speakers

Logitech (www.logitech.com) makes a range of desktop speaker systems priced from less than $25 to more than $300. But that $300 system is overkill for listening to music or video on your iPad, which doesn't support surround sound anyway. If you're looking for something inexpensive, you can't go wrong with a Logitech-powered speaker system.

I'm a big fan of Audioengine (www.audioengineusa.com) desktop speakers. They deliver superior audio at prices that are reasonable for speakers that sound this good. Audioengine A5+ is the premium product priced at $399 per pair; Audioengine A2+ is its smaller but still excellent sibling priced at $219 per pair. They're available only direct from the manufacturer, but the company is so confident you'll love them that it offers a free audition for the speaker systems.

Bluetooth speakers

Like Bluetooth headsets, Bluetooth speakers are immensely popular and let you listen to music up to 33 feet away from your iPad. They're great for listening by the pool or hot tub or anywhere else you might not want to take your iPad.

I like JBL's Pulse 3 ($230 from JBL or $120 from Amazon) and Pulse 4 ($200) portable Bluetooth speakers. Another option is the Ultimate Ears Mega Boom wireless speaker/speakerphone, which some audiophiles I know say is the best-sounding $200 Bluetooth speaker they have ever tested. The newest version, Ultimate Ears Mega Boom 3, lists for $200 but I found it on Amazon for as little as $170.

AirPlay speakers

The newest type of speakers you might choose for your iPad support Apple's proprietary AirPlay protocol, which takes advantage of your existing Wi-Fi network to stream audio and video from your iPad (or other compatible iDevice) to a single AirPlay-enabled speaker or audio/video receiver. The biggest differences between AirPlay and Bluetooth speakers are

>> Bluetooth can stream music only in a compressed form; AirPlay can stream music (and video) uncompressed. So, a speaker with AirPlay should sound better than a similar speaker with Bluetooth.

>> Bluetooth's range is roughly 30 feet; AirPlay's range is up to 300 feet. You can't extend Bluetooth's range, but Wi-Fi networks can be extended with additional Wi-Fi routers.

>> iTunes (on your computer) can use AirPlay to stream audio or video to multiple speakers or audio/video receivers, with individual volume controls for each device; Bluetooth streams to only one device at a time.

Wrapping Your iPad in Third-Party Cases

Much as I like the Apple iPad case, other vendors offer some excellent, different options:

>> Burkley Case's Turner Smart Leather Folio Cover, www.burkleycase.com

>> Griffin Technology, www.griffintechnology.com

>> Gumdrop Hideaway for iPad, www.gumdropcases.com

>> LifeProof, www.lifeproof.com

>> Otterbox, www.otterbox.com

>> Speck Presidio Pro, www.speckproducts.com

>> Targus, www.targus.com

- » Twelve South BookBook, www.twelvesouth.com

- » Vaja Cases, www.vajacases.com

- » Zero Chroma Vario, at www.zerochroma.com

Standing Up Your iPad

The Griffin Tablet Stand ($29.99) is so unusual that I just had to include it (see Figure 16-1). It's a dual-purpose desktop stand made of heavy-duty aluminum. You can open it to hold your iPad in either portrait or landscape mode for video watching, displaying pictures (a great way to exploit picture frame mode), or even reading. In upright mode, it's also the perfect companion for the Apple wireless keyboard (or any other Bluetooth keyboard). Or close the legs and lay it down, and it puts your iPad at the perfect angle for typing on the on-screen keyboard.

For sheer comfort, you can't beat the Ontel Pillow Pad (www.pillowpad.ca; $24.95), the super-lightweight and super-soft (it's made of non-slip foam) tablet holder that makes it a breeze to binge-watch your favorite shows.

Courtesy of Griffin Technology

FIGURE 16-1:
The Griffin Tablet Stand is a unique, dual-purpose tabletop stand for your iPad.

IN THIS CHAPTER

» Troubleshooting iPad woes step by step

» Rebooting, recharging, and resetting your iPad

» Fixing network and syncing issues

» Getting help from Apple's website and forums

» Restoring your stuff on a repaired iPad

Chapter **17**

Troubleshooting Common Problems

First, the good news: Your iPad is a solid, well-made device, so it should give you years of mostly trouble-free service. Now, the bad news: that word *mostly*. iPads are fiendishly complex devices running labyrinthically intricate software, so sometimes all that convolution catches up with your iPad and things go south.

Fortunately, there's more good news: Most iPad woes are quickly and easily fixed. In this chapter, you learn the most useful troubleshooting techniques that you can try to remedy the majority of iPad problems. You also learn some fixes for a few specific glitches.

After all the troubleshooting, I tell you how to get even more help if nothing I suggest does the trick. Finally, if your iPad is so badly hosed it needs to go back to the mother ship for repairs, I offer ways to survive the experience with a minimum of stress or fuss, including how to restore your stuff from an iTunes, Finder, or iCloud backup.

Troubleshooting iPad Problems: A Quick Guide

If your iPad starts behaving strangely, it's tempting to assume that the device itself is broken in some way. That's not impossible, but your iPad's innards have no moving parts, so it's unlikely that some internal component has gone belly-up. Instead, you can solve almost all iPad hiccups by following this general ten-step troubleshooting procedure:

1. Shut down whatever app you're using.
2. If you recently changed a setting, restore the setting to its previous state.
3. Shut down and restart your iPad.
4. Reboot your iPad's hardware.
5. Recharge your iPad.
6. Check for and install iPadOS updates.
7. Free up some storage space on your iPad.
8. Check your Wi-Fi network connection.
9. Reset any settings that are related to the problem you're having (such as resetting network settings if you're having connection issues).
10. Erase your iPad and restore a backup.

REMEMBER

To be clear, you don't have to run through all 10 steps for every problem. Start with Step 1 and, if that doesn't solve the glitch, proceed to Step 2. Continue working through the steps until you've solved the problem, and then move on to bigger and better things.

Troubleshooting iPad Problems Step-by-Step

The next few sections take you through each of the troubleshooting steps from the previous section in a bit more detail.

Shut down whatever app you're using

If your iPad is unresponsive, it usually means that the app you're using has crashed and has taken your iPad down with it. Most of the time, you can get your iPad going again by forcing the stuck app to quit. Here are the steps to follow:

1. **Display the multitasking screen:**

   - *All iPad models:* Swipe up from the bottom of the screen, pausing when you reach the middle of the screen.

   - *iPad models with a Home button:* Double-press the Home button.

2. **Scroll right or left as needed to bring the app's thumbnail into view.**

3. **Drag the app thumbnail up to the top of the screen.**

   iPadOS sends the thumbnail off the screen and shuts down the app.

TIP

It's perfectly okay to force-quit an app even when it's working fine. Why would you want to do that? The best reason is that it reduces clutter in App Switcher by removing apps you know you won't use for a while. Lots of iPad mavens will tell you that's a surefire way to reduce your iPad's battery life because iPadOS has to spend extra battery power the next time you start any app that you force-quit. However, the extra juice required to open an app is trivial and can be ignored.

If your iPad is unresponsive and you can't display the multitasking screen, you can follow these alternative steps if your iPad has a Home button:

1. **Press and hold down the top button until you see the Slide to Power Off screen; then release the top button.**

2. **Press and hold down the Home button for about six seconds.**

   Your iPad shuts down the current app and returns you to the Home screen.

REMEMBER

If your unresponsive iPad doesn't have a Home button, you need to restart your iPad, as I describe a bit later in this chapter.

Restore a changed setting

If you make a change in the Settings app and your iPad immediately starts behaving erratically, the changed setting is most likely the culprit. If you can still get to the Settings app, open it and restore the setting to its previous state. If your iPad is unresponsive, restart it (see the next section) and then revert the change in Settings.

Shut down and then restart your iPad

If your iPad is frozen, you won't be able to access either the multitasking screen or the Settings app — in fact, you won't be able to do anything at all with your iPad. Anything, that is, except shut down your iPad and then restart it. What good does that do? It reloads iPadOS, which almost always solves whatever glitch was causing your tablet to go haywire.

How you begin the shutdown procedure depends on which iPad model you're using:

>> **iPads without a Home button:** Hold down both the top button and one of the volume buttons until you see the Slide to Power Off slider, as shown in Figure 17-1.

>> **iPads with a Home button:** Press and hold down the top button until you see the Slide to Power Off slider.

Either way, drag the Slide to Power Off slider to the right to start the shutdown. Give the device a few seconds to turn everything off. To restart, press and hold down the top button and then release the button when you see the Apple logo.

FIGURE 17-1:
On iPads without a Home button, press and hold down the top button and a volume button.

Reboot the iPad hardware

Restarting iPadOS, as I describe in the preceding section, is usually enough to solve any iPad problem. But if the problem still exists after the iPadOS restart or your iPad won't shut down, your next step is to reboot the tablet hardware.

How you do a hardware reboot depends on your iPad model:

>> **iPads without a Home button:** Press and release the volume up button; press and release the volume down button; and then press and hold down the top button until you see the Apple logo.

>> **iPads with a Home button:** Press and hold down the top button and the Home button until you see the Apple logo.

Recharge your iPad

If your iPad is unresponsive and won't turn on, the most likely reason is that the battery is completely out of juice. Connect your tablet to a power outlet and wait for a while. If after a minute or two the device turns on and you see the battery logo, you know the tablet is charging and will be back up and running in a few minutes.

Check for iPadOS updates

Many iPad problems are caused by errors — known in programming parlance as *bugs* — in iPadOS or some other piece of your iPad's system software. There's a good chance Apple knows (or will soon know) about the glitch, will (eventually) fix it, and will then make the fix available as part of an iPadOS update.

You can check for and install iPadOS updates by following these steps:

1. **Open the Settings app.**

2. **Tap General.**

   Settings displays the General screen.

3. **Tap Software Update.**

   Settings begins checking for available updates. If you see the message "Your software is up to date," you can move on to bigger and better things.

4. **If an update is available, tap Download and Install.**

   Settings downloads the update and then proceeds with the installation, which takes a few minutes.

WARNING

Your tablet will go through with the update only if it has more than 50 percent battery life through the entire update operation. To ensure that the update is a success, plug your tablet into an AC outlet or run the update when the battery is fully charged.

Free up storage space

Your iPad uses its internal storage space to hold many things, including iPadOS, preinstalled apps, the apps you install, and the content you create with those apps.

However, your iPad uses its internal storage also as a kind of temporary work area. If the iPad's memory space gets full, iPadOS will offload some of the contents of memory to its internal storage to make room in memory for new apps or content.

All this happens automatically and *way* behind the scenes, so you never have to worry about any of it. Or, I should say, you never have to worry about any of it *until* your iPad's internal storage is nearly full and it becomes more difficult for iPadOS to manage memory and perform certain operations. When that happens, you start seeing error messages letting you know that some operation can't be completed because there is "No space left on device" or "There is not enough available storage." You might also see a message like the one shown in Figure 17-2.

FIGURE 17-2:
You see this dialog when your iPad is running low on storage space.

If you see any of these low-storage messages, you need to free up some storage space on your iPad pronto. Fortunately, iPadOS gives you several ways to free up space. To see these methods, use either of the following techniques to display the iPad Storage settings:

» If you have the message shown in Figure 17-2 on-screen, tap Settings.

» Open the Settings app, tap General and then tap iPad Storage.

Either way, you end up at the iPad Storage screen, shown in Figure 17-3. The chart at the top of the screen shows how much of your iPad's storage space is used by various categories of data, such as Apps, System (that is, iPadOS), and Photos.

FIGURE 17-3:
The iPad Storage screen shows how much storage is being used and by what.

You also usually see a Recommendations section that offers one or more suggestions for saving storage space. You should try these recommendations before trying anything else.

Next, take a look at the list of apps to see which ones are taking up the most storage space. Chances are you'll see one or more apps that are taking up an unreasonable amount of space. If so, you can take back some or all of that space using any of the following techniques:

>> **Offload the app.** Tap the app, tap Offload App, and then tap Offload App when iPadOS asks for confirmation. This method removes the app from your iPad but keeps the app's data. Use this method for large apps that aren't storing tons of data on your iPad.

>> **Delete the app.** Tap the app, tap Delete App, and then tap Delete App when iPadOS asks you to confirm. Use this method for apps that are storing a lot of data on your iPad (assuming you no longer need that data). Note that this method is not available for many preinstalled apps (such as Photos and iCloud Drive).

>> **Delete some or all of the app's data.** Tap the app to display its data usage. If you see a Documents section, such as the one shown in Figure 17-4 for the Messages app, tap a document category, and then tap Edit to put the category in edit mode. Tap to select the check box beside each item you want to delete and then tap the trash icon.

FIGURE 17-4:
If an app has a Documents section, you can free up storage space by deleting individual data items from the app.

Check your Wi-Fi connection

Some apps will stop working or will act erratically if they lose access to the internet. So, if an app is acting weird — or if you can't do any internet-related chores such as view websites or check email — it could be that your iPad's Wi-Fi connection is missing in action.

TIP

If you have an iPad that supports cellular connections and you're out of range of a Wi-Fi network, you might have problems with any app that isn't configured to use cellular data. To fix this, open Settings, tap Cellular, locate the app in the Cellular Data section, and then tap the app's switch to on.

Checking Wi-Fi means performing two separate troubleshooting steps: Check your iPad's Wi-Fi connection and check your router's connection to the internet.

On your iPad, here are a few things to go through:

>> **Check that Wi-Fi is turned on.** Open the Settings app, tap Wi-Fi, and then, if necessary, tap the Wi-Fi switch to on.

>> **Check how far your iPad is from your router.** A lack of Wi-Fi could mean your tablet is too far from the router. For most routers, the maximum range is about 230 feet.

>> **Check that airplane mode is turned off.** Open Settings and then, if necessary, tap the Airplane Mode switch to off. Alternatively, display Control Center and then tap to turn off the Airplane Mode icon.

>> **Check that your iPad is still connected to your W-Fi network.** Open Settings and check the Wi-Fi setting. If you see Not Connected, tap Wi-Fi, and then tap your network to reconnect.

>> **Renew the Wi-Fi connection lease.** When your iPad connects to a Wi-Fi network, the router gives the tablet a *lease*, which is a kind of permission to access the network. You can sometimes solve a connectivity issue by renewing your iPad's lease. Open the Settings app, tap Wi-Fi, and then tap the *i* (more info) icon to the right of the connected network. Tap Renew Lease, and when Settings asks you to confirm, tap Renew Lease.

>> **Disconnect from and then reconnect to the network.** Open Settings, tap Wi-Fi, and then tap the *i* icon to the right of the connected network. Tap Forget This Network to disconnect from the network and discard the network's saved login credentials. Tap your network and enter the password to reconnect.

>> **Restart your iPad.** See "Shut down and then restart your iPad," earlier in this chapter.

>> **Reset the network settings.** This removes all stored network data and resets everything to the factory state, which might solve the problem. See "Reset your settings," next, to learn how to do this.

On your Wi-Fi router, try these troubleshooting ideas:

>> **Turn your Wi-Fi router off and then on again.** If your network accesses the internet using a separate broadband modem, turn the modem off then on again, as well.

>> **Check for interference.** Many household devices — such as baby monitors and cordless phones — use the same 2.4 GHz radio frequency (RF) band as most Wi-Fi routers, which can interfere with Wi-Fi signals. If you have such a device near your Wi-Fi router, turn off the device or move it away from the router. Alternatively, set up a new Wi-Fi network using the 5 GHz band, if your router supports this. (See your router documentation.)

WARNING

You should keep your tablet and wireless access point well away from microwave ovens, which can jam wireless signals.

>> **Update the router firmware.** *Firmware* refers to the internal system software that runs the router. Router companies routinely offer firmware updates that fix device problems, so updating the router firmware might solve whatever connectivity issues you're having. (See your router documentation.)

>> **Restore the router's factory settings.** If the router's settings are corrupted, you can reset the device to its original factory settings. (See the router documentation.) If you go this route, once the reset is complete, you'll need to set up your network again from scratch.

Reset your settings

A common cause of iPad wonkiness is when one or more of the tablet's settings gets corrupted. For example, if you can't connect to a known Wi-Fi network, it might mean that your iPad's network settings are broken. You can almost always work around such problems by resetting some or all of your iPad's settings. Here are the steps to follow:

1. Open the Settings app and tap General.

2. Tap Transfer or Reset.

3. Tap Reset.

   Settings displays a list of reset options.

4. **Do one of the following:**

   • *Reset a specific type of setting.* Tap the corresponding Reset option. For example, if you're having connection troubles, tap Reset Network Settings.

   • *Reset every setting.* Tap Reset All Settings.

   Settings asks you to confirm that you want to perform the reset.

5. **Tap Reset.**

Erase and restore your content and settings

If you have a backup of your iPad (I talk about creating iPad backups in Chapter 3), you can solve even the most recalcitrant problems by erasing all of your iPad's settings and content and starting over with a fresh system. Then restore your backup and you're back in business.

Here are the steps to follow to erase your settings and contents and restore from a backup:

1. **Open the Settings app, tap General, and then tap Transfer or Reset.**

2. **Tap Erase All Content and Settings.**

   Settings tells you what it will erase from your iPad.

3. **Tap Continue.**

   If you have Find My and Activation Lock turned on, Settings prompts you for your Apple ID password.

4. **Type your password and then tap Turn Off.**

   Settings prompts you for your passcode. No passcode? Skip to Step 8.

5. **Type your passcode.**

   Settings asks you to confirm that you want to erase your iPad.

6. **Tap Erase iPad.**

   iPadOS erases your iPad and then restarts a few minutes later.

7. **Run through the startup steps: selecting a language, country, Wi-Fi network, and so on.**

   If you're prompted to choose how you want to restore your iPad, tap Other Options. Eventually you see the Apps & Data dialog.

8. **Tap Restore from iCloud Backup and then sign in to your Apple ID.**

   Alternatively, if you used iTunes (on Mac or Windows) or Finder (on Mac) to back up your iPad, tap Restore from Mac or PC and follow the instructions that appear.

   The Choose Backup dialog appears.

9. **Tap your most recent iPad backup.**

10. **Continue with the rest of the setup steps.**

    You eventually see the Restore from iCloud screen, which shows the progress of the restore. After a few minutes, your iPad reboots, and you see your restored content and settings.

REMEMBER

iPadOS at first restores only enough to get you back up and running. The full restore from iCloud can take quite a long time, so in the interim you might find that some content, apps, or other features are temporarily unavailable.

Getting Help on the Apple Website

If you try everything I suggest earlier in this chapter and still have problems, don't give up just yet. This section describes a few more places you may find help. I recommend you check them out before you throw in the towel and smash your iPad into tiny little pieces (or ship it back to Apple for repairs, as I describe in the next section).

First, Apple offers an excellent set of support resources on its website at www.apple.com/support/ipad/setup. You can browse support issues by category, search for a problem by keyword, read or download technical manuals, and scan the discussion forums.

Speaking of the discussion forums, you can go directly to them at https://discussions.apple.com/. They're chock-full of useful questions and answers from other iPad users. If you can't find an answer to a support question elsewhere, you can often find it in these forums. You can browse by category or search by keyword. Either way, you find thousands of discussions about almost every aspect of using your iPad.

TIP

Now for the best part: If you can't find a solution by browsing or searching, you can post your question in the appropriate Apple discussion forum. Check back in a few days (or even in a few hours), and some helpful iPad user may well have replied with the solution. If you've never tried this fabulous tool, you're missing out on one of the greatest support resources available anywhere.

Last, but certainly not least, try a carefully worded Google search. You might just find the solution.

If Nothing I Suggest Helps

If you've tried every trick in the book (this book) and still have a malfunctioning iPad, consider shipping it off to the iPad hospital (better known as Apple, Inc.). The repair is free if your iPad is still under its one-year limited warranty.

TIP

You can extend your warranty for as long as two years from the original purchase date, if you want. To do so, you need to buy AppleCare+ for your iPad. You don't have to do it when you buy your iPad, but you must buy it before your one-year limited warranty expires. AppleCare+ for iPad, iPad Air, and iPad mini is $3.49 per month for 24 months, or $69 if you pay up front. AppleCare+ for iPad Pro is $6 per month for 24 months or $129 if you pay up front.

Here are some things you need to know before you take your iPad in to be repaired:

>> *Your iPad may be erased during its repair,* so you should sync your iPad with iTunes, Finder, or iCloud and make a backup before you take it in, if you can. If you can't and you entered data on the iPad since your last sync, such as a contact or an appointment, the data might not be there when you restore your iPad upon its return.

>> Remove any accessories, such as a case or screen protector. If you have a cellular iPad, be sure to remove your SIM card.

TIP

Although you may be able to get your iPad serviced by Best Buy or another authorized Apple reseller, I recommend that you take it or ship it to your nearest Apple Store, for two reasons:

>> **No one knows your iPad like Apple.** One of the Geniuses at the Apple Store may be able to fix whatever is wrong without sending your iPad away for repairs.

>> **The Apple Store will, in some cases, swap out your wonky iPad for a brand-new one on the spot.** You can't win if you don't play, which is why I always visit my local Apple Store when something goes wrong (with my iPads, iPhones, iPods, and even my laptops and iMacs).

If you've done everything I've suggested, I'm relatively certain you're now holding an iPad that works flawlessly. Again.

That said, some or all of your stuff may not be on it. If that's the case, see the following section for a two-trick solution that usually works.

Dude, Where's My Stuff?

If you performed a restore or had your iPad replaced or repaired, you have one more task to accomplish. Your iPad may work flawlessly at this point, but some or all of your stuff — your music, movies, contacts, iMessages, or whatever — is missing. You're not sunk, at least not yet. You still have a couple of tricks up your sleeve.

>> **Trick 1: Sync your iPad with iTunes or Finder and then sync it again.** That's right — sync and sync again. Why? Because sometimes stuff doesn't get synced properly on the first try. Just do it.

>> **Trick 2: Restore from backup.** Click the General tab in Finder or the Summary tab in iTunes and then click Restore Backup. If Find My iPad (Settings ⇨ iCloud ⇨ Find My iPad) is enabled, you'll first see a message to disable it before you restore your iPad. Then the Restore from Backup dialog appears and offers you a choice of backups. Select the one you want, click the Restore button, and let the iPad work some magic.

These backups include photos in the camera roll, text messages, notes, contact favorites, sound settings, and more, but not media you've synced, such as music, videos, or photos. If media is missing, try performing Trick 1 again.

TIP

If you have more than one backup for a device, try the most recent one first. If it doesn't work or you're still missing files, try restoring from any other backups.

If you aren't holding an iPad that works flawlessly and has most (if not all) of your stuff, it's time to make an appointment with a Genius at your local Apple Store, call the support hotline (800-275-2273), or visit the support web page at www.apple.com/support/ipad.

6 The Part of Tens

IN THIS CHAPTER

» Locking your iPad with a passcode, a fingerprint, or facial recognition

» Putting your iPad to sleep automatically

» Controlling app access to your location, hardware, and data

» Checking passwords for involvement in a data leak

» Setting up restrictions for a kid's iPad

Chapter **18**

Ten Ways to Beef Up Privacy and Security

Your iPad is a music and video player, a web browser and wayfinder, an email and text exchanger, a payments device, and much more. However, although you might readily see your iPad in all these different roles, there's one role you might overlook: a vault. Perhaps you dismiss the idea because, after all, a vault is a place to store valuable things. Ah, but then you've fallen right into my trap: If your iPad had seams it would be bursting at them with valuables in the form of your precious personal data. And if your iPad were to fall into the wrong hands, those hands would also have access to an uncomfortable amount of important data (important to *you*, anyway).

In this chapter, you investigate ten useful ways to turn your iPad into a vault that safeguards your sensitive (and not-all-that sensitive) personal info. From locking your iPad to backing up your stuff to setting restrictions, read on to secure your iPad and its data.

Lock Your iPad with a Passcode

No matter what model of iPad you use, your first line of defense is to set up a passcode that must be typed before iPadOS will display the Home screen. You can set a simple six-digit passcode or a more complex one that uses any combination of numbers, letters, and symbols.

Here are the steps to follow to lock your iPad with a passcode:

1. **Open the Settings app.**

2. **Tap one of the following:**

   - *If your iPad supports Face ID:* Tap Face ID & Passcode.

   - *For all other iPad models:* Tap Touch ID & Passcode.

3. **Tap Turn Passcode On.**

   The Set Passcode dialog appears.

4. **To use something other than the default six-digit passcode, tap Passcode Options and then tap the passcode type you prefer:**

   - *Custom Alphanumeric Code:* A passcode of any length (minimum four characters) consisting of any combination of letters and numbers.

   - *Custom Numeric Code:* A passcode of any length (minimum four characters) consisting of numbers.

   - *4-Digit Numeric Code:* A passcode consisting of four numbers.

WARNING

   Whatever type of passcode you use, try to avoid easily guessed codes such as the month and year of your birthday or anniversary. Also, avoid the following overly used (and therefore easily guessed) codes: 1234, 4321, 2580, 0852, 0000, 1111, 2222, 5555, 1212, 123456, 654321, 123123, 112233, 789456, 159753, 000000, 111111, 222222, and 121212.

5. **Type your passcode and, if you're entering a complex passcode, tap Next.**

   Settings asks you to reenter your passcode.

6. **Type your passcode again and, if you're typing a complex passcode, tap Done.**

7. **If iPadOS prompts you for your Apple ID password, type your password and then tap Sign In.**

WARNING

Please don't forget your passcode! If you do, iPadOS will lock you out of your own device. You can still get back in, but the only route is a drastic one: You must restore the tablet's data and settings from an existing backup (which I describe in Chapter 17).

Lock Your iPad with a Fingerprint

If you have an iPad, iPad Air, or iPad mini, you can protect your tablet using Touch ID, the fingerprint sensor built into either the Home button or the top button (if your iPad doesn't have a Home button). By teaching the device your unique fingerprint, you can unlock your tablet merely by leaving your finger or thumb resting on the fingerprint sensor. You can use the same fingerprint to approve purchases you make in the iTunes Store, the App Store, and with retailers who accept Apple Pay.

TIP

In the following steps, you have to enter a passcode after you add your first fingerprint. Therefore, you might as well set up a passcode now; see the preceding section for the instructions.

Here's how to set up Touch ID:

1. **Open the Settings app.**

2. **Tap Touch ID & Passcode and then type your passcode to open the Touch ID & Passcode screen.**

   If you haven't set up a passcode, Settings will require you to enter one after you finish adding your first fingerprint. Therefore, you might as well set up a passcode now; see the preceding section for the instructions.

3. **Tap Add a Fingerprint.**

   The Touch ID screen appears.

4. **Lightly rest your thumb — or whatever finger you most often use when you're unlocking your iPad — on the fingerprint sensor.**

   The location of the fingerprint sensor depends on your iPad model:

   - *If your iPad has a Home button:* The fingerprint sensor is part of the Home button.

   - *If your iPad doesn't have a Home button:* The fingerprint sensor is built into the top button.

5. **Repeatedly lift and place your finger as Touch ID learns your fingerprint pattern.**

6. **When you see the Capture All of Your Fingerprint screen, tap Continue.**

7. **Once again, repeatedly lift and place your finger, this time emphasizing the edges of the finger.**

8. **When you see the Complete screen, tap Continue.**

9. **To specify another fingerprint, repeat Steps 3–8.**

Here's how you use Touch ID (for each, use the Home button instruction if your iPad has a Home button; otherwise, use the top button instruction):

» **Unlock your iPad.** Using a fingerprint-scanned finger, either press the Home button or press, release, and then rest your finger on the top button until the Home screen appears.

» **Make an iTunes or App Store purchase.** In the iTunes Store or the App Store, tap the price of the item you want to buy and then tap the Buy button. When the Touch ID dialog appears, rest your finger on the Home button or the top button until the purchase is approved.

» **Make an in-app purchase.** For apps that support Apple Pay, tap the Apple Pay button in the checkout screen and then place your scanned finger over the Home button or the top button.

» **Make an Apple Pay purchase.** You can use Touch ID to pay for goods in the real world without having to use cash or a credit card. If a merchant accepts Apple Pay, place your scanned finger over the Home button or the top button and then hold the tablet near the store's contactless reader.

Lock Your iPad with Facial Recognition

Recent versions of the iPad Pro — that is, all generations of the 11-inch iPad Pro and the third generation and later of the 12.9-inch iPad Pro — replace Touch ID with Face ID, which enables you to unlock your tablet using facial recognition. By letting your iPad learn to recognize your face, you can unlock the device just by looking at it. This works even if you are wearing sunglasses or haven't shaved for a few days.

REMEMBER

Face ID doesn't work if you're wearing a mask, such as the cloth masks so many of us used during the COVID-19 pandemic.

You can also use facial recognition to approve purchases you make via the iTunes Store, the App Store, and Apple Pay, as well as authorize the use of AutoFill passwords.

TIP

In the following steps, you have to enter a passcode after you finish scanning your face, so you might as well set up a passcode now as I describe earlier in this chapter.

Here are the steps to follow to configure Face ID:

1. **Open the Settings app.**

2. **Tap Face ID & Passcode and then type your passcode to open the Face ID & Passcode screen.**

3. **Tap Set Up Face ID.**

   The How to Set Up Face ID screen appears.

4. **Tap Get Started.**

   Settings displays a frame on the screen.

5. **Position your face within the frame and then slowly rotate your head until you fill in the circle that appears.**

   When the circle is complete, the first Face ID scan is complete.

6. **Tap Continue.**

7. **Once again, position your face within the frame and then slowly rotate your head until you fill in the circle that appears.**

   When the circle is complete, the second Face ID scan is complete.

8. **Tap Done.**

Configure Your iPad to Sleep Automatically

You can put your iPad into standby mode at any time by tapping the top button once. However, if your tablet is on but you're not using it, the device automatically goes into standby mode after two minutes. This feature is called auto-lock, and it's handy because it saves battery power and prevents accidental taps when your iPad is just sitting there.

Auto-lock is also a crucial feature if you've protected your tablet with a passcode lock, Touch ID, or Face ID, as I describe earlier, because if your device never sleeps, it never locks either unless you shut it off manually.

To make sure that your iPad sleeps automatically or to change the default two-minute Auto-Lock interval, follow these steps:

1. **Open the Settings app.**

2. **Tap Display & Brightness.**

   The Display & Brightness settings appear.

3. **Tap Auto-Lock.**

   The Auto-Lock screen appears.

4. **Tap the interval that you want to use.**

   You have five choices: 2 Minutes, 5 Minutes, 10 Minutes, 15 Minutes, or Never.

Back Up Your iPad

The data you have on your iPad might not be vital in the overall scheme of things, but there's no doubt it's vitally important to you. Therefore, it makes sense to protect your tablet's data and settings by backing up your iPad to your iCloud account. That way, if you lose your tablet or you have to erase it because of a problem, you can at least restore your data and settings from the backup. (I show you how this is done in Chapter 17.)

Follow these steps to back up your iPad's data and settings to iCloud:

1. **Open the Settings app.**

2. **Tap your name near the top of the Settings pane.**

   The Apple ID settings appear.

3. **Tap iCloud.**

4. **Tap iCloud Backup.**

5. **If necessary, tap the iCloud Backup switch on.**

   This configures iPadOS to make automatic backups whenever it's locked, connected to a Wi-Fi network, and plugged into a power source.

6. **Tap Back Up Now.**

   iPadOS backs up your tablet's data to your iCloud account.

Control Which Apps Can Use Your Location

When you launch an app that would like to use location data, you see a dialog similar to the one displayed in Figure 18-1. Here, the app is requesting permission to use the iPad's location tools to determine your location.

Note, however, that whichever permission you give the app, you can always change your mind later. Here are the steps to follow to control how an app can access Location Services:

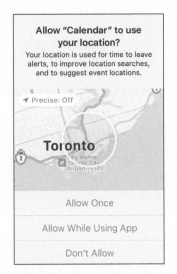

Allow "Calendar" to use your location?
Your location is used for time to leave alerts, to improve location searches, and to suggest event locations.

◀ Precise: Off

Toronto

Allow Once

Allow While Using App

Don't Allow

FIGURE 18-1:
Apps that can use location data require your permission to use that data.

1. **Open the Settings app.**

2. **Tap Privacy.**

   The Privacy settings appear.

3. **Tap Location Services.**

4. **Tap the app you want to work with.**

5. **Tap one of the following (note that not all apps offer all these options):**

   - *Never:* Prevents the app from using your location.

   - *Ask Next Time or When I Share:* Configures the app to ask for permission to use your location the next time you run the app or use the app to share your location.

   - *While Using the App:* Gives the app permission to use your location when you use the app.

   - *Always:* Gives the app permission to use your location even when you're not using the app. (Note that this setting is available only for certain apps.)

6. **If you don't want the app to use your exact location, tap the Precise Location switch off.**

Make Sure Apps Can't Track You

Some apps want to track your activity across the apps and websites of other companies. Why would they want to do that? Usually, they want to show you ads targeted to your activities, but sometimes they just want to sell your activity info to data brokers.

If it all sounds positively dystopian, you're right. That's why iPadOS not only requires these apps to ask for permission to track you but also denies these tracking requests by default. Thanks!

However, just to make sure, follow these steps to ensure that tracking it turned off on your iPad:

1. **Open the Settings app.**

2. **Tap Privacy.**

   The Privacy settings appear.

3. **Tap Tracking.**

4. **Make sure the Allow Apps to Request to Track switch is set off.**

   If it isn't, tap the switch to the off position and then say "Whew!"

Control App Access to Your iPad's Hardware and Data

Most iPad apps just go about their business and don't mess around with your privacy. However, some apps will ask your permission to use iPad data such as your contacts, calendars, and photos, and iPad hardware such as your microphone, camera, and Bluetooth radio.

If you give (or deny) permission to an app to use your iPad data or hardware, you can always change your mind and revoke (or grant) that permission. Here's how:

1. **Open the Settings app.**

2. **Tap Privacy.**

   The Privacy settings appear.

3. **Tap the app, data type, or hardware device that you want to work with.**

   Settings displays a list of apps that have at one time requested permission to use the resource you just tapped. If you granted permission to the app, the app appears in the list with its switch set to on; otherwise, the app's switch is off.

4. **Tap the app's switch off or on to deny or grant, respectively, permission to use the resource.**

Check for Compromised Passwords

iPadOS has an autofill passwords feature that, when activated, enables web browsers to save login credentials for websites. (To activate this setting, choose Settings ⇨ Passwords ⇨ AutoFill Passwords and then tap the AutoFill Passwords switch to on.)

The Autofill passwords feature not only saves you time and taps but can also make your online life more secure. How? Because iPadOS has a feature that examines known data breaches. If a password you've saved via autofill has been involved in one of those data breaches, iPadOS will alert you so that you can take action (such as changing your password on the site).

Besides getting an alert for a breached password, you can also follow these steps to check for such compromised passwords:

1. **Open the Settings app.**

2. **Tap Passwords.**

   The Passwords settings appear.

3. **Tap Security Recommendations.**

   Settings displays the Security Recommendations screen, which includes a list of compromised credentials.

4. **Make sure that the Detect Compromised Passwords switch is on.**

5. **For each breach you want to fix, tap the recommendation to see its details, then tap Change Password on Website to update your password.**

Set Restrictions on a Child's iPad

If you have children with their own iPads, you probably don't want them performing certain tasks on the tablet, such as installing and deleting apps, changing account settings, and making in-app purchases. You also might be concerned about some of the content they could be exposed to on the web, on YouTube, or in iTunes, and you might not want them giving away their current location.

For all these and similar parental worries, you can sleep better at night by activating the parental controls. Follow these steps to set these controls, and restrict the content and activities that kids can see and do:

1. **Open the Settings app on your child's iPad.**

2. **Tap Screen Time, read the overview, and then tap Continue.**

The first time you tap Screen Time, you see an overview of the feature. Screen Time asks whether this is your iPad or your child's.

3. **Tap This Is My Child's iPad.**

The Downtime dialog appears. You use Downtime to set times when the child can't use the iPad without your permission.

4. **Use the Start and End controls to set a schedule for when the child isn't allowed to use the tablet; when you're done, tap Set Downtime.**

The App Limits dialog appears. You use App Limits to set the maximum time the child is allowed to use certain app categories, such as Games.

5. **For each app category you want to limit:**

a. *Select the check box beside an app category you want to limit.* Alternatively, select the All Apps & Categories check box to set a limit on everything at once.

b. *In the Time Amount setting, tap Set and then select the maximum number of hours and minutes the child is allowed for the selected app categories.*

c. *Tap Set App Limit.*

d. *Repeat these steps for the next app category.*

The Content & Privacy screen appears.

6. **This screen is just an overview, so tap Continue.**

(To actually set these restrictions, complete these steps and then tap Content & Privacy Restrictions in the Screen Time settings.) iPadOS asks you to enter a Screen Time passcode. You use this passcode to access the Screen Time settings and to override the restrictions you've set.

REMEMBER

The Screen Time passcode is not the same as the passcode used to unlock an iPad.

7. **Type the passcode you want to use, and then type the passcode again when prompted.**

iPadOS prompts you to enter Apple ID credentials.

8. **Enter your Apple ID email address and password and then tap OK.**

You can use this information to reset your Screen Time passcode if you forget it.

Chapter **19**

Ten Hints, Tips, and Shortcuts

If someone asked me to pick my ten favorite iPad features, I'd probably say something like, "How could I? It would be like picking my ten favorite children!" (Then to myself, I'd snicker and think, "Ho, ho, I don't even *have* ten children!") However, my editor just sighed and asked once again, "Could you *please* just pick your ten favorite iPad features. Thanks!" Okay, for her — and especially for *you*, dear reader — I've put together ten of my favorite hints, tips, and shortcuts. Enjoy!

Use Do Not Disturb for Others

You probably think of the do not disturb (DND) feature as a way of keeping your iPad from bugging you while you are sleeping, in a meeting, or just don't want to be bothered. But DND can also help you be considerate to your family, roommates, or fellow office workers. If you're going to leave your iPad behind when you go somewhere, activate do not disturb to keep your notifications from bothering everyone else! You can activate DND by swiping down from the upper-right corner of the screen to open Control Center, tapping Focus, and then tapping Do Not Disturb, as I explain in Chapter 15.

Turn Off Keyboard Clicks

A *keyboard click* is a brief sound effect — yep, it's a click — that fires each time you tap a key on the onscreen keyboard. For unfathomable reasons, every iPad comes with keyboard clicks turned on by default. What's the problem? Have you ever sat near someone who does a lot of typing on the iPad? If so, you know all-too-well how annoying those incessant clicks became after even just a few minutes' exposure.

Do yourself and everyone around you a huge favor and turn off keyboard clicks by choosing Settings ⇨ Sounds and tapping the Keyboard Clicks switch to off.

Create a Website Home Screen Shortcut

You can add any web page as an icon to your Home screen, and then open the icon with a tap, like any app icon. In Safari, navigate to the page you want to save to your Home screen, and then tap the share icon near the top-right corner of the screen next to the address bar. In the Share dialog that appears, tap Add to Home Screen. You'll see a preview of the icon and its name. Edit the name, if you feel like it, and then tap Add to complete the process. Your Home screen appears, sporting your new shortcut. Tap it any time to open that web page.

Customize Your Dock with Your Most Used Apps

The dock is one of the most used elements of iPadOS. It comes with several apps by default, as described in Chapter 2, but you can also add up to 15 apps to the dock.

To add an app to the dock, long-press the app icon on your Home screen, and then tap Edit Home Screen. With the icons now wiggling adorably, drag the icon down into the dock, drag the icon horizontally within the dock until it's in the position you prefer, and then release the icon. Done! Don't be shy — add your most commonly used apps to the dock for quick access to them from anywhere.

Type on a Floating Keyboard

Have you ever wanted the virtual keyboard in iPadOS to be smaller? Why didn't you say so? In any app that uses the virtual keyboard, just pinch the keyboard using two fingers (or a finger and a thumb), and it will shrink to less than half its normal size. The keyboard will also be set to float, so you can move it anywhere on the screen.

To move your floating keyboard, tap and drag the gray bar at the bottom of the keyboard. To expand the keyboard back to its full size and re-dock it to the bottom of your screen, either spread two fingers on it or drag it to the bottom of your screen. It will automatically expand to its normal dimensions and position.

Look Up Words

I love words. Okay, I'm a writer so I'm *supposed* to love them, but I know that many of you love words, too. One of the things I love most about my iPad is the ability to look up a word any time I want.

To look up a word, long-press the word to select it. iPadOS highlights your word and displays a contextual menu with several commands (including Copy and Share). Tap Look Up to display a window that shows the definition of the word, as well as some relevant searches, Siri suggested websites, and more. After you get used to this feature, if you're like me you'll come to rely on it so much that you'll find yourself long-pressing words in print media as well!

Find Almost Anything Using Spotlight

Spotlight is a feature that can easily be overlooked. If you need to find something on your iPad or do a quick web search without opening Safari first, swipe down from the middle of your Home screen to open Spotlight. Type your search term, and you'll get relevant results from your iPad, apps on your iPad, and Siri suggestions for websites.

Long-Press Home Screen Icons

You can long-press any Home screen icon for quick access to actions specific to that app. Some apps will have more — or fewer — actions available. For instance, long-pressing the News app icon will give you quick access to some of the news sites you follow. Tapping and holding down on the Maps app gives you quick access to marking your location, sharing your location, and searching nearby. Apple's Measure app, on the other hand, has no special actions available, but every app will give you the option to Edit Home Screen or Remove App.

Lock Your Screen's Rotation

You can unlock and lock your iPad's screen rotation when needed. This feature is handy; I use it frequently. For instance, when lying down and reading, I lock my screen because I don't want my iPad rotating the screen every time I move. But when I'm doing many other activities, I usually want to be free to rotate the screen at any time. To lock or unlock your screen rotation, swipe down from the upper-right corner to open Control Center and tap the screen rotation lock icon.

Use a Volume Button as a Camera Shutter

When taking photographs with your iPad, you can use either the volume up or volume down button as a camera shutter button. Many times, I just can't reach the onscreen shutter button, and this handy trick has really helped me out. If you want to shoot a burst of photos, press and hold down either button for as long as you need.

Index

About the Author

Paul McFedries has been a technical writer for 30 years (nope, not a typo) and owns more than 1,000 iPads (definitely a typo). He has written more than 100 books that have sold more than 4 million copies throughout the known universe. Paul's books include the Wiley titles *iPad Portable Genius*, Fourth Edition, *iPhone Portable Genius*, Sixth Edition, *Alexa For Dummies*, Second Edition, *Fitbit For Dummies*, and *Teach Yourself VISUALLY Windows 11*. Paul invites everyone to drop by his personal website (`https://paulmcfedries.com`) and to follow him on Twitter (@paulmcf) and Facebook (`www.facebook.com/PaulMcFedries/`).

Dedication

For Karen and Chase

Author's Acknowledgments

The writer and poet Gina McKnight once said that "Writing is like riding a bike. Once you gain momentum, the hills are easier. Editing, however, requires a motor and some horsepower." Editing, in short, is hard work, but it's work that makes a big difference. Any errors or omissions you find in this book are all on me. But if this book reads well and is accurate (and I happen to think it's both), those are the result of the powerful motors and abundant horsepower of project editor and copy editor Susan Pink and technical editor Guy Hart-Davis. Thank you both for making me look good. I'd also like to thank Executive Editor Steve Hayes for asking me to writing this book.

Publisher's Acknowledgments

Executive Editor: Steve Hayes

Project Editor: Susan Pink

Copy Editor: Susan Pink

Technical Editor: Guy Hart-Davis

Proofreader: Debbye Butler

Production Editor: Saikarthick Kumarasamy

Cover Image: © best pixels/Shutterstock; screen-shot courtesy of Paul McFedries